MW01383327

NEW JERSEY STATE FEDERATION OF WOMEN'S CLUBS

NEW JERSEY STATE FEDERATION OF WOMEN'S CLUBS

EW JERSEY STATE FEDERATION OF WOMEN'S CLUBS

A CENTURY OF CHALLENGE

New Jersey State Federation

of

Women's Clubs

First 100 Years

Published 1994
New Jersey State Federation of Women's Clubs
55 Clifton Avenue
New Brunswick, NJ 08091-1593
(908) 249-5474

Printed in the United States of America by
Spectracolor-Reynolds
458 Third Avenue
Cherry Hill, NJ 08002-2990

Cataloguing-in-Publication Data
Williams, Grace Mathis, ed
A century of challenge: New Jersey State Federation
    of Women's Clubs—first 100 years
 I. New Jersey State Federation of Women's Clubs
II. Title 1994   367   93-086926
ISBN 0-9638106-0-X

TABLE OF CONTENTS

DEDICATION

With pride, affection and sincere appreciation, the New Jersey State Federation of Women's Clubs dedicates this story of its first one hundred years to Marina Orellana of Santiago, Chile.

In 1940 Senorita Orellana received New Jersey State Federation of Women's Club's first Pan-American Exchange Scholarship to study at the New Jersey College for Women (now Douglass College). Her generous monetary gift in 1992 made it possible to publish this book.

The Clubwomen of New Jersey are sincerely grateful to Marina Orellana.

i

FOREWORD

The gala 100th Annual Convention of the New Jersey State Federation of Women's Clubs will be a tribute to the women who have gone before us. This is a time to reflect on the many contributions our members have made over these one hundred years, members who have shown their PRIDE IN MEMBERSHIP!

It is a privilege to be President during this very special occasion. And, it is with pride that this President offers for your enjoyment and edification the chronicle of our First One Hundred Years. It is a true testimony to NJSFWC's proud heritage.

The Editor, Grace Williams, and her committee are to be commended for producing this treasure! It took endless hours devoted to researching and writing to produce this memorable piece of history. A true labor of love to be sure. Federation is indebted to these volunteers who personify TODAY'S WOMAN - FACING TOMORROW'S CHALLENGES!

Joan M. Hunt
State President

NEW JERSEY STATE FEDERATION OF WOMEN'S CLUBS
Joan M. Hunt - President   1992 - 1994

THE FIRST CENTURYANS

EDITOR   Grace Mathis Williams (Mrs. Joseph C.)
PRODUCTION EDITOR   Gail C. Shast (Mrs. Gregory)
GRAPHICS DESIGNER   Anita Rosen (Mrs. Bernard H.)

EXECUTIVE COMMITTEE ADVISORS:

Joan M. Hunt (Mrs. John A.) - President
Dorothy Lowe Greene (Mrs. James B.) - First Vice President
Cathy Southwick (Mrs. Robert W.) - Second Vice President
Phyllis W. Schneck (Mrs. Ernest J.) - EMD State Chairman

RESEARCH and EDITORIAL ASSISTANTS:

Past State Presidents
Marijane Singer (Mrs. Frederick D.)   1978-80
Gloria Malasky (Mrs. Lee J.)   1982-84
Shirley G. Goettel (Mrs. Edward C.)   1988-90
Marion Graham Arnao (Mrs. Edward C.) 1990-92

Ann Quinn (Mrs. J. Anthony)   Past Jr. Dir.   1982-84
Mary Lou Sullivan (Mrs. W. Timothy) Past Jr. Dir.   1988-90
Sharon L. Cartwright (Mrs. Donald)   Past EMD Ch. 1988-90

Irma Mirante (Mrs. A. R.)
Janice H. Paul (Mrs. Russell E.)
Mary Finley Rugarber (Mrs. Paul)
Raphael Sorbello (Mrs. Vincent A.)

PREFACE AND ACKNOWLEDGEMENTS

Creating a written record of accomplishments made possible by thousands of clubwomen volunteers during the New Jersey State Federation of Women's Clubs' first century was a monumental task. It was done through the devotion and dedication of a committee which contributed many hours from otherwise busy lives. This group named itself THE FIRST CENTURYANS when it first met in June, 1990.

Information was culled from available material which, during the early days of NJSFWC, was not always as detailed and precise as desired. It was impossible to include mention of each and every club, individual and event which was a part of the organization's extensive history. THE FIRST CENTURYANS regret any discrepancies or omissions.

A Century of Challenge includes the origin of women's clubs, the formation of the General Federation of Women's Clubs (GFWC) and the start of the New Jersey State Federation of Women's Clubs (NJSFWC) as researched and compiled by Ann Quinn.

The individual administrations of the outstanding leaders who served as Presidents from 1894 through 1958 were prepared from previous NJSFWC histories. Several active Past State Presidents (Elizabeth B. Alton, Marion Graham Arnao, Mary R. Bixby, Dorothy M. Constants, Shirley G. Goettel, Betty P. Loizeaux, Gloria Malasky, Marijane Singer and Emily Strakosch) supplied data from their own records. Joan M. Hunt, State President 1992-1994, actually found time in her very busy schedule to write her own administration story. The Past State Presidents serving on the committee and Irma Mirante researched the material used to write other administration segments.

Mary Finley Rugarber and Sharon L. Cartwright drafted the sections devoted to the Junior Clubs and the Evening Membership Department, respectively. Dorothy Lowe Greene, Cathy Southwick, Phyllis W. Schneck, Mary Lou Sullivan and Raphael Sorbello provided statistics and valuable advice throughout the project.

Janice H. Paul proofed the original manuscript and supplied valuable suggestions. Anita Rosen was responsible for the book's general layout, selected pictures and created all artwork including designs for the end sheets and dust jacket. Gail C. Shast handled production aspects, transcribed the Editor's dictation via computer and completely developed the extensive Index.

It was a privilege and pleasure to work with all of these exceptional, talented clubwomen.

GRACE MATHIS WILLIAMS
Editor - NJSFWC History

the first Centuryans

HOW IT ALL BEGAN AND GREW

As a tiny spark can ignite a flame and develop into a major fire or a small seed can grow to a towering Redwood tree, so can a moment of female frustration expand into a movement which has involved thousands of women throughout the world.

The person most credited with the growth and success of the Woman's Club Movement is Jane (Jennie) Cunningham Croly, who was born December 19, 1828 in Leicestershire, England and died December 23, 1901 in New York City. She was one of a small group of pioneer newspaper women in the middle of the 19th century who forced themselves into a male-oriented field.

Jane Cunningham Croly

Mrs. Croly's moment of wrath occurred in March, 1868 when the New York Press Club held a dinner to honor Charles Dickens at the end of his second reading tour in the United States. Men with even slight literary connections wanted tickets for this event, and so did two of the best known and most quoted women writers of the day — Jennie Cunningham Croly and Sara Willis Parton. Despite the fact that Mrs. Croly's husband was on the executive committee of the club, the male membership was outraged that she should dare to make this a "promiscuous" social occasion! They had refused to admit women! Jennie's response to the sexist treatment received from the influential male organization was to found Sorosis, the first Woman's Club of note. Her aim was to unite women to reach their potential and cultivate their place in society.

Jane Cunningham Croly had already become influential in the field of journalism. She became the first woman reporter employed by a metropolitan newspaper to write in the office on a daily basis, the first to serve as a regular correspondent for out-of-town daily papers, to manage a woman's department of a newspaper and to teach a journalism course. She perfected the "duplicate exchange agreement" (syndication), founded a New York Press Club for Women, was the editor and writer for some of the most prestigious magazines of her time and the author of nine books. For over 40 years she wrote under the pen names "Jenny June" or "Jennie June", and the women for whom she wrote were avid readers of her columns concerning fashion, food, home decorating, literature and drama. They consulted her editorials for help and advice on the changing social issues of the day. She was the wife of journalist and reformer, David Goodman Croly, and the mother of three daughters and one son who survived infancy. Her son, Herbert, became famous in his own right as founder and editor of the "New Republic" and author of "The Promise of American Life".

Although the later part of the 19th Century saw the appearance of a new phenomenon, "The Woman's Club", there had always been religious organizations among women who had banded together for charitable and missionary work. Women also worked in groups as auxiliaries to men's organizations as early as the 1820's, and fostered cultural activities in frontier communities. By the 1830's, there were attempts in the northeast by women to affect community life. These were stirred up by efforts to eliminate prostitution and were led by female moral reformers. By the mid 19th Century, a handful of women were beginning to organize on behalf of Women's Suffrage. For many women, this idea was too radical and the proponents were too strident. An alternate approach was desired.

The abrupt change to an industrial age was the hall-mark of the 19th Century. It brought a demand for the education of women, the abolition of slavery and the Civil War. These factors contributed to the formation of the Woman's Club. New labor-saving devices eased the running of a household, freedom for one class of people stimulated the thought of freedom for all, and the death and injuries suffered by men during the Civil War thrust women into a more dominant role.

Early clubs usually were comprised of ladies with interests in common. Programs were literary in character, designed to educate and cultivate self-improvement. Founders of the club movement — Jane Cunningham Croly, Charlotte Wilbur, Julia Ward Howe and Caroline Severence — envisioned something more meaningful and far-reaching than just the formation of study clubs and literature classes.

By the beginning of the 20th Century the movement had gained in scope and momentum. Clubs served to meet the pressing needs of the women of the day and became the vehicle for independence and self-determination — a way of earning women the right to an education, the right to work, the right to manage finances, the right to own property and to vote. The vision and dedication of the founders of the Woman's Club movement places them among the early crusaders for women's rights.

When "Jenny June" (Jane Cunningham Croly) and Sara Willis Parton (who wrote under the name of "Fanny Fern") were excluded from the Dickens' dinner, Mrs. Croly called upon her friends — mostly writers and career women — to help her. On April 20, 1868 the first official meeting of "Sorosis" was held at Delmonico's Restaurant. The term "Sorosis" was chosen from a botanical dictionary meaning "aggregation or collection of fruits".

Sorosis was not the first Woman's Club in existence, but is always referred to as the "Mother Club". Its location in the country's largest city, its on-going feud with the Men's Press Club and the occupation of its members generated press coverage which, if not complimentary, served to alert other women to the existence of the organization.

As explained by Mrs. Croly, "The club was a new departure for women. It involved a wider outlook, broader methods, a recognition of diversified claims, hospitality to new ideas, submission to the will of the majority, impartial examination (instead of condemnation) and the creation of absolutely new standards of respect and respectability."

Jennie Cunningham Croly and Charlotte Wilbur, thinking their club was the first, were surprised when Miss Ella Dietz, a charter member, told them that she had attended meetings of the Minerva Club of New Harmony, Indiana. They quickly discovered that another woman's club, The New England Woman's Club, had been organized in February 1868, in Boston, and had men associates. The founder of this club was Caroline Severence, assisted by Julia Ward Howe who succeeded her as President in 1871 and held that office until her death in 1910.

The earliest "Woman's Club" is probably the Ladies Society of Detroit and Vicinity organized in 1818. (The handwritten constitution and minutes can still be seen in the Detroit Public Library.) However, The Ladies Education Society of Jacksonville, Illinois, organized in October 1833 and formed to obtain funds to train women as teachers, became the oldest Federated Club. The Ladies Library Association in Kalamazoo, Michigan was the first women's group to erect a clubhouse as well as a library built, maintained and supported entirely by women.

The spontaneous appearance of the individual clubs springing up all over the country was just a beginning. Even as early as 1869, Jennie Croly dreamed of a recognized permanent institution for a great united womanhood with branches throughout the country sending delegates to an annual meeting. She realized that, only as a united group, could women hope to improve their lot in society. In May 1869, she persuaded Sorosis to sponsor a Woman's Parliament. Despite relevant subject matter discussed, the Parliament was not a great success. In 1873, Charlotte Wilbur, President of Sorosis, resurrected a simplified version of Mrs. Croly's plan and Sorosis issued a "Call" to American and

European women to attend a Woman's Congress in New York. This meeting resulted in the formation of the Association for the Advancement of Women.

Throughout the 1870's and 1880's women's clubs were forming — many influenced by Sorosis, the New England Woman's Club and the Association for the Advancement of Women.

"In the memory of every loyal clubwoman there should be a place kept green in grateful appreciation of the services rendered by Mrs. Croly. It was an uncrowned service, since she put away the honor of being the first President of the General Federation, an honor which would undoubtedly have been hers for the taking, but so long as the General Federation exists, space and time should be accorded to show honor to her memory." (Mary I. Wood)

Although born in England and a resident of New York, Jane Cunningham Croly does have some ties to New Jersey. As a newspaper reporter she traveled many times to the Jersey Shore, especially once it became a fashionable resort. Her daughter, Vida, was born in East Orange. Her brother, John Cunningham, began his congregational ministry in Boonton and Paterson. Her husband, David, spent the winters of 1887 and 1888 trying to regain his health in the dry, pine-laden air of Lakewood, a new winter health resort. On December 27, 1888, David Goodman Croly purchased plot #59 in Evergreen Cemetery for $12. This quiet place was to become the final resting place of David Goodman Croly, Jennie Cunningham Croly, her daughter Vida Croly Sidney and son-in-law, Frederick William Sidney. The NJSFWC undertook permanent maintenance of the gravesite in 1972 as a project of Dorothy Weinheimer's administration. The tombstone of Jennie Cunningham Croly marked her only as wife of David Goodman Croly, but in 1989 this oversight was rectified when the GFWC Junior Past Presidents' Club of the Fifth District collected money, mainly from clubs in the Fifth District, to add a foot marker reading:

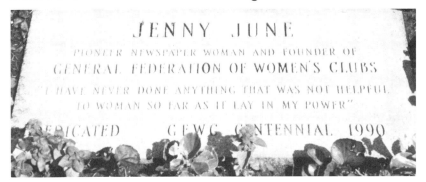

As part of the GFWC Centennial Celebration, the gravesite was beautified through monies donated by the General Federation of Women's Clubs. Special roping outlined the area and new gates were bought for the cemetery. On June 30, 1990, immediately prior to the GFWC Centennial Convention in New York City, a special memorial service to honor the founder of the organization was held at the gravesite. It was attended by 250 representatives from NJSFWC and GFWC. Mrs. Croly's contribution to the Woman's Club Movement was detailed by the International President, Alice C. Donahue, and her contributions to journalism extolled by Carol Napolitano, Bureau Chief of the Asbury Park Press.

Tributes honoring Jenny June were selected from "Memories of Jane Cunningham Croly" and were read by the GFWC Junior Past Presidents' Club of Fifth District who also prepared a 'life story' and hosted the event. Ann Quinn, currently Fifth District Vice President of NJSFWC, researched information on Mrs. Croly's life and authored the booklet, which is of interest to all clubwomen.

BIRTH OF THE GENERAL FEDERATION OF WOMEN'S CLUBS

The occasion of the 21st birthday of the founding of Sorosis prompted Jennie Cunningham Croly to suggest that a celebratory convention of all the women's clubs known to exist should be held. The "Call" to meet on March 18 - 20, 1889, in Madison Square Theater, New York was sent to 97 clubs. Each club was cordially invited to send a delegate and report on their clubs' methods and results. Sixty-one clubs sent delegates (some from uninvited clubs not even known to Sorosis) and letters were received from six other clubs.

This 1889 gathering was attended by representatives of three New Jersey clubs who reported as follows:

The Woman's Club of Orange. Charlotte Emerson Brown reported that the club formed in 1872 with 15 members had grown to a membership of 130. Since more members were expected, the meeting place had been changed to accommodate 300. The object of the club was literary and social improvement with meetings held every two weeks.

8

The Club had nine standing committees: History and Literature, Political and Social Science, Art, Education, Science, House and Home, Ethical Culture and Reform, Miscellaneous, and Lectures and Entertainment. (A representative from The Woman's Club of Fargo, North Dakota stated that her club had been founded by a member of the Woman's Club of Orange who had moved there.)

The Monday Afternoon Club of Plainfield. Elvira Kenyon reported that the club was just one year old having been founded for intellectual and social culture. The membership was limited to 75, and the admission fee entitled members to all lectures and entertainments. The club carried standing committees on Literature, Art, Science, Miscellaneous Topics and Entertainment.

Amelia Dickenson Pope reported for the El Mora Literary and Social Club of Elizabeth. The club was entering its third year. The object was literary and social. A weekly topic was selected with a leader appointed.

It was during this convention that Ella Dietz Clymer, President of Sorosis, made use of the phrase that afterwards became the motto of the General Federation, "Unity in Diversity". The closing words of her address stated: "We look for unity, but unity in diversity. We hope that you will enrich us by your varied experiences and let us pledge ourselves to work for a common cause — the cause of united womanhood throughout the world."

The convention adjourned with the appointment of a committee to draft a constitution and present a plan of organization for a permanent Federation of Clubs. The first meeting of the Federation Committee was held the day following the convention and a group of seven, called the Advisory Board, was selected for executive purposes. They were Ella Dietz Clymer, Jane Cunningham Croly, Charlotte Emerson Brown, Louise Thomas, Sophia Hoffman, Mary Hall and Amelia Wing. The committee met thirteen times in preparation for the Ratification Convention held April 23-25, 1890 at the Scottish Rites Hall, Madison Ave., New York.

At the Ratification Convention, Jennie Cunningham Croly was nominated for the office of President of the General Federation but she declined, leaving that honor to Charlotte Emerson Brown of New Jersey. Mrs. Croly possessed the ability to inspire thousands of women to unite and address the issues of the day. The General Federation of Women's Clubs can be said to be her legacy.

Charlotte Emerson Brown

New Jersey's own "First Lady" of the Federation movement, Charlotte Emerson Brown, was an ideal choice for President of GFWC. Born in 1838, she had received a broad education in her native Massachusetts. She was the daughter of Ralph Emerson, a professor of ecclesiastical history and pastoral theology at the Andover Theological Seminary. His second cousin was Ralph Waldo Emerson. She studied abroad for a while before returning to take a business course and become secretary for her brother's business in Rockford, Illinois. Her marriage to the Reverend William Brown took her to Orange, New Jersey. She joined the Woman's Club of Orange in 1887, becoming President in 1888 and delegate to the gathering of clubs in New York in 1889. Since there were no precedents for her position, her own innate common-sense, her ability to think clearly and speak well and her devotion to the cause stood her in good stead. She laid a remarkable foundation to be built on by those who would follow her.

The growth in membership as well as the huge geographical area covered by GFWC made practical work and assistance to local clubs difficult. Such was the concern of many member clubs that the idea of forming State Federations was born. (Actually this possibility had been envisioned by the 1889-90 Advisory board but had been deemed unnecessary and a detraction from the formation of the General Federation.)

Credit for the first state organization goes to the Maine Federation of Women's Clubs organized September 22, 1892, followed by the Utah Federation of Women's Clubs in April 1893. Neither took steps to join the parent organization until the newly formed Iowa State Federation with 45 clubs was admitted as part of the GFWC during the Board of Directors' meeting held in May 1893 at the World's Fair in Chicago. The "Value of the State Federation" had been discussed by delegates to the preceding Council Meeting and, despite fears of possible adverse effects on the parent organization, the need was recognized.

At the second Biennial Meeting held in Philadelphia May 9 - 11, 1894, the Secretary reported four State Federations (Massachusetts being the fourth). The idea of a State Federation as an auxiliary to the General Federation was considered inspiring. This policy was promoted under the leadership of Ellen Herotin, the second GFWC President 1894-1898, and it quickly bore fruit. Twenty-six Federations were organized in four years. The NJSFWC became the eighth to form on November 16, 1894. It was elected to GFWC membership on December 14, 1894.

Mrs. Brown recognized a need for proper business organization and persuaded the Federation to obtain a certificate of incorporation under the laws of New Jersey in 1893:

CERTIFICATE OF INCORPORATION

This certifies that there exists in the United States of America an association composed of about three hundred clubs having an aggregate membership of about forty thousand individuals from the United States and foreign countries, which said association is known and designated as "the General Federation of Women's Clubs", and has been formed to bring into communication with one another the various women's clubs throughout the world, that they may compare methods of work and become mutually helpful.

Constitutions of clubs applying for membership should show that no sectarian or political test is required, and that while the distinctively humanitarian movements may be recognized, their chief purpose is not philanthropic and technical, but social, literary, artistic, or scientific culture.

This further certifies that at a regular meeting of that association held on Friday, the thirteenth day of May Eighteen Hundred and Ninety-two, the persons whose names are hereto affixed were elected by a majority vote to the several offices provided for by the constitution of said association. Said officers, elected as aforesaid, do hereby, in pursuance to an act of the Legislature of the State of New Jersey, entitled, "An Act to incorporate benevolent and charitable associations, approved April 9, 1875," and a supplement to an act entitled, "an Act to incorporate benevolent and charitable associations, said supplement approved April 6, 1876," certify that the association has assumed and adopted the name of the General Federation of Women's Clubs as their corporate name, and we desire that this, our certificate, be filed and recorded by the Clerk of the County of Essex, and State of New Jersey.

OFFICERS

Charlotte Emerson Brown, President.
Julia Plato Harvey, Vice President
J. C. Croly, Recording Secretary
Mary V. Temple, Corresponding Secretary.
Jane O. Cooper, Treasurer
Harriet H. Robinson, Auditor.

DIRECTORS

Joseph Bates	*Mary E. Mumford*
Mary Rogers	*Octavia N. Bates*
Fanny Perdy Palmer	*Julia Ward Howe*
Cordelia I. Sterling	*Katherine Noble*

Mary D. Steele

Recorded and Filed December 29, 1893
(signed and sealed)
J.T. Wrightson, Clerk, Newark, New Jersey

To set the newly formed General Federation on a firm footing, Mrs. Brown conducted at least four meetings of the Advisory Board (known as the Board of Directors after 1892) prior to the first Council meeting. This was held in Union Hall in East Orange, New Jersey on Wednesday, May 20, 1891 and hosted by the Woman's Club of Orange on the occasion of their 19th anniversary. The purpose was to consider proposed changes to the constitution and to plan for the first convention or Biennial Meeting to be held in Chicago in 1892. Each president of a federated club was a vice president and, either in person or by written message, was permitted to share in the deliberations of the meeting. Over 200 women attended, including elected officers of GFWC, and 65 delegates representing 18 states. Luncheon, which included a visit to the inventor's workshop, was held at "Glenmont" (the home of Mr. and Mrs. Thomas A. Edison) where "upwards of two hundred ladies were seated, without crowding, at the tables in two rooms".

In response to a toast to the "General Federation", Charlotte Emerson Brown said, "In federated club life is a bond of sympathy that unites us in a common sisterhood. The solvent of all differences among us is love — love for each other and for our common cause". During another response, Mrs. Croly made a plea for the inclusion of civic activities in club life, "Is there not room in the club for outlook committees, whose business it should be to investigate township affairs, educational, sanitary, reformatory, and on the lines of improvement, and report what is being done, might be done, or needs to be done, for decency and order in the jails, in the schools, in the streets, in the planting of trees, in the disposition of refuse, and the provision for light which is the best protection for life and property".

At the first Biennial Meeting held in Chicago, in May 1892, 297 delegates representing 185 clubs from 29 states were in attendance. Work in each state was reported. Florence Howe Hall reported that the club movement in New Jersey was healthy but added, "A number of our New Jersey clubs dislike the idea of formal organization. They dread the idea of a constitution and of regularly elected officers."

Mrs. Brown was elected to a second term as President and served to the close of the second Biennial Meeting in Philadelphia in May 1894. During her remarkable farewell speech, Charlotte Emerson Brown detailed her conclusions about the organization. Among them — that as a world-wide organization the Federation would spread and grow, that the organization should not become entangled with other organizations or involve men in their work, that it should establish good business principles, and, where the want existed, that State Federations should be formed, not as rivals but as helpers in the common cause. She continued, "I would, however, impress upon those engaged in state organizations that they make their constitution very simple and flexible and that state bodies and organized groups of clubs should hold direct membership in the general body . . . Wheels within wheels is the divine order. As I have committed this work to divine guidance a thousand times, so again I commit it here and now; may God's blessings be upon it and upon us all."

Charlotte Emerson Brown continued to serve on the Board of Directors as Chairman of Foreign Correspondence. She was also commissioned to write a History of the Woman's Club Movement, but her death intervened, leaving the task to Mrs. Croly.

Mrs. Brown died on February 4, 1895 at the age of 57. A Memorial Service, at the Trinity Congregational Church in East Orange on March 22, 1895 was held by invitation of the President of NJSFWC, Margaret T. Yardley. The General Federation was represented by Jane Cunningham Croly and a large delegation, representing clubs from New Jersey and New York. Tributes were presented by many clubwomen. Letters of condolence were sent to Dr. William Brown in a white morocco case inscribed with the words, "Her children shall call her blessed".

Her successor, Ellen Herotin, said of her, "The whole success of this woman's movement was due to the devotion and the unselfishness of Charlotte E. Brown".

Now, over 100 years later, the General Federation of Women's Clubs remains strong through excellent leadership and the enthusiastic support of its members.

Ann Holland   Joan Hunt
1992-1994 Presidents of GFWC and NJSFWC

FORMATION OF THE NEW JERSEY STATE FEDERATION OF WOMEN'S CLUBS

Since delegates from three clubs in New Jersey had attended the convention to format a permanent national organization in 1889, it was a logical step for clubs in New Jersey to band together into a State Federation.

The impetus to form a New Jersey Federation came from a remark made at the Annual Breakfast of the Ray Palmer Club of Newark, a GFWC member club. Florence Howe Hall, the daughter of Julia Ward Howe, was a guest speaker at this event. Mrs. Hall, a Past President of the Monday Afternoon Club of Plainfield and a GFWC Board Member, advocated that New Jersey form a State Federation as a supplement or auxiliary to the General Federation. She stated that the club movement was growing in New Jersey (at that time there were 15 clubs with a membership of 1,900 women) and, with the formation of a State Federation, clubwomen could be brought together for an interchange of ideas and methods and for the cultivation of good fellowship.

Invitation To Convene in Orange in 1894

To the Women's Clubs of New Jersey

In accordance with the impulse and the spirit of the times, it is deemed advisable to organize a State Federation of Women's Clubs in New Jersey for the purpose of uniting them in a stronger bond of sympathy and fellowship and of bringing the benefits of organization more closely home to the individual association than can be accomplished through the General Federation, alone.

The Woman's Club of Orange has been asked to take the initiative in this movement and hereby invites every Woman's Club in New Jersey whose main object is the culture and improvement of its members and of humanity to convene for the pupose of considering a State Federation and if deemed adviseable to form such a Federation: at its club rooms in the Woman's Christian Temperance Union Building, corner of Main and Commerce Streets, Orange , on Friday, November 16th at 10 a.m.

Each club is requested to send two delegates with power to act. The Women's Club of Orange will entertain the delegatess at luncheon and provide for those who come from a distance.

It is hoped there will be a hearty response from every Club and that the smaller and younger clubs as well as the larger ones and older ones will cooperate in forming this State Federation.

(Signed) Sarah M. Johnson,
President, Woman's Club of Orange
Margaret T. Yardley
Chairman Committee of State Federation

The invitation to form a New Jersey Federation was issued by the Woman's Club of Orange, the pioneer club in the state, in the autumn of 1894. The invitation was signed by Sarah M. Johnson, President of the Woman's Club of Orange, Margaret T. Yardley, Chairman of a Committee on State Federation. Charlotte Emerson Brown of the GFWC Board of Directors and Florence Howe Hall, State Chairman of Correspondence for GFWC, endorsed the letter.

It was a cold Friday morning, November 16, 1894, when approximately 150 women met in Union Hall, Orange, New Jersey. The 65 delegates and other attendees represented 36 or 37 clubs — there has always been a slight disagreement among authorities on the number of clubs represented. To arrive on time for the 10 a.m. session, many of the women left their homes well before daybreak to travel by train, trolley or carriage. Although the majority of them were from the northern part of the state, there were representatives who came from as far south as Salem, Bridgeton, Haddonfield, Vineland and Merchantville.

To better understand the effort put forth by these women who founded NJSFWC we are indebted to Cecilia Gaines Holland for a "picture" of life in the 1890's which she provided in a speech given in 1933. Mrs. Holland said, "A typical home of the middle or upper middle class family housed a large number of people — perhaps a dozen. It would be a grandfather and grandmother, parents, sons and daughters and even grandchildren who usually gathered for morning prayers. The patriarchal grandfather would read some verses from the Bible and everyone knelt to say the Lord's Prayer. If any member of the little flock was in special trouble, a special prayer was said for him or her. Although they all lived busy lives, they had time for this ceremony which sent them out into their world each day with the conviction that 'God was in His Heaven and all was right with the World!'" She continued to describe the era . . .

"In the Gay Nineties they first had horse drawn trolley cars followed by trolley cars with stoves in them which was the last word in luxury. People rode in these for pure pleasure and took trips in them — sometimes full day trips. They had bicycles and women wore bloomers to ride on them. This was thought to be very 'sporty'. In fact, a bicycle built for two was the last word in devotion. Women wore pompadours that went all around their heads with 'rats' in them. They had very large hats and hatpins a half yard long to hold them on. There were buggies with romantic possibilities for couples who had time to ride in them. The women wore dresses with enormous sleeves and had very small waists. The country had not yet gone off the Gold Standard so the women wore substantial wedding rings, and they wore them for life! The young had not lost their capacity for wonder and for respect. Hero worship still existed for the great ones on Earth, and heroes had not yet been de-bunked. There was a belief in superior people with fine characters, and a spirit of reverence existed in Church and outside of Church in daily life."

She went on to say, "There was something called 'taste' in literature and books were thought to be a source of intellectual uplift and inspiration. To be clean and righteous did not indicate feeblemindedness on the part of authors. There were fine magazines being published which were a monthly treat. People were thrilled when a new "Century" or "Harpers" came in the mail, and editors were responsible people — the great newspapers of the day had standards and had not sold their souls to the monster called 'circulation'. In the theatre, the mechanics may not have been so good but they had moral values which have been lost by 1933. The audiences applauded the hero and cried over the unfortunate victims in plays. They had contempt and indignation for the villain in the piece. Later, when the villain became the hero, it was confusing to the audience."

Mrs. Holland also told her audience that, "In the 1890's there were qualities called 'Dignity and Decorum' — words which are still found in today's dictionaries. Also in the 90's was something called 'manners!' Well-bred people who were invited to dinner called afterwards to pay their respects, and gentlemen asked ladies for permission to smoke. Biology and birth control were not general. Babies came from Heaven and the Stork brought them! Psychology was in the same class as Astrology, and the monstrous theories of Freud had not yet degraded the human mind. New York City, which claimed Newark, New Jersey as a 'silk stocking suburb' had a '400' — A social register of the elite. American heiresses married foreign noblemen and they became the most valuable export to leave our shores. There were kings and courts and Kaisers and Czars in the 90's. It was all very glamorous and enticing at long range."

According to Mrs. Holland, "The residents of this era had many things such as parlors (which later became a term only used by Morticians) and at least one gilt chair which was apt to be shaky. They had gaslights and kitchen stoves which burned coal and they wore long thick underwear and corsets — even flannel petticoats! There were parasols for the sun and rubbers for rainy days. A few of the daring women powdered their noses, but rouge and lipstick were used only by actresses. There were not so many bathtubs, but there were things called modesty and a dignity of personality which made a woman a 'lady' — a discrimination between good taste and vulgarity as well as a delicacy of appreciation for the finer things of life. Electricity was in its infancy and there were no automobiles, no air ships and no motion pictures. That greatest wonder of all, radio, had not yet been invented. When Ed Bellamy predicted that the world would hear grand opera while sitting in their own homes, he was pitied because it was thought that his mind had become deranged. Both men and women wore long nightgowns or nightshirts. The women looked like perfectly proper angels and the men looked liked Hebrew prophets. However, in the case of a fire, one could flee the house with warmth and decency."

Cecilia Gaines Holland, who later became the second President of NJSFWC, humorously said that Russia's five year plan was nothing new for her. She was elected President in 1896, served until 1898, was married in 1899 and had her only child in 1901. As she put it, "Federation first — Family afterward." She firmly believed that the women of her time had colossal ambitions and that the work of NJSFWC proved that they had blazed a trail for those who would follow them.

By the time the November 16, 1894 meeting was concluded the New Jersey State Federation of Women's Clubs was an established fact! A President had been elected (Mrs. Charles B. Yardley of Orange) and a committee formed to prepare a Constitution for the organization. Most of the clubs sending representatives to this first meeting became Charter Clubs and the Charter was closed on March 15, 1895 with an official listing of 35 clubs:

Arlington *Woman's Club*. . . . . Woman's Literary Club
*Bayonne . . . . .Athena Club
*Bayonne . . . . Felipsa Magazine Club
*Bayonne . . . . Ladies: Political and Social Society
*Bayonne. . . . . .Woman's Musical Literary and Study Club

22

```
*Bridgeton . . . . . . . . . . . . . . . . . . . . . . . . . . . . . Friday Club
 Cranford . . . . . . . . . . . . . . . . . . . . .Wednesday Morning Club
*East Orange. . . . . . . . . . . . . . . . . . . . . . . . . . . .Fortnightly Club
*Elizabeth . . . . . . . . . . . . . . . . . . . . . El Mora Women's Literary
*Elizabeth . . . . . . . . . . . . . . . . . . . . . . . . . . . . . .Monday Club
*Elizabeth . . . . . . . . . . . . . . . . . . . . . . . . . . . .Ninety-two Club
*Elizabeth, Research Club. . . . . . . .Over The Tea Cups Literary
 Haddonfield. . . . . . . . . . . . . . . . . . Haddon Fortnightly Club
 Jersey City . . . . . . . . . . . . . . . . . . . . . . . Odd Volumes Club
 Jersey City . . . . . . . . . . . . . . . . . . . . . . . . . . Woman's Club
*Madison . . . . . . . . . . . . . . . . . . . . . . . . . . .Fortnightly Jaunts
 Merchantville, Woman's Club of. . . .Half Hour Reading Club
*Montclair . . . . . . . . . . . . . . . . . . . . . . . .Social and Literary Club
*Montclair. . . . . . . . . . . . . . . . . . . . . . . Three O'Clock Club
*Montclair . . . . . . . . . . . . . . . . . . . Wednesday Afternoon Club
*Morristown . . . . . . . . . . . . . . . . . . . . . . . .Current News Club
*Newark . . . . . . . . . . . . . . . . . . . . . . . . . . . . . . Current Topics
*Newark. . . . . . . . . . . . . . . . . . . . . . . . . . . Ray Palmer Club
*Newark . . . . . . . . . . . . . . . . . . . . . . . . . . Saturday Night Club
*Newark. . . . . . . . . . . . . . . . . . . .Traveler's Club of Roseville
*North Plainfield . . . . . . . . . . . . . . . . . . . . Current Events Club
*Orange . . . . . . . . . . . . . . . . . . . . . . . . . . . . . . Woman's Club
*Passaic . . . . . . . . . . . . . . . . . . . . . . . . .Monday Afternoon Club
 Plainfield . . . . . . . . . . . . . . . . . . . . . .Monday Afternoon Club
*Plainfield. . . . . . . . . . . . . . . . . . . . . . . . . . . . .Rasores Club
*Rahway. . . . . . . . . . . . . . . . . . . . . . . . . . . . . .Athenian Club
*Rahway . . . . . . . . . . . . . . . . . . . . . . . .Home Reading Circle
 Roselle . . . . . . . . . . . . . . . . . . . . . . . . . . . . . . . . Clio Club
 Salem . . . . . . . . . . . . . . . . . . . . . . . . . . . . . .Woman's Club
 Verona, Woman's Club of . . . . . . . . . . . . . . . .Isabella Literary
```
*Indicates clubs that are no longer members.

Italics indicate clubs that are still members but whose names have changed.

Partial List of Delegates
to the Meeting in Orange

Woman's Club of Orange
  Mrs. L. H. Johnson
  Mrs. Theodore F. Seward
Friday Club of Bridgeton
  Mrs. Oberlin Smith
  Mrs. M. K. Elmer
Half Hour Reading Circle,
Merchantville
  Mrs. Charles Silvus
  Mrs. Joseph Van Kirk
Woman's Literary Union Of
Elizabeth
  Mrs. Mary E. Hinds
  Mrs. H. A. Class
Note: The above "Union" was
composed of several clubs,
five of which sent delegates to
the meeting in Orange as
follows:
Shakespeare Club
  Mrs. Charles Silvus
  Miss Belle Miller
92 Club
  Miss Adelaide Bonnell
  Miss Mary A. Hinds
Over the Tea Cups
  Mrs. J. B. Wardell
  Mrs. J. D. Clark
El Mora
  Mrs. R. D. Colburn
  Mrs. H. de Raismes

Clio of Roselle
  Mrs. E. P. Tenny
  Mrs. E. W. Pattison
The Octagon of Elizabeth
sent no delegates
Monday Afternoon Club of
Plainfield
  Mrs. Charles Ryder
Rasores of Plainfield
  Mrs. Horace Kimball
  Mrs. H. R. Halloway
East Orange Fortnightly
  Miss Sue Taylor
  Miss L. H. Jones
Woman's Reading Circle of
Rutherford
  Mrs. C. L. Crear
  Mrs. E. C. Abbott
Ray Palmer Club of Newark
  Mrs. E. P. Dennison
  Mrs. W. H. Brown
Current Topic, of Newark
  Mrs. L. E. Palmer
  Mrs. J. D. Dewitt
Travelers Club of Roseville
  Mrs. F. A. Stokes
  Mrs. H. H. Mitchell
Woman's Literary Circle of
Arlington
  Mrs. M. D. Crowell
  Mrs. E. H. Silbus

The Three O'clock Club Montclair
  Mrs. Benjamin Strong
  Mrs. S. W. Carey
Wednesday Afternoon Club of Montclair
  Mrs. C. W. Butler
  Mrs. F. A. Hall
Madison Fortnightly Jaunts
  Mrs. A. C. Coursen
  Mrs. C. G. Davis
Jersey City Woman's Club
  Mrs. Emma Newbury
Odd Volumes of Jersey City
  Mrs. G. B. Eaton
  Mrs. Marcus Beach
Athena of Bayonne
  Mrs. J. H. Eadie
  Mrs. Ida M. Batchelor
Salem Woman's Club
  Mrs. Isabel Craven
  Mrs. Emma Bassett
Wednesday Morning Club of Cranford
  Mrs. E. D. Horton
  Mrs. L. P. Naylor
Monday Afternoon Club of Passaic
  Mrs. Benj. Mc Grew
  Mrs. Harrison Crane
Talitha Cunn of Vineland
  Mrs. J. D. Meech

The Political and Social Advancement Society of Bayonne
  Mrs. A. Christie
  Mrs. R. D. Eddowes
Felipa Magazine Club of Bayonne
  Mrs. C. C. Sleesman
  Mrs. William Collins
Isabella Literary of Verona
  Mrs. J. C. Shafer
  Miss deGrolier
Fortnightly of Summit
The Woman's Saturday Night Club of Newark
  Mrs. Elizabeth S. Hunt
  Mrs. Maretta Mahaffy
Columbian Literary Circle of Rahway
  Mrs. J. Lambertin
  Mrs. C. S. Leonard
Home Reading Club of Rahway
  Mrs. F. C. Bardwell
  Mrs. J. T. Barnes
The Monday Club of Elizabeth
  Mrs. Charles Fowler
  Mrs. Alonzo Pettit
The Ramblers of Jersey City
  Miss M. Williams
  Miss J. R. PerLee

Program of the First Annual Meeting
October 24 and 25, 1985 - Newark, N. J.

Morning Session, 9:30 - 12

Prayer, Mrs Antoinette Brown Blackwell

Welcome from Newark Clubs, Rev. Phebe A. Hanaford

Annual Reports —

> President, Mrs. Margaret T. Yardley
>
> Recording Secretary, Mrs. Laura G.S. Smith
>
> Corresponding Secretary, Mrs. Sophie C. Coursen
>
> Treasurer, Mrs. Harriet B. Miles
>
> Auditor, Miss Caroline Van Meeter

Afternoon Session, 2 - 5

Ten-minute Papers

> Mrs. Antoinette Brown Blackwell - Immortality
>
> Mrs. Florence Howe Hall - School Suffrage
>
> Mrs. Mary Philbrook,Lld. - New Jersey Laws Relating to Women
>
> Mrs. Marie Heyburn Marshall - Evelyn College
>
> Miss Cornelia F. Bradford - College Settlements
>
> Mrs. Emily Williamson - State Charities
>
> Mrs. Mary Virginia Terhune - Country Clubs, Story of a Rocking Chair
>
> Miss Adelaide Sterling - Patriotic Societies
>
> Miss Maude Fletcher - Town Improvement Societies
>
> Miss Clara Woodward Greene - Women's Relation to Public Schools
>
> Mrs. Harriet Lincoln Coolidge - The Children
>
> Rev. Phebe Hanaford - Evangelical Work among Women
>
> Dr. Emma W. Edwards - Women in Medicine

Evening Session, 8 - 10

Mrs. Talbot R. Chambers - "Open Thy Blue Eyes"
Massenet; "Love's Philosophy", *Jordan*

Mrs. George R. Seward - Violoncello Obligato

Miss Marie Hartley - Dialect Recitation

Miss Annie Beaston - Paper: Women's Place Today

Miss Nellie K. Kinnard - Recitation, The First and
Last Race

Miss Emily Burbank - Music, Its Interpretation
Chopin, Miss Helen M. Wright, Illustrator

Mrs. Talbot Chambers - "Beautiful Eyes", *Tosti*

Friday, October 25 9:30 - 12

Prayer, Rev. Phebe Hanaford

Roll Call and Presentation of Certificates to Charter Clubs

Election of Five Directors

Three-minute reports from the rest of the clubs.

Unfinished Business.

Afternoon Session 2 -3:30

Discussion - Traveling Libraries - Discussions opened
by Mrs. E. D. Horton

What Aims in Club Life Are Most Beneficial? - Mrs.
Ada Loomis McGrew.

NEW JERSEY STATE FEDERATION OF WOMEN'S CLUBS
ANNUAL MEETINGS
(SHOWING YEAR, PLACE, ATTENDANCE)

Year	Place	Attendance	Year	Place	Attendance
1895	Newark	175*	1924	Atlantic City	519*
1896	Jersey City	**	1925	Atlantic City	492*
1897	Camden	122*	1926	Asbury Park	628*
1898	Elizabeth	600	1927	Atlantic City	468*
1899	Atlantic City	**	1928	Atlantic City	394*
1900	Newark	163*	1929	Atlantic City	593*
1901	East Orange	168*	1930	Atlantic City	584*
1902	Jersey City	183*	1931	Atlantic City	696*
1903	Trenton	145*	1932	Atlantic City	660*
1904	Newark	190*	1933	Atlantic City	550*
1905	Elizabeth	164*	1934	Atlantic City	553*
1906	Asbury Park	177*	1935	Atlantic City	600*
1907	Orange	202*	1936	Atlantic City	599*
1908	Riverton	**	1937	Atlantic City	532*
1909	Atlantic City	186*	1938	Atlantic City	586*
1910	Englewood	153*	1939	Atlantic City	596*
1911	Asbury Park	337*	1940	Atlantic City	783*
1912	Montclair	339*	1941	Atlantic City	605*
1913	Atlantic City	294*	1942	Atlantic City	582*
1914	Asbury Park	391*	1943	Atlantic City	1304
1915	Atlantic City	343*	1944	New York City	1465
1916	Asbury Park	343*	1945	WAR - Mail Votes	491
1917	Atlantic City	378*	1946	New York City	644*
1918	Newark	475*	1947	Atlantic City	1257
1919	Atlantic City	349*	1948	Atlantic City	794*
1920	Asbury Park	699*	1949	Atlantic City	1141
1921	Atlantic City	431*	1950	Atlantic City	1176
1922	Atlantic City	474*	1951	Atlantic City	1207
1923	Atlantic City	428*	1952	Atlantic City	1352

1953	Atlantic City	1452	
1954	Atlantic City	1523	
1955	Atlantic City	1333	
1956	Atlantic City	1495	
1957	Atlantic City	1434	
1958	Atlantic City	1575	
1959	Atlantic City	1538	
1960	Atlantic City	1613	
1961	Atlantic City	1673	
1962	Atlantic City	1654	
1963	Atlantic City	1668	
1964	Atlantic City	1699	
1965	Atlantic City	1717	
1966	Atlantic City	1894	
1967	Atlantic City	1884	
1968	Atlantic City	1907	
1969	Atlantic City	2053	
1970	Atlantic City	1757	
1971	Atlantic City	1635	
1972	Atlantic City	1906	
1973	Atlantic City	1763	
1974	Atlantic City	1737	
1975	Atlantic City	1754	
1976	Atlantic City	1812	
1977	Atlantic City	1795	
1978	Atlantic City	1735	
1979	McAfee	2176	
1980	McAfee	1711	
1981	McAfee	1518	
1982	McAfee	1600	
1983	McAfee	1390	
1984	McAfee	1592	
1985	McAfee	1277	
1986	McAfee	1392	

1987	McAfee	1120
1988	Atlantic City	1504
1989	Atlantic City	1143
1990	Atlantic City	1065
1991	Parsippany	1335
1992	Parsippany	1245
1993	East Brunswick	1251

*Voting Delegates
**No Figures Available

HEADQUARTERS - NJSFWC

Although progressive women of the 20th Century have long ago disproved the old adage that "Woman's place is in the home", the concept of "home" is a vital one to all women. The thousands of clubwomen in New Jersey share this feeling, and a home for NJSFWC has always been an important issue. The detailed story of "Headquarters" is one that deserves to be told.

For the first six years of its existence - from 1894 to 1900 - New Jersey State Federation of Women's Clubs was "homeless". The Board of Directors met on alternate months at members' homes, most often at the home of the State President. The hostess provided luncheon during which the members enjoyed a social hour. Officers and chairmen arrived at the meetings carrying the books and papers concerned with their activities. These were vital Federation records and equipment. Since many of the women came from a distance and transportation was anything but speedy, it was customary to complete Board Meetings promptly at 5:00 P.M.

As the Federation grew larger and more complex, the

situation grew intolerable and in 1900 a room at 885 Broad Street, Newark was acquired to be used as a central meeting place and for storage of some of the voluminous material. Although this improved the situation to some extent, conditions were not ideal and in 1906 - 1909 the need for a real headquarters became evident. Plans were begun to secure a suitable site, but the dilemma continued. State President Catherine C. Warren had stated that the Federation "still needs a club home and field secretary" in 1913. Jessie Alexander Ropes, the new State President, announced in 1914 that the Hotel McAlpin in New York City would provide a room free of charge which would be suitable for small meetings. Traveling to New York, especially from the southern part of New Jersey, was anything but convenient. In 1917 the Robert Treat Hotel in Newark, New Jersey placed a room at the Federation's disposal. The work of the Federation was steadily increasing and the organization continued to grow.

In February, 1919 a room in the Y.W.C.A. Building, 53 Washington Street, Newark was obtained for $200 per year. Each member of the Board of Directors contributed $5 from her miniscule expense account to cover the first six months' rent and necessary equipment. The Y.W.C.A. Building became the Federation's "home" for the next 40 years. In 1927 a larger room in the building was secured and a permanent secretary was employed.

In 1959 Rutgers University, which had owned the Y.W.C.A. Building for a number of years and used its facilities for classrooms etc. for students at its Newark College Campus, found it necessary to politely, but firmly "evict" NJSFWC because they needed the space which the Federation occupied.

Rutgers suggested a vacancy in the nearby Griffith Building at 605 Broad Street, Newark. On inspection, it proved to be a four room suite appropriate and even more comfortable for the Federation's purposes. The new location required renovations and new furniture was obtained with $500 received as a National Award for 100 percent participation of clubs in the Community Achievement Contest (CAC). During the administration of Elizabeth B. Alton, every club in New Jersey had entered the contest!

The furnishings consisted of chairs, tables and office equipment carefully purchased with shopping skills inherent in the clubwomen.

With an Executive Secretary on the job to answer the telephone inquiries and respond to personal visits from club members, the Board of Directors had a meeting place which - for a time - was adequate for its needs. But the Federation was still a growing business and, with growth and expansion of interests, came ever-increasing details and additional "paperwork". The number of Board members grew constantly, and the quarters became increasingly cramped. Working together in a limited space promoted cameraderie.

By this time the automobile had come into its own, and many New Jersey clubwomen were accustomed to driving long distances. New Jersey highways were improving, but with more people taking to the road the traffic situation often left much to be desired. Parking space in Newark was uncertain and expensive — $1.25 per day. For active members of the Board of Directors, who had to attend many meetings at Headquarters, this could amount to many dollars annually just for parking! With more than fifty members on the Board of Directors, it was necessary to move the secretary's desk out of the Board Room and into one of the storage rooms when everyone attended a meeting — even then, late comers had to spill out into the corridor.

For many years, the clubwomen had suggested and discussed the idea of building a headquarters which would be more centrally located for the convenience of all members, and which would provide more adequate facilities for the operation of Federation affairs. A woman of purpose and courage, Levenia S. Taylor had decided that (should she ever be given the opportunity) she would do something about building a truly permanent Headquarters for NJSFWC. When Mrs. Taylor was installed as President on May 15, 1964 she announced in her acceptance speech at Convention that the primary project of her administration would be just that! She was given a standing ovation, a vote of confidence which lasted for several minutes.

Less than one month later, Lavenia Taylor appointed a Headquarters Committee headed by Mildred Hollenbeck and composed of a Past State President, two members of the State Executive Committee and six clubwomen from various parts of the state. The Committee met on June 9, 1964 to formulate plans for implementation of the new Headquarters Project. The Committee was assisted by the remaining members of the Executive Committee and the State Chairmen of the Evening Membership Department and the Junior Membership Department in ex-officio capacities.

Earlier in June Mrs. Taylor had discussed her dream with Elizabeth B. Alton, Past State President. Mrs. Alton advised that, if the building was to be completed during Mrs. Taylor's administration, work should begin on the project immediately. She was also able to offer expert advice on the cost of construction. Mrs. Taylor believed that a building could be constructed for about $40,000 since she had seen a clubhouse in southern New Jersey recently built for that amount of money. Mrs. Alton felt, that if the Federation built a Headquarters in the central part of the State, $40,000 wouldn't begin to cover the cost . And, she was right about that!

As a member of the Board of Governors for Rutgers University, Mrs. Alton had served on the Building and Grounds Committee. Rutgers was in the process of expanding its facilities, having benefited by millions of dollars from a higher education bond recently passed by the State of New Jersey. In her Building and Grounds Committee work, Mrs. Alton had been involved in interviewing and selecting architects and contractors, studying bids and handling problems related to construction for the University.

A knowledgeable member of the Rutgers Board of Governors in this field was Philip Levin, a building contractor, lawyer and entrepreneur. Mr. Levin agreed to meet with Mrs. Taylor and Mrs. Alton to discuss the Federation's plans for a Headquarters building. The meeting took place during a lunch break at the Board of Governors session and included Mrs. Hollenbeck and Miss Geraldine V. Brown. Mr. Levin brought with him an architectural drawing of a colonial style building which he had had an architect prepare without charge. It conformed in size and space to the specifications "Vinnie" Taylor had provided to Elizabeth Alton. The sad news was that a building of that type in the New Brunswick area would cost not less than $100,000. Undaunted by the mammoth question of financing such an expensive project, Mrs. Taylor proceeded to appoint her committee.

The Headquarters Committee brought to the Board of Directors three recommendations: (1) the establishment of a fund for a new Headquarters Building; (2) the proceeds from Strawbridge and Clothier Day for 1964 were to go to the Headquarters Fund and (3) the raising of funds through the saving and redeeming of trading stamps. These recommendations were approved, and Anita Nussbaum, who had suggested the trading stamp idea, was appointed chairman of the "Stamp of Approval" Project. The unique fund-raising idea of trading stamps was one which was painless and fun. It was accepted by the clubwomen throughout New Jersey without complaint or criticism. Each of the 44,000 members of NJSFWC was asked to contribute one filled book of trading stamps or give the equivalent of $2 in cash. S & H Green Stamps, Plaid Stamps, Merchants' Green and Triple S-Blue Trading Stamps were all acceptable. Arrangements had been made to redeem the filled stamp books for cash. By July 29, 1964 Mrs. Taylor had written to all Club Presidents in the state urging them to become active participants in this Stamp Project.

The Headquarters Committee appointed three teams to explore and investigate possible sites and/or possible existing buildings in the Trenton, Princeton, and New Brunswick areas. The teams were headed by Elizabeth Bittel, Mrs. William Buchanan and Elizabeth B. Alton. Mrs. Alton, who had been delegated to investigate the New Brunswick area, spoke to Dr. Mason Gross, President of Rutgers University, about the Federation plans. Dr. Gross had been a professor at Rutgers long before becoming President, and was familiar with the work of the Federation and its strong support for Douglass College which had been founded by NJSFWC. He had a deep respect and affection for the Federation which he exhibited by showing Mrs. Alton the two acres of land on which the current Headquarters Building now stands. At that time it was a slight hill, overlooking a wide open expanse of land. U.S. Route #1 was visible from the area as was the beginning of a mall-like construction of commercial property which Dr. Gross believed would expand to the Douglass College Campus borders. He saw the possible building for NJSFWC as a buffer between the two. Mrs. Alton was satisfied that Dr. Gross, at least, approved the presence of the Federation adjacent to Douglass College and she was well pleased with the land he suggested. The Headquarters Committee subsequently agreed that New Brunswick should be the site.

On July 13, 1964 the Board of Governors of Rutgers University authorized negotiation with NJSFWC for a long-term lease of land on the Douglass College Campus, subject to the Rutgers University Trustees' decision. The close connection of the Federation with Douglass College was, undoubtedly, instrumental in overcoming any resistance of the Board of Governors. Their question had been one of precedent, and they were concerned that approval given to the Federation could establish an embarrassing precedent should other organizations (desirable or undesirable) ask for or demand the same privilege. On October 15, 1964 the Rutgers University Board of Trustees gave its final approval for leasing the land to the Federation, and on December 11, 1964 the NJSFWC Board of Directors gave its official approval to build on this selected site.

The Headquarters Committee approved a modified colonial style of architecture to be constructed on Clifton Avenue near the intersection of Ryders Lane, New Brunswick. James S. Jones, AIA was engaged as the architect to draw a floor plan and pictured frontage of the proposed building at a cost of $300. It was agreed that, if sufficient funds were raised to go forward with the project, Mr. Jones would be employed to perform all architectural services for a fee not to exceed 7% of the total cost of the building. On January 8, 1965 the architect was asked to have preliminary floor plans ready for perusal on March 8.

On January 18, 1965 a brochure was sent to the Evening Membership and Junior Membership Departments urging their support of the Headquarters Project. On February 6, 1965 the Evening Membership Department voted to include the project in their 1965 - 1966 State Project plans. By February 24, 1965 nearly $17,000 had been collected through the Stamp Project and other means of raising funds through Memorials, Honors, and special Gifts from business and industrial firms were discussed.

A rally was held in Voorhees Chapel at Douglass College on March 8, 1965 to give Club Presidents and club Stamp Chairmen information on the Headquarters Project and to present future plans. Speakers included Raymond Jubnyik, who had been retained as legal council, Mrs. Alton, Mrs. Nussbaum, Dorothy T. Weinheimer and Geraldine V. Brown, members of the Headquarters Committee. Mrs. Taylor opened the meeting and Mrs. Hollenbeck presided as Headquarters Committee Chairman. This session was attended by more than 500 clubwomen. Attendees were able to view floor plans and drawings, and were given directions to find the site for an on-the-spot inspection.

On May 12, 1965 the delegates to the Annual Convention ratified the actions taken by the Board of Directors to build the Headquarters. The Headquarters Awards Luncheon was held on this date and certificates were presented to all clubs who had reach 100% of their quota — one book of trading stamps or the $2 equivalent from each member. It was announced that the Stamp Project would be continued by popular request through the 1965 Fall Conference. The Junior Membership Department voted at their 1965 Convention to include the Headquarters in their 1965 - 1966 projects.

On May 14, 1965 the lease was officially signed by President Taylor and the Recording Secretary, Mrs. James B. Roberson, as the officers designated in the Federation Bylaws. The lease was for 50 years with a renewal clause and an annual rental of $880. Rutgers University retained the Right of First Refusal to purchase the building should the Federation decide to leave New Brunswick in future years or to move elsewhere on the college campus. The architect, at this time, estimated that the cost of construction would be between $73,000 and $157,000. (Actual cost was nearly $145,000)

Over $53,000 had been received by July 1965 from Trading Stamps alone, and all seemed to be going extremely well. A bombshell was dropped in the form of a new Zoning Ordinance adopted by New Brunswick which effectively made building the Headquarters in that particular location impossible. The area had been zoned residential! By August 10, it was decided that a delegation should attend a meeting of the New Brunswick Board of Adjustment to plead the Federation's case. Mrs. Taylor, Mrs. Hollenbeck, and Miss Brown went to the meeting accompanied by Mrs. Alton who was a member of the Headquarters Committee and also a member of the Rutgers University Board of Governors. Mrs. Alton remembers this event well. She says, "We must have been a picture to the three men of that board! We were all dressed 'women's club style' with hats, gloves, and fancy purses — all in the latest fashion and surely quite different as a group from those who usually attend such meetings." Mrs. Alton's notes go on to tell us that she was reasonably certain that Dr. Gross had cleared the way for them before they arrived. The men of the New Brunswick Board of Adjustment were courteous, friendly and listened to the Federation's appeal as if they had not already made up their minds in favor of the project. She felt that they might really be enjoying the presence of the delegation since she caught an occasional chuckle or a quickly hidden grin. The permit to build was granted with little or no discussion by the Board of Adjustment.

By September 9, 1965 the architect had submitted building plans to nine contractors for bids. Six of the nine contractors returned the bids and all were higher than expected. The lowest bids were retained for further study.

On September 18, 1965 the NJSFWC Fall Conference was held in Voorhees Chapel, Douglass College. It was a very special day for GROUND BREAKING was held in an appropriate ceremony at the site of the proposed Headquarters. President Taylor lifted the first shovel of dirt. Special guests for the occasion were the former Governor Alfred E. Driscoll, best known to the Federation members as the son of Mrs. Alfred Robie Driscoll who was a Past State President; Dr. Mason Gross, President of Rutgers University and Dr. Ruth Adams, Dean of Douglass College. The Federation had not yet hired a contractor, but this Fall Conference was a perfect time to hold a Ground Breaking Ceremony.

On September 22, 1965 the Headquarters Committee met with the three lowest bidders. Melvin P. Windsor was selected as the contractor with a bid of $122,286. Completion of the Building was promised by June 1, 1966. Since it had been decided that construction would not begin until the Federation had at least $60,000 and that goal had been reached, construction began on October 8, 1965. Mrs. Alton's notes tell us that she felt "pretty good" about the selection of the contractor because she had asked many questions about the quality of construction and material. He had answered her with a smile and said that we should not worry since his wife was a member of a Woman's Club and she wanted it built right. Early in October General Electric (courtesy of a Mr. Wall) offered to install the kitchen appliances free of charge. This offer was quickly accepted, despite the fact that the Headquarters Committee did not then know that a prominent and influential member of Rutgers University Board of Governors was a top-ranking Vice President of General Electric. Elizabeth Alton felt that he recognized the publicity value in the Federation's use of GE appliances.

On November 29, 1965 the Headquarters Committee learned that Public Service Gas and Electric Company would install the gas free of charge, courtesy of the efforts of Frederick Holman, husband of a committee member.

The Stamp Project aiming for 100% participation by clubs was continued to April of 1966 and $2500 was received in Honors and Memorials. The Drama Department raised $1500 for the Public Address system. In a state of shock, the Federation learned that the cost of connecting the sewer system would be $10,000.

On December 10, 1965 the Board of Directors authorized the sale of bonds in the Endowment Fund investment portfolio with the proceeds to be transferred to the Headquarters Fund. The Board also authorized the transfer of $5,000 from the Girls Citizenship Institute Restricted

Funds. These financial maneuvers were necessary to keep the project moving steadily forward.

On January 12, 1966 the Headquarters Committee met at the site where the building was taking shape. The walls had been closed in and the tile roof was on. Decisions on important interior items were left to a subcommittee under the supervision of Mildred Hollenbeck. Dorothy B. McGlade was Subcommittee Chairman with Jan Denniston, Evening Membership Department Chairman, and Mrs. James D. Roberson, Recording Secretary, assisting her. Their responsibility was to select the wood paneling, floor tile and linoleum, lighting fixtures and other necessary items.

By February 28, 1966 rapid progress was being made in construction and plans were made with Richard Hale, contractor, to grade the ground, construct driveways and a parking lot to be finished by May 1, 1966. The parking lot was finished by April, 1966 and the very next day the Federation moved into the building. Peg White, Executive Secretary, and her volunteer assistants moved all of the accumulated records and equipment to the new building from Newark. A steel flagpole and a flag which had flown over the Nation's Capitol in Washington, D.C. were presented by a New Jersey Congressman. (Unfortunately, the name of the Congressman does not appear in the available records.)

The Headquarters Building, as it stands today, consists of 3735 square feet on the main floor with a partial basement. Entering the foyer from the Clifton Street entrance the main meeting room, measuring 83 by 45 feet, is on the right. This room can be divided by a folding partition when it is necessary to hold two meetings at the same time. The fully-equipped kitchen is adjacent to the meeting room with louvered doors which can be closed when sound shielding is necessary.

On the left of the foyer is the Secretaries' Office, behind which is a work room containing duplicating equipment and mailboxes for members of the State Board. The horizontal hall bisecting the building has entrances to the President's Office, the work room and two rest rooms — a larger one for women and a smaller one designated as the "Men's Room". Next to the President's Office, with entrances to it and to the hall, is a smaller room originally intended as a bedroom for the President in the event that she should be required to stay overnight at Headquarters. When this need did not arise, this room was converted to a small meeting room and, more recently, became the Federation Library. A small powder room also opens off of this room.

The vertical hall leading from the foyer to the rear door opening on the parking lot is equipped with storage cabinets for folding tables, chairs, and various larger food preparation articles. [The large wood-paneled assembly room seats 150 persons. Walls of the rooms are now painted in light colors and carpeting has replaced the original buff vinyl tile on most floor areas.]

The exterior of the building is colonial brick. The parking lot is paved in asphalt with parking for more than fifty cars and the grounds are beautifully planted with shrubs and seasonal flowers.

On May 1, 1966 at 2 p.m. the Headquarters Building was formally dedicated and the cornerstone laid with appropriate ceremonies conducted by Mrs. Taylor, Mrs. Hollenbeck and the Chairmen of the Junior and Evening Membership

Departments. Others who had worked diligently during the twenty-two months since the project was initiated also participated in the ceremonies. Over 300 people attended this Dedication and learned that $134,228.46 had been raised for the Headquarters Fund. The dream of nearly 45,000 clubwomen (to which Mrs. Taylor had given impetus) had become a reality. New Jersey State Federation of Women's Clubs had a permanent home especially designed and built to fit its needs!

Lavenia Taylor, Mildred Hollenbeck

Anita Nussbaum, Elizabeth Alton

A side note to the Dedication Ceremony comes from Mrs. Alton's memories. She served as Master of Ceremonies for this occasion which was also attended by Dr. Mason Gross of Rutgers University and Dean Ruth Adams of Douglass College. When Mrs. Alton arrived she was given an agenda for the event. The agenda listed Ruth P. Sanborn (Burrill) as the person who would open the occasion with a prayer. Ruth Sanborn gave an eloquent, beautiful prayer which called for blessings upon the new building, the Federation and its Officers. It was a superb invocation, given with all the dignity of her many years of public speaking experience. It was not until later that Mrs. Alton learned that, through an oversight, no one had asked Ruth to perform this function in the ceremony. As always, she had risen to the occasion beautifully. Later, she expressed her great shock at being called on quite "out of the blue"; however, no one could have known that she had not prepared her prayer long in advance. This is truly a testimony to Ruth's intellectual capacity and experience.

As women through the ages have known, building a new home is one thing but equipping it, moving into it and maintaining it is something else. The bulk of this task, as a new administration took office, fell to Geraldine V. Brown, the new State President and Dorothy McGlade, Southern Vice President and new Headquarters Chairman, and to Dorothea Kinney who was the newly-appointed Chairman of Building and Grounds. The settling in process included finalization of any unfinished construction tasks and costs. In 1966 it was necessary to withdraw $10,300 from Unrestricted Funds to complete payment to the contractors. Many conferences were held with contractors and workmen and careful shopping was done to obtain office furniture, equipment and chairs for the assembly room — all of which were high on the list of priorities. A Committee of Past State Presidents was appointed to select furnishings for the foyer, a task which they accomplished with dispatch and excellent taste. Additional outside lighting was installed to meet building code regulations.

Fall rains and winter snows brought unexpected problems (often related to new construction) which necessitated repair of leaks, loose floor and ceiling tiles, peeling paint, cracked plaster, warped doors and bent spouting. A cleaning service and maintenance of the heating and air conditioning systems was obtained, as was snow removal for the driveways and parking area. An underground sprinkling system was installed, draperies hung throughout the building, additional electrical work completed, wood paneling installed in the halls and offices for easier maintenance and many other minor repairs finalized. The landscaping of the grounds was a major project of the Conservation and Garden Department. Clubs contributed many plantings to memorialize outstanding clubwomen. The redemption of Trading Stamps was continued for landscaping work with the slogan being "Plant with Stamps".

Early in the game, it had been determined that a maintenance fund was of absolute importance so 400 clubs throughout the State sold 78,503 boxes of notepaper featuring scenes of New Jersey during 1966 - 1968. The project raised $6,380.24 to provide for the building upkeep. The individual clubs also profited from this project. The sale of 19,000 boxes of New Jersey pictorial placemats earned $3,800 for the Headquarters Maintenance Fund in 1968 - 1969.

In April 1967, the Trading Stamp Institute of America, Inc. presented the Federation with the first American Homemakers' Achievement Award for raising more than half the funds for the Federation Headquarters by the collection of Trading Stamps. "Gerry" Brown was honored at a dinner held at the Waldorf-Astoria Hotel in New York and presented with a citation and a passbook redeemable for 1,000,000 trading stamps as a gift from all of the trading stamp companies belonging to the Institute. Much nation-wide publicity resulted from this event and the Trading Stamp Institute received inquiries from other states interested in this method of building a federation headquarters in their areas. The stamp gift was used to purchase the Sarouk oriental rug in the foyer at Headquarters. Today the foyer is beautifully furnished and includes many cabinets housing gifts given in honor or memory of the many dedicated clubwomen who have served the Federation so valiantly over the years.

The Federation Headquarters has music in it. A beautiful piano was a gift resulting from a Music Department project in 1966 - 1967. More recently a television and VCR were added, and the Library became a reality, through generous contributions.

It is impossible to itemize here all of the many gifts given to Headquarters by clubs, districts, individuals, departments and business firms and the list grows daily. All contributions and gifts, including those given in honor or memory of clubs or individuals, are carefully recorded in appropriate books on display in the foyer.

The first club to hold a meeting at Headquarters was Sewaren History Club which met there on October 5, 1966. Since then many clubs have met and innumerable committees, departments, board meetings, workshops, conferences, Presidents' Councils, institutes and other activities have taken place at Headquarters. On May 1, 1991 a special celebration of the 25th Anniversary of the Headquarters Building, chaired by Cathy Southwick, had an overflow crowd in attendance.

Today, the building is in constant use and has proven to have been one of the Federation's wisest investments. "Home is where the heart is", and the clubwomen of New Jersey fully appreciate having a home for the heart of the Federation's operations. With current real estate values in the New Bruswick area, the NJSFWC Headquarters is worth more than $600,000. This is added proof that women in New Jersey are good investors. as well as good planners and managers.

Over the years from the cramped offices in Newark to the current building, many women have served as employed secretaries and executive secretaries for NJSFWC. Although they work for salaries well below the "current rate", they do a superlative job and their dedication is unsurpassed. They are listed below in tribute.

Executive Secretaries	Date
Carolyn B. Payson	1927-29
Alice S. Hall	1939-1946
J. Adele Puster	1946-1961
Peg White	1961-1967
Grace Emerson	Feb. 1967-June,1967
Olga Mackaronis	June, 1967 to Present

Secretaries	Date
Betty Rethy	1971 - 1978
Jane Smith	1978 - 1980
Carol J. Sas	1980 to present

FEDERATION OFFICE STAFF

Alice S. Hall

Peg White

Olga Mackaronis   *Carol Sas*

49

FEDERATION PUBLICATIONS

This volume is the sixth history to be published by NJSFWC. In 1917 Ada D. Fuller presented the first history when she was Historian of the State Ex Club. In 1927 Miss Fuller was named as Historian of the Federation and prepared an expanded history covering the years from 1894 to 1927. Helen E. Marsh, NJSFWC Historian 1945 - 1947 prepared the history covering the years from 1927 to 1947. The next volume was published in 1958 under the direction of Mrs. Frederick C. Wurtz, Historian from 1955 to 1958. This was a hard-bound volume of 127 pages which provided information on each State President's Administration from 1894 through 1958. Federation Milestones was published in soft cover in 1969 in conjunction with NJSFWC's Seventy Fifth Anniversary. This was formatted to provide information concerning the achievements of the Federation under specific categories related to its accomplishments. It was prepared by Grace Mathis Williams and a committee of six researchers.

Since 1897 the Federation has published a State Yearbook. The original Yearbooks provided clubs with lists of Officers and Committee chairmen. As the years rolled onward and the Federation grew in size, the State Yearbooks were expanded to provide additional information to the clubs. Current Yearbooks now run to nearly 400 pages which include not only information on Federation personnel, but NJSFWC Bylaws, Fall Conference and Convention minutes, reports of Officers and Chairmen, Outlines of Departments and Committees, Programs/Projects/Activities and extensive additional information important to the clubs. The State Yearbook is an essential tool industriously used by all clubs in New Jersey.

From the beginning a need was felt to communicate regularly with the clubs. The "Club Owl" appeared in 1900 and in October, 1916 the "New Jersey State Bulletin" was issued as a twenty-four page publication. This 8 1/2" by 11" news bulletin was available to all club members for twenty-five cents per year.

By October 1926 "The New Jersey Club Woman" magazine was born to be the carrier of New Jersey club news. This magazine was published in a 10" by 12" format, and the first editor was Mary S. Daniels. State President Edith Duff Gray Hubbard lent sufficient funds to the Federation to underwrite the first year's publication expense. With paid advertising and subscriptions at fifty cents per year the loan was repaid in eight months. The "New Jersey Club Woman" continued successfully with the Evening Membership Department adding a section called "Even'tide" in 1947. "Even'tide" had previously been a separate publication issued by the EMD since 1937. The Junior Membership Department started a newsletter of their own called "TeleJunior" in the early 1950's. It was combined with "The New Jersey Club Woman" for one year in 1958; however, the Juniors decided to return to a separate newsletter in 1959. It was later renamed Tel-A-Junior.

THE NEW JERSEY CLUB WOMAN

Volume 4
No. 3

December
1929

"The New Jersey Club Woman" went through many changes in size and appearance over the years of its existence, depending upon available funds. One of the cover designs which is most remembered was a picture of a woman seated in a chair reading a book and simultaneously rocking a cradle. This was symbolic of Federation founders, who gleaned information and education even while they attended to home duties.   Unfortunately, "The New Jersey Club Woman" disappeared from the Federation scene in 1988 due to a lack of funds to continue its publication.

In 1969 a newsletter called the "Anniversary Almanac" was issued as a supplement to "The New Jersey Club Woman". This provided an additional source of communication to clubs and has been continued as a monthly publication used as a vehicle by Officers and Chairmen to disseminate information to all clubs. It is now called "The Almanac".

During the 1930's several supplements were included in "The New Jersey Club Woman" magazine to publish original work of club members submitted to the Creative Writing Contests. In 1969 a paperbound book of such material was published under the title Diamond Harvest. In 1979, when the Federation observed its Eighty-Fifth Anniversary, clubs were asked to submit individual club histories. These were published in a soft-cover volume called From the Beginning — A Page of History.

Many other publications have been available to Federation clubs throughout the years. After the "Club Owl" and "The New Jersey State Bulletin" a "Newsletter" was published in 1922. The Legislation Department published the "Clip Sheet" to keep clubs informed of activities in the New Jersey Legislature. There was also a booklet called "Verses by New Jersey Clubwomen" published in 1929. In 1931 a handbook containing information on duties and privileges of Board Members was printed and distributed. It was revised four times. In 1951, the material was split into two booklets — one for elected Trustees and the other for Committee Chairmen. These were known as the "Buff and Blue" books. These manuals of information are constantly updated and provided to elected and appointed members of the Board of Directors. Wisely, the current format is "loose-leaf" so that additional material can be added easily.

The late Grace Schongar, when she was General Federation Parliamentarian and Parliamentary Consultant to the NJSFWC Board, published many books. One of these entitled Procedure, Policy and Protocol is still in use and made available to clubwomen. Other booklets of this nature, including "Protocol for Club and District Meetings", were prepared in 1956 -1958 for the use of clubs. In 1960 - 1962 basic information to be used at District Conferences was compiled. In March 1961 the Federation Policies from 1894 to date were reviewed and revised. Other printed material includes Federation Song Sheets, Handbooks on Parliamentary Procedure, Program Listings, and a wide variety of informative items provided to build leadership and participation. Beginning in the 1950's the Juniors combined their Department and Committee outlines into a folder called EUREKA which is provided to the Junior Club Presidents.

Since 1965 NJSFWC has published appointment calendars or "Date Books" of a size convenient for carrying in a pocket or purse. Preprinted with Federation Event Dates spanning a two year administration, this handy item makes it possible for busy clubwomen to appropriately schedule their active lives. For the 1993 Convention a catalogue of items available for purchase at Headquarters was distributed.

The written word has always been important to NJSFWC whose members are proud of its publication record. Although some of the older documents are now "collector's items", copies of them are in the Federation archives housed in the Library at Headquarters.

INSIGNIA — SIGNS AND SYMBOLS

Members of NJSFWC should never suffer the trauma of an Identity Crisis. At the first meeting of the Board of Directors on December 4, 1894 it was decided that a badge should be made available to the clubwomen of the Federation. Mrs. Brooks of the Monday Afternoon Club of Passiac suggested a design based on the New Jersey State Coat of Arms. By February, 1895 an emblem had been adopted. On a shield-shaped background of light blue enamel was placed a plow and a rising sun, with the words "Unity" and the letters NJSF. These little blue badges were owned by a large number of the clubwomen and this was the official pin of the Federation until 1914. At that time a new pin was made from the same design but in the two shades chosen by the Federation as its official colors — Continental Buff and Blue. At the first Annual Meeting in October, 1895 attendees sported ribbon badges in buff with New Jersey emblazoned in blue. After much discussion and consideration of many flowers, the Lily of the Valley was chosen as the Federation flower in 1895. To this day, bowls of this fragrant flower grace the head table at many Federation events.

During the 1917-1920 Administration it was decided that the NJSFWC State President should wear a distinguishing pin while she was in office. This was a gift from the NJSFWC State Ex Club who also, in 1926, designed a Past State President's Pin to be worn after the President completed her term of office. State Ex Club presented the former Past State Presidents with these pins at that time. This type of pin was presented to all Past State Presidents until 1958, and Ruth Sanborn Burrill is still proudly wearing hers. It is thought that something must have happened to the die for the 1926 Past State President's Pin since a GFWC emblem surrounded by appropriate embellishment to distinguish it as NJSFWC was used until 1992. At that time Anita Rosen designed a new Past State President's Pin specifically for NJSFWC. The die for this current pin was also presented by the State Ex Club.

*State
President's Pin*

In 1928 an oval-shaped pin was made available for women who had served as Presidents of the individual clubs. Gold bars are available for attachment if she serves as President of her club more than once, or if she serves as President of another club. In 1959 a square pin was designed for use by club Presidents while they are in office. This pin is purchased by clubs and passed on to successive presidents. Similar pins for current and former presiding officers of Junior Clubs and Evening Membership Departments were also designed in this era. Special gavel guards are available for attachment to pins worn by women who founded their clubs. It is evident that New Jersey clubwomen enjoy this meaningful jewelry since they proudly wear membership pins, Federation charms on bracelets and — if eligible — a charm which indicates that their name has been place on the Federation Honor Roll. A unique diamond-shaped pin is available to members of the State Ex Club and proudly worn as a symbol of having served NJSFWC as a member of the Board of Directors. There are pins for members of the Federation State Board, the Junior State Board, District Vice Presidents, District Chairmen and Vice Chairmen within the Federation's structure. The EMD State Board members wear a charm denoting their status. Women who have been members of the Federation for twenty-five years have a sterling silver pin available to them and fifty year members may have a gold pin.

Club President's Pin

Club Past President's Pin

In the 1970's pins, lapel buttons and charms became popular in connection with Special State Projects and awards for bringing new members into clubs. These ranged from gold teddy bear stick pins and enamel pins in the shape of the State of New Jersey to angels and bunny rabbits. Active club women acquire many pins and often wear them on a ribbon banner with as much pride as military personnel wear their ribbons and battle stars.

There are other symbols dear to the hearts of federated clubwomen. In 1918 the Newark Retail Merchants presented a banner of buff and blue when the Federation held a Convention in their city. At the 1922 Convention the Woman's Club of Montclair presented a silken banner, and in

1936 the Junior Membership Department supplied a new Federation flag to replace the worn one which had been flown from the Convention hotel's flagstaff each year. In 1968 a new banner was presented by the Oradell Book and Needle Club in honor of Annette Brickmann. In 1993 the Past Presidents' Club of Fourth District presented a new banner with gold lettering on a dark blue background. It was made by Doris Psak and Dorothy Berrien to hang at Headquarters. The NJSFWC Centennial emblem, designed by Anita Rosen, has been used for a pin, currently being worn by many clubwomen. The Centennial symbol has been embroidered on a tablecloth used at Headquarters. The symbol is also being used on the cover of the State Yearbook and is imprinted on a white satin lectern cover with the Centennial emblem embossed in dark blue.

Eileen Becker, 11th District VP, and Evelyn Barton, 11th District Centennial Chairman, presented a centennial flag from all the clubs in the District on January 6, 1994. This gift given at the Centennial Premier Event will be flown over Headquarters for the 1994 Centennial Year.

The first official gavel was presented to the Federation by Margaret Yardley, the first NJSFWC President. It was lost during the second night of the 1917 Convention and replaced at the Silver Anniversary Convention in 1919 with a gavel of interesting construction. This gavel was made by Bayonne High School students and featured a head made of wood from the famous "Salem Oak" which was then hundreds of years old with the handle of wood from the Trenton Barracks of Revolutionary War fame. It was banded in silver in recognition of the 25th Anniversary. Records also state that in 1906-1909 another gavel was presented to the State President. This was fashioned from a Hickory Tree grown on the grounds of Andrew Jackson's Nashville, Tennessee home. Later the East Brunswick Woman's Club gave the Federation a gavel made from the wood of the tree under which Joyce Kilmer allegedly composed the poem "Trees".

All organizations experience sad occasions and the Federation is no exception. In 1993 a "grieving flower" in purple and black was made by Marie Drake and Rose Schmitt to be hung on the door of Headquarters mourning the death of a Past State President, Junior Director or EMD State Chairman. It was first used in May, 1993 when Laura Teachman, EMD Chairman 1968-1970, died.

Mrs. Drake and Mrs. Schmitt also designed and made banners for each of the eleven Districts which were carried by Presidents from the Districts in the 1993 opening banquet processional at the Annual Convention. The banners were a gift from Marie Drake, Headquarters' Chairman 1992 - 1994 and were placed in the care of DVPs at the close of the 1993 Convention.

All of the emblems are of historical and current importance to the clubwomen of New Jersey. They denote "a glorious past and a brilliant future".

IN THEIR HONOR

During the first seventeen years of NJSFWC's existence women serving as Officers and in other state-wide leadership positions were expected to defray expenses incurred in the organization's operation. This created an increasing financial burden for which a solution was sought. On October 22, 1910 at a semi-annual meeting in Westfield the Endowment Fund was authorized for this purpose. Letters were sent to clubs in May 1911 to solicit support. When the first report was given on December 15, 1911 stating that $1,200 had been received, it was referred to as the "Department of Prosperity". Trustees were appointed to administer the funds and the Endowment Fund was incorporated on March 18, 1912.

On May 2, 1913 the retiring President, Catherine C. Warren, suggested that a Founders' List be established to encourage contributions to the Endowment Fund. On May 8, 1914 the first Founders' Book was presented to the Federation by the State President, Jessie Alexander Ropes. This volume bound in navy blue was dedicated to the Federation's first State President, Margaret Yardley. Clubs were invited to contribute money for pages in the book on which the names and deeds of the women to be honored or memorialized would be inscribed. The first volume was filled in a few years and a second book was presented by the State Ex Club.

The Endowment Fund contained $25,000 by 1930 and had grown to nearly $60,000 by 1956. In May, 1956 the Endowment Fund was closed, and the idea of paying special tribute to those "who have been of special service to clubs, community or Federation" was continued as the Federation Honor Roll. The Founders' Books became known as the Honor Roll Books and a page may be dedicated for a $50 contribution.

Several years ago Memorial Books were created that contain tributes to deceased clubwomen. The Honors Books and Memorial Books are on display at Federation Headquarters and at the Annual Convention. Each honoree receives a certificate that has been inscribed in calligraphy. Honor Roll tributes are read at the Annual Conventions and often come as a complete surprise to the recipients. By 1972 more than one thousand women had been honored in this way and the number continues to grow each year. Being placed on the Federation's Honor Roll is a supreme accolade to be accorded to a New Jersey clubwoman who has provided outstanding volunteer services.

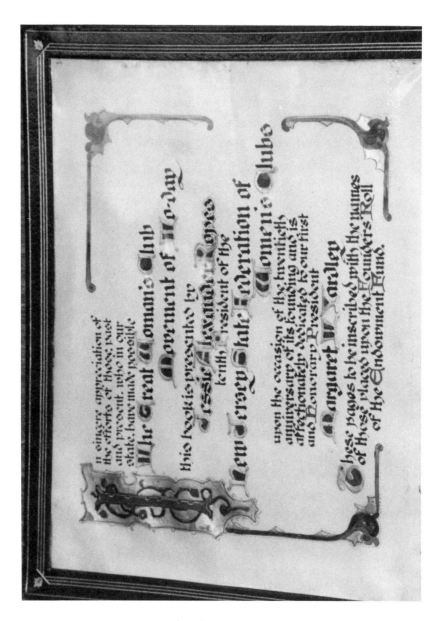

A page from the Honors Book

STATE PRESIDENTS

NEW JERSEY STATE FEDERATION·

OF WOMEN'S CLUBS

*1894-96	Margaret Tufts Yardley (Mrs. Charles B.)
*1896-98	Cecilia Gaines Holland (Mrs. John A.)
*1898-00	Emily E. Williamson (Mrs. Benjamin)
*1900-02	Johanna Hartshorn (Mrs. Stewart)
*1902-04	Mary McKeen (Miss)
*1904-06	Emma W. Newbury (Mrs. Andrew J.)
*1906-09	Ida W. Dawson (Mrs. Henry H.)
*1909-11	Mary Pattison (Mrs. Frank A.)
*1911-13	Catherine C. Warren (Mrs. Howard C.)
*1913-15	Jessie Alexander Ropes (Mrs. William T.)
*1915-17	Lillian J. Stockton (Mrs. Charles W.)
*1917-20	Agnes A. Schermerhorn (Mrs. John R.)
*1920-23	Sara S. Proal (Mrs. Arthur B.)
*1923-26	Etta Gould Lee (Mrs. Clayton D.)
*1926-29	Edith Duff Gray Hubbard (Mrs. L. V.)
*1929-32	L. Ethel Heine (Mrs. M. Casewell)
*1932-35	Adele J. Grimley (Mrs. Thomas H.)
*1935-38	Mattie Eastlack Driscoll (Mrs. Alfred Robie)
*1938-41	Helen Purdy Adams (Mrs. Patrick Henry)
*1941-44	Elizabeth Middleton Maddock (Mrs. Charles S.,Jr.)
*1944-47	Louie C. Francisco (Mrs. Stephen J.)

*1947-50   Alice L. Cornelison (Mrs. Robert W.)

*1950-53   Marion S. Spain (Mrs. Batt L.)

*1953-56   Grace Y. Christian (Mrs. Wilson Y.)

1956-58   Ruth P. Sanborn Burrill (Mrs. Charles M.)

1958-60   Elizabeth B. Alton (Mrs. John M.)

*1960-62   Lucille M. Dangremond (Mrs. Harley L.)

*1962-64   Margaret D. Wagner (Mrs. Douglas G.)

*1964-66   Lavenia S. Taylor (Mrs. S. Herbert)

1966-68   Geraldine Brown Sentell (Mrs. Douglas P.)

1968-70   Dorothy B. McGlade (Mrs. Thomas H.)

1970-72   Dorothy T. Weinheimer (Mrs. George F., Jr.)

1972-74   Mary R. Bixby (Mrs. Donald T.)

*1974-76   Marjory Bonynge Fielding
                (Mrs. Robert Winton)

1976-78   Virginia E. Zanetich (Mrs. Anthony T.)

1978-80   Marijane Singer (Mrs. Frederick D.)

1980-82   Emily Strakosch (Mrs. George T.)

1982-84   Gloria Malasky (Mrs. Lee J.)

1984-86   Dorothy M. Constants (Mrs. Alfred C., Jr.)

1986-88   Betty P. Loizeaux (Mrs. Jerry B.)

1988-90   Shirley G. Goettel (Mrs. Edward C.)

1990-92   Marion Graham Arnao (Mrs. Edward C.)

1992-94   Joan M. Hunt (Mrs. John A.)

Past State Presidents' Pins

Margaret Tufts Yardley
(Mrs. Charles B. Yardley)
1894 to 1896

On May 14, 1844, while living in Auburn, New York, Dr. Samuel Swan and his wife Lucretia Green Swan (nee Staniels) celebrated the birth of a daughter, Margaret Tufts. At the moment of her birth, there was no way that her parents could have realized the effect that their new daughter would have on the future of women in the world, and particularly women in New Jersey.

The Swan family moved to Montgomery, Alabama when Margaret was a year old. After passing the governess period, she attended private schools in New York and Philadelphia.

Unfortunately, many details concerning Margaret's early life are elusive; however, it is known that she lived in Wilmington, Delaware during the Civil War and cared for the wounded there. The Swans returned to New York where in June, 1866 she married Charles Burleigh Yardley. They lived in Yonkers, New York where she became a member of Sorosis of New York City in 1871. When they moved to East Orange, New Jersey in 1876, she joined the Woman's Club of Orange . This was the oldest Woman's Club in New Jersey, and the fourth oldest in the United States. Margaret Yardley served as Vice President of the Club, and later became President.

Active in community life, Mrs. Yardley served on the Board of Managers of the Columbian Exposition in Chicago, Illinois in 1893. A collection of her writings about New Jersey women was exhibited. She received a medal for her efforts. Locally, she served as Director and President of the Orange Orphans Society, helped start the first Homeopathic Hospital of the Oranges, championed the improvements of New Jersey's child labor laws and remained active in political work in East Orange until she was over 80 years of age.

Mrs. Yardley also founded the Essex Chapter of the Daughters of the American Revolution (DAR) and briefly served as a Regent of the National DAR. She was also a member of Nova Caesarea Chapter of the DAR and, as the great-granddaughter of Major Samuel Swan of the Continental Army, a member of the Colonial Dames of America. Margaret Yardley was a charter member of the Charlotte Emerson Brown Club founded in 1895. She later was made an honorary member.

As one of the founders of the New Jersey State Federation of Women's Clubs (NJSFWC) Margaret Yardley with Sarah M. Johnson, President of the Woman's Club of Orange, issued a "Call" to other women's clubs in New Jersey. One hundred and fifty women from the entire state responded to the invitation and met in Union Hall, Orange, New Jersey on November 16, 1894. One of the speakers, Florence Howe Hall, advocated the formation of the state society or federation as a means of bringing women together for interchange of ideas and methods, and for the cultivation of fellowship.

Before the meeting adjourned that day a Constitution and Bylaws had been written and adopted and officers had been elected. The New Jersey State Federation of Women's Clubs object or purpose as stated in the Constitution was "to bring the women's clubs of the State into communication for acquaintance and mutual helpfulness." Mrs. Yardley was elected as the first President of NJSFWC.

Five Vice Presidents were elected, including the Reverend Antoinette Brown Blackwell who had the distinction of being the first woman ordained as a minister in the United States. Others were Miss Cecilia Gaines, Mrs. Edward Horton, Mrs. Horace Kimball and Mrs. Benjamin McGrew. The committee which formulated the Constitution and Bylaws included Charlotte Emerson Brown, Mrs. Hall, Mrs. E. P. Denniston, Mrs. McGrew and Mrs. H. A. Glass.

Original Shield

The Board of Directors, consisting of the Officers and nine elected representatives from the Clubs, met on December 4, 1894 at Mrs. Yardley's home. A badge designed after the State Coat of Arms was submitted for consideration by Mrs. Brooks of the Monday Afternoon Club of Passaic. A shield with a plow, a rising sun, the word unity and the letters NJSF done on a pale blue enamel was accepted at the next meeting in February, 1895. This badge or pin was not to exceed sixty cents ($.60) in cost.

The February meeting had been saddened by an announcement of the death, on February 4, 1895, of Charlotte Emerson Brown of Orange, the first President of the General Federation of Women's Clubs. A memorial service was held on March 19, 1895 in Trinity Church in East Orange.

Subsequent meetings of the Board of Directors authorized opening a bank account at the First National Bank of Elizabeth and a recorded balance of $25.45 was deposited. Incorporation was discussed and papers drawn. One hundred certificates of membership were printed to give to each new club upon admission to membership in the Federation. At that time dues were $2 per club plus $1 for each delegate to be sent to an annual meeting which was under consideration. A chairman was appointed to arrange for publicity through the news media.

The lily of the valley was decided upon as the Federation flower when it received more votes from the clubs than the other suggested flowers. Buff and blue were chosen for Federation colors, and a badge was designed for use at the first annual meeting held in Newark on October 24 and 25, 1895. The continental colors were used—a buff ribbon with New Jersey printed in blue. This meeting was attended by one hundred seventy five women who heard ten minute reports by thirteen chairmen of various committees. With a special ceremony, the Charter certificates were presented to The Charter Clubs. Papers were presented on health, forestry, and traveling libraries, and the Treasurer reported a balance of $21.97. At this point the President ordered that the bills for dues be sent to the clubs.

Organization work gave way to civic action projects. Clubs were joining in satisfactory numbers, and Mrs. Yardley had an urge to demonstrate women's organized strength to the New Jersey Legislature. She called for a public gathering of clubs in Trenton on March 20, 1896. Three hundred women listened to papers on New Jersey's forests and the beautiful Palisades which were threatened with distruction by commercial enterprise. A plea was directed to the Governor to appoint a commission to create state traveling libraries like the type that had originated in Scotland in 1810. Health Culture, Household Economics and "Women's Place Today" were subjects of other papers presented at this meeting that was called Literary Day. The guests included the Vice President of The General Federation of Women's Clubs and the State Federation Presidents of Maine, New Hampshire and New York as well as the President of Sorosis. Each guest discussed "the Scope of the State Federation".

The second annual meeting (now called a Convention) was held in Jersey City on October 29-30, 1896. The speaker's topic was "What the Legislature of 1896 has done for women". Important business at this gathering was the election of new officers. As her administration closed, Margaret Yardley was named Honorary President. Margaret Yardley's influence and interest in NJSFWC continued long after her presidency. As the "Federation Mother", her pleasant smile, her fine bearing, her skill in argument and her wide, human sympathies made her a conspicuous success. She firmly believed in the use of the clubs to correct many existing evils and she thought that all women of intelligence should recognize the obligation resting upon them to help their less fortunate sisters. She continued to be known as a philanthropist and a civic leader who was one of the most energetic and aggressive women in the country. On June 4th, 1927 the New Jersey College for Women (now Douglass College) honored Margaret Yardley with a Master of

Philanthropy degree. The citation read in part "pioneer leader in the first women's club in the eastern United States... one of the first to discern the potential contribution of women in civic life... and one of the wisest in using women's influence for public good."

Margaret Yardley died on September 3, 1928 at the age of 84 while staying at her summer home at Burkehaven, Lake Sunapee, New Hampshire. Although not entirely recovered from pneumonia in the spring, she was in fair health and her death was unexpected. She was buried in Greenwood Cemetery in Brooklyn, New York.

In 1929, at the State Convention of the NJSFWC in Atlantic City, the Margaret Yardley Fellowship Fund was established to provide a fellowship for a qualified woman to do graduate work in her field. The first contribution to the fund, in the amount of $5,000, was given by her son Farnham Yardley in his mother's memory. Along with all of her other accomplishments, Margaret Tufts Yardley also raised five children.

Cecilia Gaines
(Mrs. John A. Holland)
1896 to 1898

Born January 12, 1861 in Jersey City, Miss Cecilia Gaines of the Odd Volumes Club of Jersey City was an attractive and vigorous young woman when she became the second NJSFWC President. Shortly after finishing her term of office she became the bride of Dr. John Arnold Holland. The Vice Presidents for this administration were Isabel Craven, Florence H. Hall, Madge McClary, and Adeline Sterling.

With the Federation's formative years now becoming part of history, there were several committees firmly established. These included Town Improvement, Kindergarten, Traveling Libraries, Education and Reciprocity. The Reciprocity Committee was formed to provide an exchange program service with the Chairman having on file copies of papers and lectures to be loaned to clubs.

From the beginning, the clubwomen realized that achievement of their ambitions would require aid and support from the officials in the state government. The

Federation began to appeal to the Governor asking that a Commission be appointed to draft legislation establishing Traveling Libraries. Legislation was also sought to include Kindergartens in the public school system. It was not until 1898 that a Bill was introduced in the State Legislature to establish Kindergartens, if requested by parents.

By now, clubwomen were accustomed to prolonged discussions and numerous delays when dealing with the Legislature. A sub-committee was formed under the Forestry Committee which sought to revive the interest of government in preventing the threatened destruction of the Palisades. In 1895 the New York and New Jersey Legislatures had appointed a Commission to solve the problem by attempting to establish a military park for government purposes, but this effort was dropped. A chairman was authorized to take preliminary steps toward founding, outside of the Federation, a League for the Preservation of the Palisades.

While waiting for governmental action on Traveling Libraries, clubs began to sponsor and support libaries in their own communities.

Although some women were serving on school boards in New Jersey at this time, the Resolution permitting women to vote for members of school boards was rejected. Meanwhile, clubwomen continued to discuss the needs of schools, and they became very vocal on this subject.

A further Resolution designed to improve conditions on New Jersey's race tracks was approved.

Requests were received to help furnish the New Jersey Room at Mt. Vernon and for cooperation with the Woman's

Health Protective Association. Request for aid sought by the George Washington Memorial Association in establishing a "well endowed University in the City of Washington" was endorsed.

The next Annual Meeting of NJSFWC in 1897 was held in Camden, and the following Annual Meeting was held in Elizabeth in 1898. At the 1898 meeting there was an audience of 600 women who heard Julia Ward Howe deliver the invocation. In the invitation to this meeting, President Gaines stressed that the subject would be sociology "from the practical economic, philanthropic, ethical, physical and aesthetic standpoint." She also said that "life is but a unit; society but one body, and as long as misery or disease exists anywhere the whole can not be healthy. This revelation of the solidarity of humanity is the great lesson of our age."

In 1897 a State Year Book which contained lists of officers, directors, member clubs and reports of committees was published for the first time. This annual publication has since become known as the "Federation Bible" to clubwomen throughout the state.

The New York Journal had announced that it was the official organ of The General Federation of Women's Clubs. The New Jersey Directors protested to both the General Federation and the Journal because it was considered a "sensational publication". A Resolution was adopted which refused the use of the New York Journal or any other newspaper or magazine as an official organ.

During this administration 16 new clubs had joined the Federation, making it 74 clubs strong with 2500 members. The Federation was now united in an ambitious program —

much of which depended on actions of the Legislature. The determination to succeed was much more impressive than the balance in the treasury, which was $31.85 at the close of Miss Gaines' administration.

Cecilia Gaines Holland who died in 1944 bequeathed the sum of $1,000 to be invested by the Board of Directors . The income from the investment was to be given annually (either in the form of cash or as a medal) to a clubwoman doing outstanding civic work in New Jersey. This award is still given annually at the NJSFWC Convention.

The following is an excerpt from an article appearing in the November 1, 1900 issue of "The Home Journal". ..."Miss Cecilia Gaines, of Jersey City, who is now Mrs. John Arnold Holland of Cold Springs, New York, has infused the Federation with some of her own radiant personality. She has the good fortune to be one of the positive blonds whom Dr. Holmes immoralitized, and has moreover, a keen sense of humor. While in power her bright speeches were often quoted in editorial paragraphs of the New York papers. She has been a potent factor in developing the dormant literary aspirations of Jersey City. Her pet club is the unique "Odd Volumes" of which she is now president for the tenth time. Just now her influence is mainly directed toward the preservation of the Palisades, as she is one of the Palisades and Forestry Committee, recently appointed by the state. Mrs. Holland is said to be the best loved clubwoman in New Jersey."

Emily E. Williamson
(Mrs. Benjamin Williamson)
1898 to 1900

Born Emily Hornblower in England in 1869, this third NJSFWC President was educated by tutors and through extensive personal reading. After coming to the United States, she married Benjamin Williamson, a lawyer, and lived in his family mansion in Old Elizabeth, New Jersey. The couple had no children, and Mr. Williamson died on March 12, 1900.

Long before becoming president of NJSFWC Emily E. Williamson was active in charitable work with many of her efforts concentrated on improving the lot of women and children. She founded and was Secretary of the State Charities Aid Association (SCAA). In 1888, she became the Secretary of the Home for the Care and Training of Feeble-minded Women at Vineland which is now know as Vineland Development Center. She visited alms houses throughout New Jersey, observing the poor quality of care provided. Determined to save children housed in these facilities, she went before the State Assembly to speak on their behalf—

something which few, if any, women had done in the past. As a result of her efforts, the State Board of Children's Guardians was created in 1899, a forerunner of agencies for child welfare established at later dates. With some modification, the system of foster homes in use today was a direct result of her efforts.

Mrs. Williamson was interested in correctional institutions and President Theodore Roosevelt named her a delegate to the International Prison Association which met in Budapest in 1904. She was a founder of the probation system in New Jersey, and lobbied constantly for laws to establish probation. It was largely because of her efforts that Rahway State Prison was founded. She is pictured to have been a beautiful woman. Her verbal skills were well known, and she was described as a fluent and inspiring speaker.

Mrs. Williamson was a member of the Woman's Civic Federation of Elizabeth when she became State President. Serving with her as Vice Presidents were Miss Elizabeth B. Vermilye, Mrs. Edward B. Horton, Mrs. Frank J. Taylor, and Mrs. Francis W. Kitchel.

By 1899 the Federation reported a membership of 6,000. The reorganization of the General Federation patterned after the Massachusetts plan was endorsed, and on April 4, 1900 the bill providing for the preservation of the Palisades was finally passed in the New Jersey Legislature. New Jersey clubwomen received acclaim (not only at home but over the entire country) for their perseverance and patience which contributed to this successful conclusion of one of their initial projects. The culmination of "saving the Palisades" had resulted from earlier activities when the New York Legislature appointed a Commission and joined New Jersey in its work. The Palisades League had been formed and funds raised to provide a suitable memorial to be placed in the area. Clubs had donated $1500 and the League matched this amount.

NJSFWC had formed a Department of Education. More than half of the towns having Women's Clubs now had kindergartens. The Federation supported a bill introduced into the Legislature to establish kindergartens in the public schools when requested by parents.

The State Mosquito Extermination Commission seeking to eradicate or control New Jersey's famous pest received the support of the Federation.

A protest was registered against B. H. Roberts, a Utah polygamist who served in Congress. A Resolution was adopted to outlaw polygamy. "Family Values" was always a concern of the Federation.

The long sought legislation to provide funds for Traveling Libraries was passed in 1899. Many books were given by the clubs and the first boxes of books were purchased with state money. The State Librarian asked the Federation to prepare a list of suggested books, about 50 percent of which were fiction. In February 1900 the Board of Directors donated a library to be circulated under the name of NJSFWC.

The Board members were continuing to personally finance their Federation activities. Clubs donated $143 to send the President to the General Federation Convention in Denver.

The amount of club news printed in newspapers was not sufficient to properly publicize the activities of NJSFWC; therefore, a small bulletin called the "Club Owl" was printed and adopted as the official publication.

Semi-annual and annual meetings continued to be held in the spring and fall. Margaret Sanger, early advocate of family planning, gave the innovation at one of these meetings, and 250 State Year Books were printed for the October 1900 meeting. The interest in the Year Books was disappointing, and the President urged the delegates to promote their use in clubs as guides in planning. She also emphasized the steady growth of the Federation and the need for additional income.

In March 1899, the New Jersey Society of the Daughters of the American Revolution (DAR) joined the Federation as a State Organization.

The subject of household economics was still important to the clubwomen and led to the observation that "if a boy needs a commercial high school, a girl needs a domestic high school". The Federation agreed to work for the inclusion of Domestic Science in the public school curriculum.

Emily Williamson, who was also a member of Sorosis, was well known as an author of magazine articles throughout her lifetime. As she concluded her administration she held a dinner in her home for 500 NJSFWC members. She died of apoplexy, at age 60, on September 13, 1909 at her home in Elizabeth. She was buried in the Evergreen Cemetery in Elizabeth, and her obituary appeared in the New York Times.

Johanna Hartshorn
(Mrs. Stewart Hartshorn)
1900 to 1902

At the turn of the Century, Johanna Randall Hartshorn of the Short Hills Reading Club assumed leadership of the Federation as its fourth President. Increased activity necessitated additional personnel from all parts of the state which increased the size of the Board of Directors. It was no longer feasible to hold meetings of the Board in the homes of members, and the quantity of papers and records which had been carried from meeting to meeting and passed from one officer to another had grown tremendously. A central location to serve as an office, meeting place and site for storage of Federation property was desperately needed. A suitable place was found at 885 Broad Street in Newark. At that time, this was considered a central location which could be reached by the Board members regardless of the mode of transportation used.

The times were changing. An entirely new trend was developing when women, whose work for the most part had been teaching, nursing or home-making, were entering industry in positions formerly occupied solely by men. The

79

question most debated in the early months of the new Century was how to protect such women workers. The Federation was active in seeking legislation to require employers of factory help to appoint female inspectors wherever women were a part of the work force. It was felt that only such inspectors could have a sympathetic approach to the working women. Most of the clubwomen of this era had some form of domestic help in the home. They recognized that they had a responsibility for the welfare of these employees.

Other fields of concern and study were the Mother's Congress, the Consumers League and Juvenile Delinquency. The national movement for a juvenile court was endorsed to eliminate the prevailing custom of placing young offenders beside adult criminals in the same court room. Already on record as opposing polygamy, a committee was appointed to investigate the proposed Constitutional Amendment outlawing plural marriages.

During 1900 and 1901 sixty-two Traveling Libraries had been assembled by the State of New Jersey and were available to any community by application. At that point only five libraries had been circulated. It was believed that insufficient publicity, unfamiliarity with the procedure on acquiring a library and lack of interest may have accounted for this fact. This result was a disappointment to the Federation after its strenuous effort to secure the legislation which established the libraries. The clubwomen were not easily discouraged and began in earnest to promote library use. Nearly every club meeting devoted some time to discussing ways to arouse enthusiasm. At Federation meetings exhibits concerning the State System of Traveling Libraries were brought by a State Library official who explained the simple method required for obtaining a library.

At the seventh Annual Meeting of the Federation in 1901 a motion to tax each Federation member five cents ($.05) to pay the expenses of the State President to the General Federation Convention was vigorously opposed. Voluntary contributions provided the necessary funds.

Revised Bylaws were adopted at this meeting. The Revision had been authorized primarily because the growing organization required additional income. The annual dues for clubs with 50 members or less were raised to $3.00; $4.00 for clubs with 50 to 100 members and for larger clubs an additional dollar for each 100 members. Representation at the Annual Meetings had been limited only by the payment of $1.00 for each delegate the club desired to send. The new Bylaws specified that clubs with 50 or less members were entitled to two delegates; 50 to 100 members, three delegates; one delegate for each 100 members thereafter.

Johanna Hartshorn, who had been born in the back woods of Nova Scotia, was noted for her love of nature. She advocated vacation school, home and school gardens and devoted much of her time to the study of birds. She was considered an authority on ornithology, and at the Spring Meeting in 1902, she presented a report of the Audubon Society.

The 1902 Annual Meeting was held for two days in Jersey City. One thousand programs were printed for this eighth Annual Meeting with papers and speeches devoted to the topic of securing A State Reformatory for Women which would provide intellectual and physical training. William R. George was a guest speaker. He delivered an address on Juvenile Delinquency. Pamphlets containing the revised Bylaws were distributed to the delegates.

Mrs. Hartshorn and the four vice presidents: Miss Mary McKeen, Mrs. W. H. Houghton, Mrs. Richard Gnade and Mrs. John L. Scudder had successfully completed their terms of office.

Early in the following administration it was determined that the "Office" was no longer large enough for permanent storage of the vast quantities of material accumulated in the first eight years of the Federation's life. It was decided to evaluate and discard material of no further use. The papers which were retained were placed in Mrs. Hartshorn's care. Undoubtedly, much of this data (if available now) would provide deeper insight into the daily lives of the earliest clubwomen.

Mary McKeen (Miss)
1902 to 1904

Mary McKeen, from the Woman's Club of Camden, was the first President elected from a club in the southern part of New Jersey. She had served as a Vice President for two years prior to her election, and had rendered distinctive service as Forestry Chairman. With this background she was well acquainted with the aims and purposes of the Federation, and she realized that it was more permanent in character while growing in strength and scope. The Vice Presidents were Emma W. Newbury, Mrs. Allen B. Endicott, Miss Ann Tichenor and Miss Ella Mecum.

From the original 35 Charter Clubs the Federation had grown to 100 clubs, and new membership certificates were printed. Associated organizations, with no privilege to vote, were accepted into the body. The State Nurses' Association joined in 1903. Attention was focused on providing more extensive communication and information to the clubs through the State Year Book which was becoming more valuable to the membership. Plans were made to print the Bylaws in the Year Book; however, since finances prohibited large sums for publication, it was decided to omit the reports of the Chairmen. As another means of keeping clubs informed a Press Committee was appointed with the stipulation that all press notices were to be reviewed by the Board before publication.

During this administration fourteen meetings were held in various places within New Jersey. Clubwomen were alerted to their responsibilities in such fields as education, legislation, community improvement and libraries. Members were asked to become interested in the Teachers' Retirement Fund and the teaching of Domestic Science in the public schools.

Success in helping to establish and maintain libraries and the many suggestions for town improvements made the general public realize that clubwomen were trying to bring about desirable changes for the benefit of all. The clubs were asked to send reports of their work to Federation. The information obtained from such reports helped other clubs avoid pitfalls and to handle situations comparable to their own. The Departments of Sociology and Household Economics were formed to do research work and to offer suggestions to clubs interested in those fields.

The Reciprocity Bureau which had been formed in 1899 for the purpose of exchanging papers presented at clubs to assist other clubs had expanded considerably. By 1902 it was decided that a Program Chairman should be appointed to coordinate this work which would broaden another field of service to the clubs.

The work begun in 1897 by the Federation to preserve the Palisades from distruction by commercial interests was still growing. Money was being collected by clubs and set aside to purchase a suitable memorial, a piece of land to be used as a park. Because of the important and efficient work being done by NJSFWC for this cause it became an all absorbing topic and even received special commendation from the General Federation of Women's Clubs. The work and ideals of the Federation were being woven into a colorful fabric which resulted in the accomplishments of united women being recognized everywhere.

In close cooperation with the Audubon Society the Federation endorsed the law prohibiting live pigeon shooting.

It was decided to help the George Jr. Republic of Freeville, NY. This was a home and school organized by Mr. George for the rehabilitation of boys aged 14 to 17. Clubs raised funds to send a boy of their selection who, through such help, could mature and learn what a good life had to offer him.

An important area that required close attention was legislation in which many vital questions called for the reaction of an interested public. A Resolution covering an important topic that aroused the clubs to action was the Pure Food Bill which was so controversial at that time. Miss Alice Lakey, President of the Cranford Village Improvement Association was nationally recognized as an advocate of this legislation, finally passed in 1906. The Civil Service Reform and the much discussed Child Labor Laws were also given attention. Factory inspection was definitely needed and the Federation endorsed the Swaze Bill. Assistance was given to a movement by the Orange Charities Association to promote the establishment of a State Reformatory for Women. The NJSFWC Department of Sociology realized that, by supporting this movement, clubwomen who were interested in helping other women learn how to live better lives could offer their services. Another Resolution urged the women to use their influence in obtaining the privilege of voting on all school questions. An Advisory Committee, whose work was to prepare a skeleton of all Resolutions, was appointed by the President.   This eventually became today's Resolutions Committee.

The value of contact with GFWC became more noticeable each year. Attendance at its Biennial Meetings afforded an opportunity for the New Jersey clubs to broaden their scope of achievements and much benefit was derived from the personal contacts with clubwomen from other states. The problem of the financial status of NJSFWC reared its ugly head again since it could not meet the expenses of sending its President to the GFWC Convention. It was recommended that clubs send a voluntary contribution every two years for a fund which was set aside for that purpose.

The Federation completed its first decade of service with the close of Mary McKeen's administration. Records proved that much had been accomplished in improving woman's place in her community. The old concept that woman's place was in the home was giving way and club work was providing inspiration and means of broadening the activities of individuals and groups of civic-minded women.

Emma W. Newbury
(Mrs. Andrew J. Newbury)
1904 to 1906

Emma W. Newbury of the Jersey City Woman's Club assumed the Presidency in 1904. By this time it was apparent that the club movement was growing rapidly. There were now 104 clubs with approximately 1100 members. At that time there were 36 cities or towns in New Jersey where there were no clubs, so a definite effort was made to establish new clubs in these communities. A Chairman of Organization, forerunner of a later Membership Department, was appointed to help form and acquaint new clubs with the Federation plans. The State Year Book was expanded to contain the names of the Past State Presidents.

Mrs. Newbury expressed her faith in the value of clubs at every opportunity and said, "Surely man, in the future, can not say that he is worse off for his mother or grandmother having learned to debate. Clubs are a good thing. They make women unselfish and appreciate their husbands better since they find how difficult it is to have things go just as they would wish them. The same genius that can guide a club can easily conduct a model home." Continuing along these lines, the object of the Home Economics Department was to gather data from various sources and disseminate information concerning better house keeping, the means of meeting the high cost of living and the domestic servant question. A circular explaining the Department's recommendations was prepared and sent to all clubs. In the early 20th Century the executive ability required of women was seldom recognized. Clubwomen were being given credit as those "amiable mortals" who can, if need be, "knead bread with energy, mend rents with cheerfulness, nurse the sick with skill and gentleness, put witchery into a ribbon and genius into a stew."

The Education Department absorbed the Department of Libraries and increased the study of the greater need for Traveling Libraries. At this time clubs could borrow libraries for an annual fee of $2.00. Instruction in sewing and basketry for young people was suggested "to brighten long winter evenings and bring new life into what is now a monotonous existence." Interior decoration of schools was recommended. Mrs. Newbury asked members to interest themselves in education and said, "In the coming year we trust every mother will interest herself in at least one school and one teacher— her child's—that he, instead of being a nuisance in the school and a torment to his teacher, as is too often the case, may be a credit to both." She also quoted a recent speaker at one of the clubs as saying, "Some beautiful quality can be found in every pupil and that teaching under all circumstances may be made a pleasure." To this Mrs. Newbury added, "A cheering faith, it will move mountains. We need more of it."

The Federation was appreciative of the service rendered to

humanity by President Theodore Roosevelt by his part in the Peace Conference which resulted in the signing of a treaty and the close of the Russo-Japanese War. The Federation sent a letter to President Roosevelt stating that they felt the Peace Conference had taught the nation that, in this age of civilization, war is not necessary. As an auxiliary to the Federation work, a Peace Society was formed at a meeting in Elizabeth in 1905. In doing so, New Jersey clubwomen displayed a united effort for promoting universal peace.

Community betterment, under the guidance of the Town Improvement Committee brought about many changes throughout New Jersey. Clubs purchased drinking fountains for parks, helped clear up the unsanitary conditions of railroad stations and streets and offered prizes where contests were held for the best kept yards. More sanitary removal of ashes and garbage was encouraged. In some towns, where no means of refuse collection was established, clubs provided the needed funds for equipment and service.

Cooperation with the Palisades Park Commission continued by setting aside collected funds for a suitable memorial to be established on the ground offered by this Commission.

The Sociology Committee was especially interested in helping discharged prisoners to rehabilitate themselves. Another boy was sent to the George Jr. Republic in Freeville, NY. Greater interest in the welfare of young people was displayed when the Federation tried to get the State Legislature to abolish night labor for boys in glass factories. This placed our state side by side with those who "favor boys above bottles." This Committee was also instrumental in finding good homes for many homeless children.

New Jersey clubwomen were becoming more interested in legislation. It was suggested that a Legislation Committee be formed. Interest was not confined to state matters, but was noticeable on the national level. The Federation requested Albert J. Beveridge (Chairman of Territorial Committee of the United States Senate) to use his influence to amend a bill forming the states of Oklahoma and Arizona. This bill classified women with the illiterate, felons, and insane. Senator Beveridge replied to this request by stating that the Committee had voted to strike out the objectionable language. Emma Newbury spurred the clubs to more active work in proper legislation on food laws when she asked, "Are we as interested in what we eat as in what we wear? Settle the question in your attitude toward the Pure Food Bill."

Demonstrating early advocacy of "animal rights" the Federation expressed its disapproval of wearing coats made from baby lamb skins because of the cruelty of killing the baby lambs for such skins. They urged the discontinuance of such garments by manufacturers. The Audubon Society asked the Federation to refrain from the use of Aigrette, the plumage of Egrets widely used in hat decoration.

The Reciprocity Committee was still active. The number of such documents submitted was gradually increasing, although not to the extent anticipated. A special request was put out to the clubs for papers on noted New Jersey men and women in the fields of history, art, literature, and science. Detailed information on New Jersey landmarks was sought. A list of reference books for study was provided and, whenever possible, the committee arranged programs on these subjects.

The prejudice which had existed against the formation of

clubs for women was gradually disappearing, and taking its place was a growing respect for the self-sacrificing devotion shown by Federation members.

Practical work, united with genial fellowship, described the clubs of this time period. When Mrs. Newbury was asked what made a happy club, she replied, "It is a happy club where nine-tenths are doing the work and one-tenth is criticizing." She continued, "Someone defines criticism as moral vaccination to avert more serious disease." At another time she had said, "There was a time when comments, not always kindly and too often audible, were made in club meetings. A clubwoman told me that she has been frequently tempted to pass to her seatmate a written request—'don't criticize; the speaker's relatives are seated near you'." Emma Newbury always emphasized the object of the Federation which is to bring the women's clubs of the state into communication for acquaintance and mutual helpfulness. She and her Vice Presidents: Mrs. Henry P. Bailey, Mrs. John Meeker, Mrs. Robert H. Dodd and Mrs. R. A. Tusting accomplished this object well during the sixth administration of NJSFWC.

Ida W. Dawson
(Mrs. Henry H. Dawson)
1906 to 1909

Ida W. Dawson of the Contemporary Club of Newark with the Vice Presidents: Mrs. Thomas S. Henry, Miss Elizabeth Demerest, Miss M. Louise Edge and Mrs. James M. Maxwell headed the seventh administration of NJSFWC. Mrs. Dawson opened her first Board meeting by saying, "The twelve years since Federation began have presented a fine piece of weaving, not withstanding its imperfections, and the pattern for the most part has been distinct." This administration was characterized by several organizational changes including that of districting the state by existing counties with a new office of County Chairman put into operation. This change had been recommended by the previous President, and proved useful in binding the clubs more closely together for community effort.

County Committees were the out growth of this new formation. Each member of the Committee was assigned a certain number of clubs in which to arouse interest in club projects. Later County Chairmen asked for membership on the Board. Since that would enlarge the Board to undesirable size, the Federation was redistricted along the lines of the Congressional Election Districts with the ten leaders being called District Vice Presidents. Each of these was appointed to head a Department. Board meetings were changed in number from five to three each year, and the President's term of office to three years. The Annual Meeting was changed from October to May and was to last for two days.

The always-strong connection with GFWC was emphasized during this administration. Clubs were urged to join GFWC with the dues of that time being twenty-five cents per club. Reading the "Club Bulletin", GFWC's official publication, was stressed and the clubwomen were encouraged to utilize the services of the General Federation. In compliance with a request of the national organization to conform with departments of that body, the new departments of Civics, Literature, Art, and Civil Service were added and the name of the Sociology Department was changed to Industrial and Child Labor. The General Federation President, Mrs. Decker, asked that State Year Books be modeled after the Illinois Year Book. Each state was asked to appoint a member on the Public Health Committee, and clubs were urged to hold a civic meeting on March 10 of that year.

Clubs were studying such topics as standards for American citizenship and whether or not politics would be purified by Women's Suffrage. NJSFWC went on record as endorsing the principle of equal suffrage for women and of taking action to secure laws to give the working women the needed protection of the ballot.

Club women felt the need for public identification so a pin was designed and a membership card was prepared for this purpose.

A gavel made from a hickory tree at Andrew Jackson's home in Nashville, Tennessee was presented to Mrs. Dawson.

Home Economics was still being stressed throughout the clubs. Through the Federation's efforts the subject of Domestic Science was now being taught in seven city schools. Books dealing with Home Economics were donated to libraries, and school lunches were suggested as a "nerve saver" for teachers as well as pupils and parents. The problem of making housework as attractive as working in factories to young immigrant girls was discussed. Mrs. Dawson said, "Clubwomen should see that home-making as a career becomes a fashion." A pamphlet entitled "Hints to House Keepers Without a Maid or Easy Methods of House-keeping" was compiled to make housework less of a hardship. Among many Resolutions presented at annual meetings, clubs recommended the teaching of Home Economics and Domestic Science in all High Schools.

Members were urged to work for compulsory school laws for well-built and well-equipped schools, and for better paid and better prepared teachers. Instruction for the blind, deaf and defective children was advocated. A special effort was made to have Civics taught in all schools.

Libraries were still an important aspect of club work and many small towns established libraries through the efforts of clubwomen. Sixty-one libraries in New Jersey were assisted by clubwomen who emphasized the need to train library workers.

Library established by the Woman's Library Club at Bound Brook, 1903.

Tuberculosis was a grave peril of this era and the Federation acted in forming an Association for Prevention and Study of Tuberculosis. A State Sanitarium opened in Glen Gardner in October, 1907 and clubwomen urged those afflicted with Tuberculosis to seek help there.

Health situations in factories, public buildings and streets; a safe and sane Fourth of July celebration, abolition of billboards along railways, child labor, the proper licensing of midwives and other current problems were addressed in the Federation's zeal for civic betterment.

The Audubon Society advised the Federation that Queen Alexandra had joined their crusade and abandoned the use of Aigrette feathers.

The Town Improvement Department suggested periodic clean up days and was anxious to have something done about the smoke nuisance. The President said, "Some people think that a bank of smoke hanging over a city is a sign of industrial prosperity. It is a sign of industrial stupidity." The Federation began investigating laws concerning the use of soft coal in factories and by railroads.

Clubs demonstrated their alertness to current problems by passing Resolutions in opposition to the Institute for Vivisection, seeking state help for blind babies and endorsing a bill to establish a Woman's Reformatory. They also advocated a night school for convicts at the Trenton Prison.

Although local newspaper editors would publish local club news columns in their area, they did not care to publicize Federation matters. The Federation Board voted to have an official column each week in a selected newspaper, "Jersey City Journal". The column existed for two years and informed the public of many valuable projects about which they would not otherwise have become familiar.

Ida Dawson made a significant psychological impact during her term of office. Her enthusiasm spurred many to action and her hope of gaining recognition for the value of clubs in the communities was noted in her speech, "When women shall have learned to work together, and when they add to their natural gifts of warm heartedness, ready speech and sociability—that culture of intellect and cool reason which club life brings—there will be a tremendous influence upon public opinion in our homes, our schools and our public assemblies."

Mary Pattison
(Mrs. Frank A. Pattison)
1909 to 1911

Mary Stanahan Hart Pattison (known as "Molly"), a "Domestic Engineer", was born on September 7, 1869 in Brooklyn, New York. The only child of Diantha and George William Hart, "Molly" claimed French and English heritage reaching back to John Hart, a signer of the Declaration of Independence, and to various other early New England colonists. Shortly after her birth, she moved with her parents to New Brunswick, New Jersey and soon after to Metuchen. On June 6, 1893, she married Frank Ambler Pattison. They spent the first years of their marriage in New York where their two children were born—a daughter, Diantha in 1896 and a son Maynicke in 1905. In 1908 they returned to New Jersey and settled in Colonia, near Metuchen.

The Pattisons shared a common outlook on life as defined in the early Twentieth Century by the Progressive Party. This included supporting general improvement in living conditions for the poor, better working conditions and fewer work hours for laborers, prison reform, abolition of child labor and more direct participation in government including women's suffrage and foreign policy that would lead to world peace. Through her community activities, Mrs. Pattison was instrumental in founding the Borough Improvement League of Metuchen. As a member of this club she was elected to the NJSFWC Presidency in 1909. The Vice Presidents of this administration were Mrs. Edward S. Robinson, Mrs. Spencer Weart, Mrs. Clarence K. Binder, Mrs. Edward Livingston, and Mrs. J. A. MacClary. The Federation boasted 123 clubs with a membership of over 12,000, representing many walks of life.

At the first meeting of the new Board of Directors held in the President's Colonia home opening remarks by the President included plans for County (District) meetings, a Music Festival and an Art Exhibit.

The major goal for the administration was to establish a Household Experiment Station. This was accomplished on June 9, 1910 when Mrs. Pattison opened the Experiment Station in a wing of her home. The four rooms used for this purpose were equipped with all of the latest cooking and cleaning devices which were tried and tested thoroughly. Of particular fascination was an electric motor that powered everything from a coffee grinder or a vacuum cleaner to a dishwasher. Denatured alcohol, coal, gas and electricity were all studied to determine which energy source was best suited for household use.

A focus of the Experiment Station was the concept of Time-Motion Study. Whether scraping a dinner plate or folding a bed sheet, the objective was to perform the task with the least amount of labor in the shortest time possible. Another important element of the experiment was promoting aesthetic values of the work environment. Each room was designed to provide ample space in comfortable, pleasing and safe surroundings with the walls, curtains, carpets and furnishings of each room coordinated to complement each other. Oriental rugs in the kitchen and broadloom in the laundry room were two of the extravagances proposed to achieve a pleasant effect.

Mrs. Pattison and NJSFWC were "ahead of their time" in addressing three major problems of the day—high cost of living, the servant shortage caused by the movement of domestic workers to higher paying jobs, and the elimination of drudgery. Thousands of women from New Jersey and surrounding states visited the Experiment Station while it was in operation. Regardless of their individual financial situations, the visitors took home with them many new ideas to make them more efficient and creative in their roles as homemakers.

This project received recognition and in 1914, Mrs. Pattison wrote her book, The Principles of Domestic Engineering which received wide acclaim. Her article entitled "Domestic Engineering: the Housekeeping Experiment Station in Colonia, New Jersey" was published in Scientific American in 1912. An avid writer, Mrs. Pattison remained active all of her life and in 1949 at age 80, she wrote Colonia Yesterday which was one of the earliest town histories ever written.

Another accomplishment of this administration was the creation of the Endowment Fund in an effort to relieve the injustice of the Federation Officers having to meet necessary expenses from their personal funds. In a sense, this was the beginning of "budgeting" for the Federation.

Thirty clubs sent contributions to the George Jr. Republic, and Mr. George announced that a branch of the Republic would soon be started in New Jersey. A farm near Flemington Junction had been given by the Lehigh Valley Railroad and the substantial stone farm house would become an ideal home for ten or twelve boys who would be placed there within the year.

The interest of clubwomen in the work of probation officers, juvenile courts, and improvement of penal institutions received more attention. Members visited the night school for convicts at the Trenton Prison, and wrote letters to the State Legislature urging the continuation of the $1600 appropriated for the school. This request was granted by the legislature.

Women's clubs were like vigilante committees in the communities. They studied conditions in shops and factories as well as investigating laws concerning employment of women and children. The Federation endorsed building a reformatory for women and a law prohibiting white slave traffic in New Jersey. It urged inspection of slaughter houses and restriction of child labor at night in factories. Building the Henry Hudson Boulevard along the Palisades was supported.

The cultural side of life was not neglected as clubs made an effort to advance Municipal Art which would make schools, public buildings and homes more attractive places. The Art Department urged women to work for the suppression of the comic newspaper supplements, which, with their bad drawings and atrocious coloring, not to mention the vulgarity of text, were perverting the art tastes of children. Since New Jersey was one of the great pottery centers of the country and women were the principle consumers of their products, members were urged to become more informed on the manufacture of these items. The Music Department urged clubs to establish classes in sight reading of music and to form choruses in their communities. They also continued to take advantage of circulating libraries. Self improvement became more important and, as someone said, "Can a time ever come when we will know enough where can we expect to interest others in things we do not know well ourselves?"

Mrs. Pattison was widowed in September 1946. She died at home on June 28, 1951 at age 81 and is buried in Mountain Grove Cemetery, Bridgeport, Connecticut. This was a woman politically active all of her life who had served in many capacities in the state and the nation. Her obituary appeared in the New York Times on June 29, 1951.

Catherine C. Warren
(Mrs. Howard C. Warren)
1911 to 1913

A dark-haired woman, Catherine C. Warren came to the presidency of the Federation from The Province Line Club of Princeton. During her installation, she remarked that her sole qualification for office was "Faith in Organization". The fact that she was well-endowed with the prerequisite capacity for leadership became increasingly evident in her administration. An organizational change implemented in 1911 was to elect only one Vice President-at-Large instead of the previous five Vice Presidents. This position was filled by Jessie Alexander Ropes. The ranking officers in the Districts were called District Vice Presidents. They reported monthly to Mrs. Ropes.

When the new Board of Directors convened for the first time it was presented with a bill for $12 from the Jersey Central Railroad. This represented fares for eleven passengers to the previous meeting in Asbury Park. The Federation had an agreement with the railroad to run a special train provided that there were 110 passengers. Unfortunately, only 99 delegates used the special train. Fortunately, there was just enough money in the Federation funds to pay this bill immediately.

The semi-annual meeting held in October of 1911 was at the Haddon Fortnightly in Haddonfield. At the opening session the President read a "Collect for Club Women" by Mary Stewart. Mrs. Warren said, "It is a beautiful sentiment for every woman whether she belongs to a club or not." Apparently, this is the first time that the Collect was used at a Federation meeting.

COLLECT

Keep us, O God, from pettiness; let us be large in thought, in word, in deed.

Let us be done with fault-finding, and leave off self-seeking.

May we put away all pretense and meet each other face to face without self-pity and without prejudice.

May we never be hasty in judgment and always generous.

Let us take time for all things, make us to grow calm, serene, gentle.

Teach us to put into action our better impulses, staightforward and unafraid.

Grant that we may realize it is the little things that create differences; that in the big things of life we are at one.

And may we strive to touch and to know the great common human heart of us all, and, O, Lord God ! let us forget not to be kind.

The fame of the Federation had spread sufficiently to attract notable speakers to state meetings. Two of these were Rabbi Stephen S. Wise and Lucia Ames Mead of Boston. Mrs. Mead addressed a fall meeting on the topic of "Women and the War System". Clubwomen had worked for better food (the Pure Food Law), better drinking water, housing, factory laws, parks, playgrounds and civic conditions in general. The Employers' Liability Law received a great protest as it was considered a mixture of justice and injustice. Many women feared it would give greater power to insurance companies.

Pioneering an effort to help the public appreciate citizenship, the Civics Department urged clubs to study national and state laws, especially those affecting women and children in jails and station houses. They stressed the appointment of a resident woman physician on the staff of every institution where women were confined. Surveys were made of vital issues governed by the Board of Health. Clubwomen continued to concentrate on baby saving, milk inspection and medical inspection in schools. A law had been passed banning public drinking cups, and the Federation declared that it opposed any attempt to repeal this law. The Secretary of State Charities and Prison Reform, who spoke at Alexander Hall, Princeton University, suggested a study to be made for better care of the feebleminded and insane. The Federation agreed to support this movement. In 1913 Mrs. Warren was appointed by Governor Woodrow Wilson to serve on the Board of the State Home for Girls.

The Endowment Fund which had been authorized in 1910 now held nearly $1200 —and this was only the beginning. This Fund was incorporated and governed by the Board of Directors.

The clubwomen had a vision of a state college for women. Efforts resulted in the appointment of a committee on May 18, 1912 to work on a project of this magnitude - the establishment of a college.

Federation members began to study municipal budgets and school appropriations, believing that school laws should be amended to include women serving on school boards. Governor Woodrow Wilson, speaking on the subject at a club meeting in Madison, voiced his approval and suggested that the Education Committee refer the matter to the proper Commissioner. At the Spring Convention Mrs. David Kirk, the first woman Superintendent of Schools in the United States, gave impetus to the creation of recreation centers in public schools. Mrs. Warren called for an appropriation of $300 to be given by school boards for the use of auditoriums for school dances. The Education Department Chairman urged a law making it obligatory to open the schools for social centers and concerts.

The Congress of Mothers suggested cooperation with the Federation for an exchange of views and experiences which would be invaluable in the solution of sociological problems.

Several organizations had expressed a desire to be part of the Federation. On March 20, 1913 the Board of Directors passed a motion that the Federation would take in "affiliated bodies" that would have no vote, pay no initiation dues, but would pay fees at the discretion of the Board.

Continually concerned with the responsibilities of citizenship, clubwomen gave serious thought to bills presented by the Legislation Department. A few of these were: The Age of Consent, Weights and Measures, Minimum

Wage Bill, the Kenyon Shepherd Bill and the Hat Pin Bill.

At the 19th Annual Convention held in Atlantic City in May of 1913, the Recording Secretary of GFWC reminded delegates of "the honesty in office" that in club work it was necessary to give more than to receive and not to accept office for personal aggrandizement.

Minutes written in 1912-1913 provided interesting facts. At the Spring Convention in 1912 the Treasurer reported a current fund balance of $374.97. Box luncheons were popular when people got together for District Meetings. The Nominating Committee experienced difficulty in filling vacancies and asked that clubs send in names of women who were capable of serving in offices. The Chairman of the Civics Department requested a "less commercial Christmas". As a demonstration of economy in the home, thirty people were fed for $5. In 1913 the cost of printing 500 State Year Books was $150, and the cost of printing 600 Calls to Convention was $5. One club had a clause in its Constitution stating that "it is a misdemeanor to criticize a fellow club member."

During her term of office, Mrs. Warren had recommended a club home (Headquarters), a paid field secretary, a leaflet to report active work (especially legislative work), a budget for spending an income of $700 and a new type of State Club where former officers could go on to further welfare work. This suggestion may have been one which eventually led to creation of The State Ex Club, which was organized in 1915.

Mrs. Warren's theme "What is Real Club Work?" was characterized by admirable achievements during her administration. The Federation was more firmly established than ever at the end of her term of office.

Jessie Alexander Ropes
(Mrs. William T. Ropes)
1913 to 1915

Jessie Alexander Ropes, of The All Round Club of Montclair, became the 10th President of NJSFWC, bringing to the job a wealth of experience in club work. Mrs. Thomas B. Stillman was the Vice-President-At-Large for this administration.

With the continued growth of the Federation, organizational changes were a necessity. The Federation was redistricted and Departments were reorganized, reducing them to five in number. Department titles were: American Citizenship, Applied Education, Fine Arts, Legislation and Public Welfare. Each department included subdivisions. The Department Chairmen became known as Trustees and were elected to office. District Vice Presidents became voting members of the Board of Directors.

Until this time the Federation had been known as an unincorporated association. The need for incorporation was obvious. At the May 1914 Convention, held in Asbury Park, it was "duly moved, seconded, and carried that the

107

association be incorporated as the New Jersey State Federation of Women's Club, that the Board of Directors be authorized to make changes in the Constitution that they had recommended, and that the Constitution so changed be used as the Charter of Incorporation."

As suggested in the previous administration a Founders Book — later designated as the Honor Roll book — was established in connection with the Endowment Fund. The purpose was twofold, to perpetuate the names and deeds of women who aided the Federation or their clubs and to increase the Endowment Fund. The first book was affectionately dedicated to Margaret T. Yardley, and was presented by Mrs. Ropes. At that time she said, "It is a pleasure to put it in permanent form."

A contest was held for a new Federation song. The one chosen, "On, New Jersey Daughters", was written by Mrs. Allen B. Smith who was a member of the Ridgefield Park Woman's Club. It was sung with much enthusiasm at Convention to the melody of "Onward, Christian Soldiers."

Clubwomen were becoming more interested in literature and drama. The use of Traveling Libraries was encouraged to circulate knowledge. A new committee called Pageantry was set up under the Drama subdivision. Aligned with the Civics Committee, it gave club women opportunities to serve in community celebrations and patriotic events. This generated greater participation in the study of drama in many clubs.

Until this time, activity in art groups consisted mostly of exhibitions of local and visiting artists. It was not until several years later that clubwomen, through the Federation, came to a full realization of their need for creative expression.

In 1915, an exhibit of ceramics was held at Convention.

Promotion of Home Economics Programs was still wide spread. One chairman traveled up and down the state, carrying along labor-saving devices and lecturing to groups on the conservation of food and time. The word "safety" was emphasized, especially in the kitchen. A campaign for safety was conducted in the schools, with club members circulating pamphlets and buttons.

As war clouds gathered over Europe prior to the start of World War I, the people of the United States were still aimed at preserving peace. The Federation had given support to the Peace Movement, an organization advocating the education of youth toward peace — not war. A Resolution was presented at this time by the Legislative Committee in regards to the Court of Nations. It included the establishment of (1) A Court, or courts, for settlement of disputes, (2) an International Congress with legal and administrative powers, and (3) an International Police Force. Without realizing it, these forward-thinking clubwomen were designing the United Nations which would not become a reality for several generations.

Things that needed doing more locally were not neglected. The Federation advocated providing police women and matrons for jails where women were incarcerated, limiting the work of children under the age of 16 to an eight hour day, setting up a Commission on Industrial Welfare, etc. The Legislative Committee sent out 1,000 circulars and 800 form letters (at a cost of $90) to aid in the study of the proposed measures. In 1915 the Police Women's Bill became a law. History has proven that the intensive work of the Federation did get results.

Publicizing the work of the Federation continued to be a problem. Although many columns of club news were started, most media editors preferred to carry only local club news. Because of these policies, many Federation plans and programs never appeared in print. For a brief time the State Chamber of Commerce gave a page to club news, but it was dropped after several months.

Beautification of New Jersey was of prime concern to the clubwomen. The Garden Department urged planting of private and public gardens for beauty and recreation. In 1915, laurels were set out along the Lincoln Highway, the first of many plantings by clubwomen. One laurel honored Mrs. Woodrow Wilson who had endorsed this plant as the National Plant.

An outstanding achievement of Mrs. Rope's administration was the actual launching of a movement to establish the New Jersey College for Women. A Committee had been appointed in 1912 to consider such a project; however, it was not until 1915 that the Resolution to attempt this endeavor was adopted. Under the slogan, "Wanted - a State College for Women" and with the President as an enthusiastic leader, clubwomen worked unceasingly to arouse public interest in this enterprise. Funds were greatly needed, but the first successful step had been taken and with thousands of women concentrating on this as a definite project, it could not fail.

In 1915 the Federation reached its majority — it was 21 years old and still growing. Mrs. Ropes' contributions to the Federation were many and varied. Her constructive record of service and her deep perception of the needs of people will long be remembered.

Lillian J. Stockton
(Mrs. Charles W. Stockton)
1915 to 1917

Lillian J. Stockton of the Woman's Club of Ridgewood chose as her administration theme Three S's — Simplicity, Sincerity, and Service. "Simplicity" — not extravagance of time or money or effort — a sane perception and a poise of thought and action which accomplishes fine things. "Sincerity" — the gold without the alloy which tried in the hottest furnace of adversity or prosperity comes out the brighter. "Service" — to so live, to so serve that we leave the world better for our living.

Sara S. Proal served as Vice President-at -Large during Mrs. Stockton's administration.

One of the first things to demand attention from the Federation was a request from the General Federation of Women's Clubs asking assistance in the campaign against illiteracy in the United States. A recent census had disclosed that more than five million adults in the United States could neither read nor write. Clubs were alerted to the importance of establishing classes for foreigners in their communities to teach both English and the duties of American citizenship. A Resolution was presented asking the establishment of non-English classes for immigrants wherever possible in evening schools.

The area than known as the "Pines of South Jersey" housed many illiterate residents. This resulted in the Federation sending a Social Service Worker to that area. Clubs were asked to support a well trained Social Worker in the Pines so that she might teach the mothers in the home, help teachers in the schools and make social centers of the little one-room school houses. This work in the area now known as the "Pine Barrens" continued successfully for two years and resulted in the appointment of a Social Worker by the Board of Education as an attendance officer for that section. The Federation paid her salary while this was in the experimental stage. In January 1920, after this project had proven worthwhile, the work in the Pines passed into the hands of the State Board of Education.

Two notable achievements from the work in the Pines resulted during Mrs. Stockton's administration. One was the purchase of a fully-equipped dental ambulance for use in the rural school districts and the other was the raising of funds to endow a bed for the use of children in Burlington County Hospital.

Many Resolutions regarding schools, child labor, worker's compensation, and the representation of women on governing boards of all state institutions concerned with woman and juveniles were acted upon. The Federation also urged the adoption, by communities in New Jersey, of a

Fourth of July ordinance prohibiting the indiscriminate and dangerous use of fireworks. A "Bird Day" proclamation set on John Burroughs' birthday — April 3 — devoted the day to observation of birds and the study of bird literature. The erection of bird shelters by children and adults interested in conserving our song birds was also part of this project.

Reports from forty-five clubs indicated an interest in art, and twenty-nine clubs had Art Departments. The Shakespeare Tercentenary was recognized by a "Shakespeare Day" in many clubs and by the presentation of "Masque of Psyche."

Public Health became a department of the Federation in 1917. This committee surveyed and listed all alms houses in New Jersey and urged that women be appointed to serve on Boards of Managers of all institutions where women or children were wards of the state. It also petitioned the state to make changes at Clinton Farms so that women under the age of 35 who had been committed to the Trenton Prison would be transferred there.

"Better Babies Campaign", a request made to New Jersey by both the Children's Bureau in Washington, DC and the General Federation, became a project of the Civics and Public Health Departments. New Jersey, led by its women's clubs, realized that more than 7,000 of the babies in the state died during their first year. Sincere efforts were made to stop this tragedy through a "Baby Week" which was held in 70 communities. It taught how to take the next step in baby saving; it showed how to turn mother love and maternal instinct to intelligence; it taught how much intelligent mothercraft can do to make the home a safer place for babies and how much a visiting nurse could do to extend home care over the entire community.

The concentrated effort was made to make Visiting Nurses an integral part of the health services in every community. The Federation also urged that a woman be put on every local Health Board and on the State Board of Health in Trenton. As a result of the work done by the Federation, the Division of Child Hygiene and Nursing was created at Trenton with a woman physician as its executive. She was placed at the service of the State Federation and individual clubs.

Unfortunately, The George Jr. Republic work had ended and the farm at Flemington was closed. This project to help young boys had long been supported by the Federation.

In 1915 there was a movement to have the Legislature submit to the voters the question of Women's Suffrage. In 1917, the New Jersey Federation supported the General Federation Resolution.

Recognizing the central need for communication between the Federation and its clubs, the "Bulletin" an official organ of NJSFWC, was issued in October 1916. The subscription price was twenty-five cents. In one year the list of subscribers grew from 200 to 1800.

Always in need of a "Home", the Federation established headquarters at the Robert Treat Hotel in Newark.

In June 1916 New York entertained the General Federation at its Biennial Convention. The Hotel McAlpin was the New Jersey Federation's Headquarters. In appreciation of the fact that New Jersey had asked to host this Convention, it was arranged that NJSFWC would have one day for itself.

General Federation Officers were luncheon guests at the Essex County Country Club. Following the luncheon a reception at Glenmont, the home of Mr. and Mrs. Thomas A. Edison, was held for 1,000 delegates who represented all of the states plus Alaska and Canada. Two hours later a second reception for the 1,000 guests took place at the Woman's Club of Orange. During this Convention New Jersey had the honor of presenting the name of Mrs. Charles B. Yardley as an honorary Vice President of the General Federation. Margaret Yardley was elected unanimously.

Despite the concentrated efforts made to keep the United States out of the war that had engulfed all of Europe since 1914, the "Impossible Dream" ended on April 6, 1917 when war was declared against Germany. The Federation's twenty-third Annual Meeting held in Atlantic City that year brought recognition to Lillian J. Stockton for the accomplishments of her administration as the clubwomen of New Jersey geared up to meet the greater challenges of World War I.

Agnes A. Schermerhorn
(Mrs. John R. Schermerhorn)
1917 to 1920

Agnes A. Schermerhorn of the Woman's Club of Orange was the second President of NJSFWC to serve a three-year term. Two Vice Presidents, Mrs. Charles F. Dewey and Mrs. William H. Teters, served with her during this administration.

The clouds of war, which had finally blown across the Atlantic Ocean, set the tone for this time. The watchword of Mrs. Schermerhorn's administration was "A sane and steady service". "Sane", for we will keep our sense of proportion in all matters and "Steady", for we will permit no hysterics over any situation, but give calmly and gladly the day in and day out "service".

The slogan of the day was COS which stood for "Conservation or Starvation". This led to the development of the Committee of Food Economics which stressed the best, most thrifty ways of learning and practicing cooperative food patriotism. Eighty-seven thousand children were enrolled in school garden work and many memorial trees were planted.

The war brought patriotism to the forefront and the needs

of the times called for work along new lines. The Espionage Committee was established as a Bureau of Information and Patriotic Services. Members of this committee were asked to be the "eyes and ears" for the government to report suspicious actions, seditious remarks, interference with government meetings and the circulation of false reports concerning war organizations. Information reported was sent through this committee to the Department of Justice in Washington, DC. They were of material assistance to the government. New Jersey had the honor of being the first state in which the women's clubs were asked to give such assistance. The Federation "went to war" in other ways by supporting three Liberty Loan Drives, selling thrift stamps and engaging in Red Cross and war relief work in response to the call for patriotic services. Several of the larger clubs who owned club houses gave these buildings over to Red Cross work during World War I.

Camp Dix (later known as Fort Dix) in Burlington County was a primary site for shipping soldiers overseas. The Federation equipped and maintained a Soldiers' Club there during the War. It was known as the "Haversack" and recognized from coast to coast and overseas as a home to thousands of men. During its twenty-one months of operation, the Haversack was visited by over one-half million soldiers. The clubs throughout New Jersey fully supported this project and the Federation received a unique citation from the War Department of the United States. The Haversack was spoken of "as the only soldiers' club of its kind on record". Mrs. Schermerhorn and the Chairman of the Haversack project were decorated with the coveted War Service Pin that they accepted in the name of the Federation. The Haversack Club was enlarged by the addition of a lounge which was built by the Twenty-Sixth Army Engineers.

The Haversack closed on July 1, 1919 and, through the sale of the building and furnishings, $4,000 was realized. It was agreed that this sum should be used for a scholarship at Stevens Institute for the male descendants of New Jersey soldiers and sailors serving in World War I. The sum was not quite sufficient for this purpose, so the Trustees of Stevens Institute generously added the necessary amount and designated the scholarship as the "New Jersey State Federation of Women's Clubs Scholarship".

The cultural aspects of the Federation were also used for wartime activities. The Department of Pageantry (Drama) proposed that the Federation work for the better use of national holidays to increase historical knowledge and develop a deeper patriotism. The Bureau of Play Exchange was kept open with all income to go to war relief. Clubs secured members for the war service classes which included training in arts and crafts and equipped them to become Reconstruction Aids for the rehabilitation of military personnel in hospitals. The Department of Industrial and Social Conditions took "Americanization" as the keynote for its efforts to promote better mental, moral and social conditions for women in industry.

Health care was still an important part of the Federation's work. Cooperation was given to the Health Department of the General Federation in its division of Child Hygiene, Anti-Tuberculosis, Social Hygiene and Adult Hygiene. It also actively cooperated with the State Department of Health, The Public Health Education Committee of the American Medical Association, the State Nurses' Association, the New Jersey Branch of the Anti-Tuberculosis Society, the Society for the Prevention of Blindness, the Housing Commission and all other such organizations for the advancement of public health. In recognition of the Federation's work with the blind, the Governor appointed the State President to the Commission for the Blind.

A survey was made in 18 of the 21 counties to investigate the care of the feeble-minded and the routine for committing patients. Two women were appointed by Governor Edge to each of the Boards of the State Hospitals for the Insane.

Resolutions presented for action included the passage of the Federal Suffrage Act as a war measure, the advisability of bestowing rank on Red Cross nurses serving in the army, safe guarding the welfare of the race by the protection of women and children in industry, protesting the singing of German songs and the teaching of the German language in schools and support of wartime alcohol prohibition (which was urged by the General Federation of Women's Clubs).

After 15 years of persistent effort, the New Jersey College for Women became a reality. It opened in September, 1918 with the first class containing 54 students. A $50,000 appropriation was secured from the New Jersey Legislature to fund the following year. The chairman of the College Committee, Mabel Smith Douglass, became the first Dean. The college was later named Douglass College in her honor.

In 1919 the Federation's Music Department voted to build and present to the MacDowell Colony at Peterboro, New Hampshire a studio for the use of any composer, artist, or writer who might wish to occupy it under the rules of the Colony. During this administration $1500 was collected for this purpose.

Again "on the move" the Federation established a

permanent headquarters at the YWCA in Newark in 1918. This consisted of one room at an annual rental rate of $200. To obtain the first six months' rent each Board Member contributed $5.

At the invitation of the Newark Board of Trade, the Federation held its 1918 Spring Convention in Newark. A banner in the Federation colors of buff and blue was presented by the Newark Board of Trade. During this administration it was also agreed that a President's badge (pin) should be made in the model of the State of NJ befitting the dignity of the Federation. A committee of two members was appointed to prepare and purchase such a badge.

The silver anniversary of NJSFWC was observed at the Annual Convention held in Atlantic City in 1919. The Conservation Department presented the President with a gavel made from the wood of the "Salem Oak" and the Trenton barracks. The gavel had been made by high school boys from Bayonne. It had a silver band in recognition of this special anniversary.

When Agnes Schermerhorn completed her term of office in 1920 she was elected Second Vice President of the General Federation. She served for two years and was chairman of a committee to establish a permanent GFWC Headquarters in Washington, DC. In this capacity she helped to raise the necessary funds in 1922 for purchase of the present GFWC Headquarters. The Woman's Club of Orange pledged the preliminary payment of $1000 which made it possible to purchase the building. The New Jersey Federation was congratulated for being the first state to pay its quota of $3500 toward the General Federation Headquarters.

Sara S. Proal
Mrs. Arthur B. Proal
1920-1923

Sara S. Proal of the Woman's Club of Nutley became President of NJSFWC while the country was experiencing the throes of reconstruction following World War I. The reaction from strenuous war activities performed by clubwomen was swiftly passing away, and they came together in a new spirit of comradeship devoted to peacetime. Mrs. Proal was assisted by two Vice Presidents — Etta Gould Lee and Kathryn K. Worcester.

Two new Departments were created by the Board of Directors. The Department of Institutional Cooperation was organized in response to a petition from the Glen Ridge Woman's Club. This club had been cooperating with other clubs in work for institutions in Essex county, and they believed that the good accomplishments in one county could be duplicated elsewhere if the movement was organized within the state. When activated this Department had 34 committees working for 51 institutions concerned with social welfare.

Practical Finance was the name of the other new Department. This was designed to provide an outline for new and comprehensive study of finance as it involved the home, municipality and state. Its aim was to make possible intelligent cooperation from women in these areas.

The New Jersey Legislature passed the Port Authority Bill without a dissenting vote. The Port Commissioners felt that this result was due, in part, to the active interest evidenced by the women's clubs in the State. It concerned the issue of food stuffs raised in New Jersey which were shipped to New York, trucked to market and, many times, trucked or ferried back to New Jersey with an increase in price and deterioration of quality. An effort to secure better distribution of food stuffs and a better scale of prices to the consumer was endorsed by the Federation which joined the Port Authority in intensive activities including lectures and motion pictures. The Federation was also largely responsible for the passage of the New Jersey Pure Milk and Pure Ice Cream Bills.

By now the New Jersey Legislature had realized that the clubwomen were active and vocal in expressing thier opinions. Much of this was done was through letter writing. The Civics Department made sure that letters were written in favor of the Vice-Repressive Act and opposing the release of the state from equal responsibility with local school districts in maintaining manual training in the vocational schools. Legislation which would have lowered nursing standards and placed hospitals under political control was steadfastly opposed. A Bill concerning "No Night Work for Women" was lost. The Federation devoted efforts to raising the standards of motion pictures, and stressed attention to the interests of native-born American boys and girls while at the same time doing everything possible for immigrants.

The Departments of Education, Industrial Social Conditions, and Legislation held District Conferences concerning the field of education. It was resolved that clubwomen be aggressively active in securing the right type of women to enter the teaching profession and to acquaint the communities of importance of public school education as preparation of citizenship in a democracy.

Small in size, but large in number, the mosquitoes for which New Jersey was notorious were still of interest within the state. At the Mosquito Convention in Atlantic City men from all over the country congratulated the New Jersey Commissioner on obtaining the valuable cooperation of clubwomen.

Conservation, which had been an interest of the Federation since the initial efforts to "save the Palisades", continued to be foremost in the minds of clubwomen. Trees were planted and protected, birds and natural flowers were preserved and statewide aid was sought in the prevention of forest fires. A call went out for volunteers among motorists and Boy Scouts, in communities close to woodland areas, suggesting they be marshalled under the Fire Districts in those locations. Local authorities were asked to forbid the dumping of inflammable material and to order that it be burned in suitable places. Safe disposal of dangerous waste substances began early in the life of the Federation.

Cultural pursuits continued among clubs with work in their communities to assist in spreading art appreciation among children and to express concern about living painters and sculptors, especially American artists. The Penny Art Fund begun in 1919 under Nellie Wright Allen was continued. Mrs. Allen had originated the custom of presenting a painting costing not less than $100 to the club which had done the most to stimulate art, particularly among young people. Many clubwomen affiliated themselves with art clubs and the Metropolitan Museum of Art. Art Department members were honored guests on several occasions at the exhibits of the National Academy of Design, the American Water Color Society, and the New York Water Color Society.

The Original Work Department conducted contests that received a great deal of support, especially in the form of manuscripts. Advice and help were given to clubs which either studied or produced plays. The Pilgrim Tercentenary was celebrated with "A Pilgrim's Canticle". The dedication of the studio given by NJSFWC to the MacDowell Colony in Peterboro, New Hampshire generated a trip to that area. The President and the Music Department Chairman had the pleasure of placing a plaque on the door of the studio which bore the inscription "The Gift of the New Jersey State Federation of Women's Clubs".

NJSFWC was invited to participate in the formal opening of the Hendrick Hudson Drive, a part of the Palisades development. Cecilia Gaines Holland, who had been President of NJSFWC when the first committee was appointed to work for saving the Palisades, was a speaker at this occasion.

A highlight of Mrs. Proal's administration was the first commencement held at the New Jersey College for Women in 1922. Many of the graduates planned to enter the teaching profession, and five of them had been elected to Phi Beta Kappa. Sixteen Hundred Dollars had been raised to provide and furnish a generous library of excellent fiction as a "browsing room" in one of the buildings set apart for the college. The young college had rapidly outgrown all of its buildings and needed additional housing facilities.

At the NJSFWC Annual Convention in 1921 it was voted to raise $25,000 to build a Science Hall for the college. Eight Thousand Dollars was raised in four months. Added to the money already on hand, this sum made it possible to accomplish the project. Science Hall, free of any financial encumberments, was dedicated on June 8, 1922. This gift to the college bears the inscription "This Hall of Science is presented by the New Jersey State Federation of Women's Clubs in Commemoration of the Vision Which Led to the Founding of the New Jersey College for Women. May the Spirit of this Place Inspire High Endeavor and Great Achievement". A portrait of Margaret Yardley was hung in Federation Hall as a gift of the clubwomen to the college students. By the close of Sara Proal's administration plans were already underway for a more ambitious project. It was voted to raise money for a Music Studio at the college.

Communication to the clubs was still a primary objective. The "News Letter" was published five times a year with two free copies of each issue sent to clubs. It provided a "direct wire" between the Board of Directors and the clubs.

An unofficial theme during Mrs. Proal's term of office was "Information, Inspiration, and Dedication", prioritized in this order, making it possible to move steadily forward toward the goal of equal opportunity and social justice for all.

Etta Gould Lee
(Mrs. Clayton D. Lee)
1923 to 1926

Having served as a Vice President in the previous administration, Etta Gould Lee from the Woman's Club of Maplewood brought to the presidency solid experience and innovative ideas. The Vice Presidents for this term of office were Mrs. George A. Smith, Miss Mary S. Daniels, and Mrs. John Hawes. This team of officers was to take the Federation into several new areas.

At the 1923 Convention the Federation voted to take the amount of cash and Liberty Bonds left in the Science Hall Fund and increase it until it reached an amount sufficient for a Music Studio building at The New Jersey College for Women. A variety of unique fund-raising events resulted in $100,000 being presented to the College within five years. With the Federation office as "Campaign Headquarters" a committee of 1000 women was urged to raise $100 each.

Contributions were given as memorials or in honor of loved ones. Aeolian Hall Company provided the use of Aeolian Hall for a concert by massed choruses (sixteen choruses composed of 300 singers) with proceeds applied to the fund. Hahne and Company contributed 5 percent of its profits on one week's sales. A collection of old gold and silver was made and sold to augment the fund. The building was dedicated on October 3, 1928 when the College celebrated its tenth anniversary.

"The Lifeline of the Federation" was inaugurated when Etta Lee appointed Mary S. Daniels as Chairman of a Committee to explore the idea of "junior" women as members. The idea was extremely popular with 61 Junior Clubs organized by the end of Mrs. Lee's administration. NJSFWC now had a Junior Membership Department headed by Miss Daniels .

There were organizational changes during this time with the Third Vice President elected to specialize in organizing new clubs. A tenth district encompassing Warren, Sussex and Morris Counties was created with a District Vice President. This promoted the development of club growth and interest in a section of the state, primarily Sussex County, where it seemed to be most lacking. By 1926 New Jersey was 100 percent organized by Counties. Sussex County had entered the Federation through the Lafayette Woman's Club.

Veterans of World War I were in need of assistance. A special committee called "Friendly Cooperation with the Ex-Serviceman" accomplished a great deal and received favorable comment from the GFWC. A Resolution was presented to President Calvin Coolidge asking that women be put on Boards of Veteran Relief. President Coolidge received this Resolution favorably and other states helped to publicize this plan.

A clubhouse for disabled servicemen was furnished in Newark. Club members responded generously to this project. The library and reading room, completely furnished by Federation Board members, became known as the Melvin Spitz Memorial Room.

There was a need for a hospital for disabled veterans and members assisted in selecting a site for the $3,000,000 hospital later constructed. Gifts were distributed to New Jersey veterans in fourteen hospitals and convalescent homes scattered throughout the country as well as to local hospitals where there was a need for holiday cheer. Names and addresses of New Jersey veterans were sent by the Veterans Bureau in Washington, and gifts were sent to "Hospital 42" for strangers in the state.

The chairman of the International Relations Department attended a conference in Washington, DC on the "cause and cure of war". The meeting had been organized by nine national women's organizations.

The Education for Peace Committee emphasized the need for arousing public sentiment in favor of peace. Literature was distributed and cooperation was with schools, libraries and other organizations. The chairman represented the Federation at the Fourth International Congress of the Woman's International League for Peace and Freedom. The Federation also passed a Resolution urging that the United States enter the Permanent Court of International Justice.

Outdoor beautification continued to be of interest to the clubwomen. Working through the Art Department, 53 clubs took part in the "protest by letter campaign" against signboards threatening to destroy the beauty of the country. As a result of 1,000 form letters and as many individual letters sent to a list of fifty national advertisers, twenty-five firms agreed to refrain from advertising along rural highways and in residential districts. Tree conservation was of increasing concern with many clubs taking advantage of the opportunity furnished by the State Department of Conservation and Development whereby they could obtain trees in lots of 1,000 for planting in their communities. The world of insects was still being observed, and a $10 prize was awarded to a boy who collected 800 tent caterpillar nests. The mosquito conflict was supported with the State Experiment Station at New Brunswick sending a mosquito film to any club which could supply an audience. The Mosquito Manual was distributed in schools by clubwomen.

A concentrated letter writing campaign to Congress resulted in a Bill to grant $2,500,000 toward a National Gallery of Art. Art receptions which interested clubwomen in the work of American painters were well attended. Several were held in New York City and others in Philadelphia.

Popularizing good plays which would appeal to the general public was the aim of the newly-organized Drama Department. A Little Theater Tournament movement was started, and all clubs interested in dramatic activities were urged to enter the tournaments.

A Chorus Contest was conducted by the Music Department, and eleven choruses competed before a large audience for a beautiful silver cup, awarded for a prize. A result of the contest was the organization of thirty-five new choruses in clubs. MacDowell Week and Music Week were set aside as special times for musical activities. Another contest was held for a State Federation Song with a $50 prize awarded by Mary J. S. Moore of Haddonfield.

Interest in education continued with clubwomen being asked to visit their local schools and get to know the teachers both professionally and socially. They studied New Jersey School Laws and became familiar with proposed educational legislation from an unbiased viewpoint. It was recommended that Normal School training be increased from two to three years in order to better prepare teachers.

Women had *finally*, been given the right to vote with the ratification of the 19th Amendment on August 26, 1920. The Federation established the American Citizenship Department aimed at having each club conduct a training camp for citizenship so that clubwomen would measure up to their new voting responsibilities. Many clubs worked with foreign-born citizens, and through their efforts admission to citizenship became a more dignified procedure for immigrants receiving their "papers".

These years saw a national call for economy which increased the clubwomen's interest in practical finance. Thirty-seven women responded to an invitation to visit the New York Stock Exchange and see it in operation. Data relative to ownership and financing of club houses was of great interest with statistics showing a large increase in the building of club houses. GFWC received permission to use an outline issued by the Practical Finance Department and recommended that such a Department be formed in all State Federations.

Clubwomen continued to increase their knowledge of institutions housing women in New Jersey. The monotony of institutional life was reduced with articles being made by the inmates and marketed. Efforts were made to have the names of "alms house" and "poor house" changed.

The welfare of children in tuberculosis sanitoriums and the problems of juvenile offenders were subjects on the minds of clubwomen. There was a State Board of Health campaign for "a Health Examination on Your Birthday" and NJSFWC cooperated in this nationwide effort to awaken individuals to responsibility for their health.

The Public Welfare Department held a Child Welfare Luncheon in an effort to reduce the great number of undernourished children in New Jersey. An appeal was also made for a Psychiatry Clinic for children. The Federation supported bills for more uniform marriage laws, worked for compulsory examination of both sexes before marriage licenses could be obtained, and also worked for the prevention of marriage of the mentally deficient and those with venereal diseases. President Lee attended a Senate Committee Hearing on Uniform Marriage and Divorce Laws.

At the closing Convention of her administration Etta Lee presented to the Past Presidents of NJSFWC pins designed for them as gifts from the State Ex Club and the Federation. She said, "We believe that there are great tasks ahead of the women of the state. We believe they are being prepared for these tasks and responsibilities and we firmly believe that they will measure up to them."

Edith Duff Gray Hubbard
(Mrs. L. V. Hubbard)
1926 to 1929

The fifteenth president of NJSFWC was Edith Duff Gray Hubbard from the Woman's Club of Upper Montclair. Serving with her as Vice Presidents were Mrs. B. C. Wooster of Hackensack and Mrs. Luther Ogden from the southern tip of the state, Cape May.

This administration began with an exciting event when NJSFWC served as co-host with the Pennsylvania Federation for the Eighteenth Biennial of the General Federation held in May, 1926 in Atlantic City. The business sessions were held on the world-famous Steel Pier, and New Jersey Night was observed with a dinner served to 465 New Jersey women and two guests — a Pennsylvania Federation officer and a delegate from Australia.

The ever-present need for more publicity was apparent when the President approved a proposal to publish a magazine as the official organ of NJSFWC. A monthly publication, the "New Jersey Club Woman", was first published in October, 1926 with the expenses for the first year being underwritten by Mrs. Hubbard.

More space was needed for Headquarters, and a larger room was secured at the Newark YWCA building. A full-time secretary was employed and placed in charge of magazine circulation along with a multitude of other duties.

The State Ex Club presented a design and a die for a pin which would be worn by Club Presidents upon their retirement from office. The Historian, Ada D. Fuller, was authorized to prepare a small history of the Federation recording events from 1894 to 1927. The paper bound 88-page volume was published in 1927.

Departments of NJSFWC were regrouped to conform to the General Federation plan. They included American Citizenship, Applied Education (American Home), Fine Arts (Art, Drama, Literature and Music), Legislation and Public Welfare. The special committees, College and Junior, were joined by a new International Relations Committee. This new committee participated in the national conferences held on the cause and cure of war. These conferences resulted because, only 10 years after the end of World War I (fought to end all war), misunderstandings among nations again threatened the peace of the world.

In fact, by 1929 the attendees of the General Federation Convention were warned on the dangers of Communism— being advised to "watch schools, churches, young people, and especially the very young children."

In May 1927 the New Jersey College for Women paid tribute to the Federation's honorary president, Mrs. Charles

B. Yardley, by conferring a Master of Philanthropy degree upon her. The College Committee realized a dream when, after 5 years of hard work, the Music Studio Building was dedicated on October 3, 1928. Funds totalling $100,000 had been raised through many projects, gifts from clubs and generous donations from Friends of the Federation. During this era NJSFWC took a firm stand that the New Jersey College for Women should maintain its individuality as the only college founded though the vision and effort of a State Federation. The college was now ten years old.

The Junior Committee conducted a special program to inform clubs of the value of organizing the younger women and sponsoring Junior Clubs. As a result of this effort, 17 new clubs joined the Federation. The First Junior State Convention ever held in the United States was planned by the New Jersey Juniors and convened in 1928 at the New Jersey College for Women in New Brunswick. The Junior Braille Fund, an early project of New Jersey Juniors, was given the status of a permanent fund and renamed the Florence L. Robinson Braille Fund in honor of the Junior Committee Chairman.

The invested capital of the Penny Art Fund was named the Nellie Wright Allen Fund in honor of the founder, who had the foresight to recognize that a Penny-a-member could go far toward encouraging young artists by purchases of their work. This type of fund was another "first" for NJSFWC, and the General Federation Art Chairman saw that other states began to adopt the Penny Art Fund Project.

By 1928 the Drama Department had held three Little Theater Tournaments, and they were established as annual events. On November 21, 1928 the first radio program under the auspices of the Federation was presented over station WOR as a result of a request for a series of broadcasts interesting to women.

The Legislation Department had been circulating the "Clip Sheet" to keep clubwomen informed on current legislation. Clubs contributed regularly to fund this informative small publication. Competition in Get Out the Vote contests became exciting as clubs vied with each other to have 100 percent of the members exercise their hard-won right to vote. Practical Finance was still being studied and correct Parliamentary Procedure was demonstrated at seminars.

The Margaret Yardley Fellowship Foundation Fund was established in 1929 to enable a selected woman to do graduate work in her chosen field. The first award was given in 1930.

During this administration the Federation protested the prevailing type of motion pictures using lurid titles, and endorsed production of better pictures. Clubs still supported efforts to conserve trees, water and soil. The use of billboards by outdoor advertisers in non-commercial areas was firmly opposed. Uniform New Jersey traffic laws were sought since each community had had its own traffic regulations in the past. Supervision of the sale and use of firearms was urged, and cooperation was extended to the World Conference on Narcotics. The Kellogg-Briand Pact (which denounced war) was endorsed.

Creative writing entries reached a new high when 1,000 poems were submitted to the contest. One hundred of these poems were published in book form under the title <u>Verses by New Jersey Clubwomen</u>.

The Watch Tower in Federation Park was erected as a monument to the successful Palisades project. This edifice was dedicated on April 30, 1929.

Mrs. Hubbard had advised the clubs that "Whatever thy hand findeth to do, do it with thy might." The concentrated actions taken by the women of NJSFWC during this administration truly demonstrated "might"!

L. Ethel Heine
(Mrs. M. Casewell Heine)
1929 to 1932

An eventful three years began as L. Ethel Heine of the Woman's Club of Maplewood took office. She was, by nature and experience, very well equipped to lead the Federation through the critical period ahead. The stock market crash of 1929 and the subsequent years of the "Great Depression" added new responsibilities to the complex and time-consuming duties of the President. Four Vice Presidents backed up her efforts. They were Mrs. William H. Osborne, Mrs. Oakley W. Cooke, Mrs. Ernest H. Boynton and Mrs. C. B. Baseler. The thoughtful theme of these years was "Balanced Thinking".

Relief for the elderly and ways to ease the increasing unemployment situation were concerns of the times. Federation representatives participated in weekly Economic Adjustment Conferences sponsored by L. Bamberger and Co. of Newark. Immigrants annually swarmed into New Jersey for seasonal jobs which were now becoming scarce, and migrant children suffered loss of schooling because of inadequate planning for these temporary workers. Clubs cooperated with State Institutions, Veterans Hospitals and other agencies which needed assistance. Clubwomen studied the proposed unemployment insurance legislation which was being planned to help the situation.

Billboard legislation was finally passed after many years of watchful waiting and hard work. Efforts to amend or repeal this Bill were opposed with grim determination. A Resolution was adopted opposing any legislation tending to break down the National Park System, and the Highway Commission was asked to hire a landscape engineer, plant along New Jersey roads and budget a regular sum for beautification.

Eugenic sterilization was endorsed as a practical, sure and humane way to stop certain hereditary mental defects and epilepsy. Along with the International Museum Committee and Pope Pius XI the Federation demanded protection of treasures of culture so that they could be designated as "Inviolable and Neutral" in times of peace or war. The League of Nations was enthusiastically approved, and the Roerich Peace Pact was endorsed. As a result of these concerns the International Relations Committee became a Department of the Federation and the chairman became an elected Trustee.

Mrs. Heine had been Chairman of the College Committee when the Music Studio was built at New Jersey College for Women. She anxiously watched developments at the college. To ensure the status quo, NJSFWC adopted a policy statement declaring that it not become co-educational, but remain a unit of the State University devoted to the education of women.

138

The Interstate Park Commission began the restoration of Cornwallis Headquarters at the foot of the Palisades. The Federation agreed to appropriately furnish the building when the work was completed.

In 1930 the first Margaret Yardley Fellowship of $500 was awarded to Dr. Lillian Milgrim to continue her studies in Pediatrics.

The Junior Committee continued to increase its activities, and the chairman was given the status of a non-voting member on the Board of Trustees. The age limit for Juniors was 30 years at which time these young women were expected to join their senior clubs. There were so many entries in the Little Theater Tournament that it was voted to organize a separate Tournament for the Junior Clubs.

The battle with the mosquitoes continued and the work done by the Mosquito Control Committee of the Civics Department was observed throughout the country. The interest and demand for information was so great that 10,000 Mosquito Manuals were printed and distributed.

The editor of "The New Jersey Club Woman" had a goal of 10,000 subscriptions; however, a 10 percent loss in subscriptions was suffered. The excellent quality of work submitted in the Creative Writing Contest sponsored by the Literature Department sparked the publishing of a literary supplement to the magazine. The compositions of the top award winners were featured in this special supplement. A decrease in income necessitated clever planning to finance the supplement, and a benefit matinee was held for this purpose.

Members of the Board of Directors needed guidance so a

small book was compiled and distributed. It contained the specific duties of each Trustee and Committee Chairman. This type of publication has been continued and expanded regularly.

Mrs. Heine realized that only 25 of the 300 clubs held direct membership in the General Federation of Women's Clubs. Some states had universal membership which meant that each club, as a member of a State Federation, was also a member of the General Federation. She did not recommend that New Jersey adopt universal membership, but she said, "It is always disastrous for an individual or an organization to feel so self-sufficient that no outside influences are needed for development." NJSFWC later adopted universal membership in 1937.

GFWC was trying to set up a huge capital fund, the income of which would support its headquarters and provide the expenses of personnel and various projects. The NJSFWC President expressed the sentiment of her Federation declaring that problems involved in administering so large a sum of money would be numerous; future clubwomen should have their opportunity to contribute; and a pay-as-you-go plan was much to be preferred.

The General Federation made an appeal for books for the GFWC Library at its Headquarters. New Jersey clubwomen contributed whole-heartedly and, of all the states, New Jersey made the largest contribution of books.

The observance of the George Washington Bicentennial Year began during the closing months of this 16th administration. Outstanding, among the many ways used by clubs to observe the birth of our country's first President, was the planting of commemorative trees and patriotic programs which were presented in every community under the sponsorship of the Women's Clubs.

As L. Ethel Heine's term of office concluded, the economic welfare of the country was uppermost in the minds of the clubwomen. Even a major Depression could not halt them in their pursuit of "mutual helpfulness".

This bookplate, which is to be used to identify all books that have been or will be presented by New Jersey clubs to the General Federation Headquarters Library in Washington is the result of a contest offered by the Art Department. The winner, as announced at the May 1928 Convention, was Miss Phyllis Staib of Hackensack.

Adele J. Grimley
(Mrs. Thomas H. Grimley)
1932 to 1935

The grave economic condition of the country was foremost in the minds of everyone, including clubwomen, when Adele J. Grimley assumed leadership of NJSFWC. Mrs. Grimley was from the Woman's Club of Ridgewood and the Vice Presidents serving with her were Helen E. Marsh and Mattie Eastlack Driscoll.

Thanks to the foresight of the women who created the Endowment Fund, which continued to grow and yield dividends, there was little or no interruption in Federation interest or activity. The magazine, "New Jersey Club Woman," keenly felt the effects of "The Depression" when advertising became difficult to secure. Hahne and Company of Newark, who had been helpful in supporting the fund for the building of the Music Studio at New Jersey College for Women, offered to share a percentage of one day's profit if the clubwomen would spend the day in the store as assistants and shoppers. This monetary reward on April 9, 1935 kept the magazine in operation and this event became an annual one for several years. In order to finance the Literary Supplement of the magazine, contestants entering the Creative

Writing Competition were required to pay a small entrance fee. Financing the Annual Convention posed another problem, and to solve it a registration fee was put into effect for the first time.

Restoration of Cornwallis Headquarters was nearing completion. The Northern Vice President, Mrs. Marsh, was appointed to find donors who had, or were willing to obtain, early American furnishings for the building. Many months were spent in the search for the collectors' items which would represent the period of General Cornwallis' occupancy. Gifts were received from 149 clubs and from 22 individuals. The most precious relic, the sea chest of Henry Hudson, was donated by the Interstate Park Commissioners. The building was officially opened on June 8, 1933 with 500 clubwomen and their guests attending the event. A picnic in the Federation Park was followed by a program honoring the women who had worked so hard to save the Palisades. Special recognition was given to Cecilia Gaines Holland.

The Federation continued its efforts to cooperate with state agencies. The Board of Directors met at the State Home for Girls in Clinton to better understand the needs of this institution. A meeting was held at the Wilburtha Headquarters of the State Police whose organization was Federation-sponsored. Clubwomen visited the veterans at Lyons Hospital to determine ways to assist in their physical and mental rehabilitation program. The Public Welfare Department worked directly with the New Jersey Commission for the Blind, arranging for the sale of articles made by the blind. In addition to sale of these items at Federation meetings, many clubs sponsored exhibits and sales in their own communities. Funds were donated for the purpose of "talking books" (phonograph records) which made the blind independent of people to read to them.

As a result of modest profits received from choral contests, the Meta Thorne Waters Music Scholarship at the New Jersey College for Women was founded in 1933. At the invitation of the college several hundred women visited there for the first time on October 29, 1933.

The Vineland Woman's Club invited the Federation to join them in what had been a local project — providing funds for research at the Vineland Training School. The objective was to determine causes of mental retardation in children. In 1934 the Vineland Training School project was adopted as a responsibility of the Public Welfare Department of the Federation. Funds are still contributed annually to this facility which is now the Vineland Developmental Center.

This era found women increasingly more interested in the creative arts, especially painting. Exhibits of their work became a feature of the District Conferences. The Art Department published a calendar of events which interested these artists. Drama was being studied in more clubs each year and the Little Theater Tournament had so many entries that District Drama Festivals were established. The winners competed for the honor of appearing at the Annual Convention of NJSFWC.

A thorough acquaintance with legislation was expanded, and the Legislature was kept fully informed of the action taken by the clubwomen. Federation approval was now considered an asset by the lawmakers. NJSFWC endorsed a Federal Survey of Education, and asked for improvement in motion pictures presented as "Children's Programs" in theaters. A Bill to shift taxation from towns to the state for education was approved, and legislation was urged to establish a uniform system of narcotics control. A Resolution was adopted requesting the simplification and coordination of government. The position of the Federation was reaffirmed by expressing opposition to any amendment affecting the Billboard Law.

As disarmament became a chief topic for discussion, clubwomen continued to participate in conferences on the cause and cure of war. A Resolution to cooperate with all world peace and reduction of arms movements was adopted. An observer for NJSFWC attended the Women's Conference on Disarmament in Geneva. As the world became more and more restless, peace was the foremost desire of all women.

The United States was still not "out of the woods" as far as economic conditions were concerned when Mrs. Grimley completed her presidency. However, the clubwomen of New Jersey were using their experiences and efficient home-making skills to good advantage. Their training in thrift and family management was being utilized as signs of hope for economic recovery began to appear on the horizon.

Mattie Eastlack Driscoll
(Mrs. Alfred Robie Driscoll)
1935 to 1938

From the Haddon Fortnightly of Haddonfield came Mattie Eastlack Driscoll whose son, Alfred E., was later to become a Governor of the State of New Jersey. A petite woman with boundless energy, Mrs. Driscoll greeted the delegates of the 1935 Convention by stating, "An aroused citizenry is America's greatest need." There were many problems facing the clubwomen who considered all problems important, whether simple or complex. Serving with Mrs. Driscoll were three Vice Presidents: Mrs. Sherman L. Warren, Elizabeth Middleton Maddock, and Helen Purdy Adams. These women were to lead NJSFWC through the declining years of the economic depression and into better financial times.

A new Federation flag was presented by the Chairman of the Junior Committee. This was to replace the worn flag which had been flown from the flagstaff of the hotel during the Annual Conventions. The First District Junior Past Presidents' Club was given a warm welcome as the first such club to join the Federation. In 1938 the Junior Committee became a Department and the Chairman became an elected Trustee. The Juniors had chosen a Student Exchange Plan as their project with the object to raise $500. This would provide "travel scholarships", one for a student from New Jersey College for Women and one for a student from a foreign college. The exchange would take place during the student's junior year in college.

It was noted that several clubs contained groups of women who, for business or other reasons, were meeting at night. Some were not eligible for Junior Membership and were unable to attend daytime meetings. Mrs. Driscoll observed that the Federation could be of some service if these groups were organized with a Chairman to represent them on the Board of Directors. A proposal was approved to make a survey determining whether such clubs would be interested. The Committee which investigated this situation found ten groups representing about 400 women as "Evening Sections" of their clubs. Several other clubs were ready to include an Evening Department in their organization to accommodate teachers, business women and mothers of young children. The survey resulted in authorizing the Evening Membership Committee in 1937. Clubs sponsoring Junior Clubs were urged to consider Evening Membership to provide for "graduating" Juniors who were not quite ready for daytime club work. In March, a Supper Conference was attended by 54 women from 14 groups representing 516 members. The President and several Trustees addressed the Conference during which each Chairman reported for her group. This new entity agreed on a desire to unite in a single undertaking while all continued to do their part in community affairs and contribute both time and money to worthwhile causes.

The General Federation of Women's Clubs conducted an

extension program with the object of increasing membership. Twenty-six new clubs joined NJSFWC. Mrs. Driscoll presented the subject of universal membership in the GFWC for consideration, emphasizing the advantages. The clubs debated this question for many months and, at the 1937 Annual Convention, a change in Bylaws authorized Universal Membership. It was approved by a vote of 344 to 160. When activated, each club member would automatically become a member of the General Federation.

The Chairman of the Public Welfare Department was a Doctor of Medicine. She introduced an educational program on venereal diseases and urged clubs to support any action which would tend to halt the alarming increase of cases. She also exhibited the common hemp weed (marijuana) in its various stages of growth and described the tragedy and danger resulting from its use as a drug or in cigarettes. She asked clubwomen to support a campaign to completely destroy the obnoxious weed which grows freely in fields, vacant lots and even in the back yards of many homes.

The Garden Department was concerned with eradicating poison ivy which caused much misery; fighting the tent caterpillar which was destroying trees and shrubs; and ending pollution in the Delaware River which was a threat to health.

In cooperation with the Near East Foundation both Junior and Senior International Relations Departments helped to rebuild communities in Macedonia, Greece. With their contributions many families were rehabilitated in this demonstration of international good will.

Many Resolutions were considered during this

148

administration. Some were reaffirmations of positions previously taken. The Hull Reciprocal Trade Treaties were endorsed as was a Resolution to foster the habit of reading good literature. The relationship of the United States to belligerent nations surfacing in the world was a subject for study, and the Federation supported in principle the request to establish uniform marriage and divorce laws. Convention delegates voted to cooperate with the Roadside Council which was opposing the use of billboards in a state promotion to publicize New Jersey's industrial, agricultural, residential and recreational advantages.

After a year's absence, the radio broadcasts were resumed on station WOR during Mrs. Driscoll's final year as President. The program was called "Woman's Club of the Air" and was found to be both informative and entertaining. Thirty "meetings" of this novel, simulated club were broadcast. The program was once pre-empted to permit Benito Mussolini to voice his approval of Adolph Hitler's actions!

As Mattie Driscoll was completing her term of office an invitation was extended by the Director of Women's Participation in the New York World's Fair for a special NJSFWC "Day at the Fair". This event was to be held in June, 1939, and the delegates voted to accept the invitation with enthusiasm. The Convention delegates also voted to invite GFWC to hold its 1941 Triennial Convention in Atlantic City.

As she retired from office, Mrs. Driscoll's admonition was, "Prove all things; hold fast that which is good." She continued to participate actively in NJSFWC events during the rest of her life time. She was an excellent speaker and never failed to voice her sincere opinions which continued to guide the Federation's future.

Helen Purdy Adams
(Mrs. Patrick Henry Adams)
1938 to 1941

The Woman's Club of Maplewood provided its third President to NJSFWC when Helen Purdy Adams took office for the years which would led up to the beginning of World War II. The Vice Presidents for this administration were Mrs. Clarkson A. Cranmer and Mrs. Walter L. Schroeder.

A definite objective was set by Mrs. Adams, "Effective citizenship through an awareness of individual responsibility." Full-day conferences with the District Vice Presidents and Department Chairmen were instituted to develop an esprit de corps in the Federation and to clarify each member's responsibility as to her part in the total organization.

The General Federation presented two prizes to New Jersey for the largest gains in membership and percentage of clubwomen in the state. Special mention was made by GFWC of the instructional sheet for speakers which had been prepared by New Jersey's Chairman of Radio Communication, and the Margaret Yardley Fellowship was also praised.

A wide range of interest was the Evening Membership concept which resulted in this Committee attaining national recognition through articles appearing in the General Federation magazine, submitted by the editor of the "New Jersey Club Woman." In the third year of existence the Evening Membership groups were growing by leaps and bounds.

For the first time in the annals of the Federation the Junior Chairman marched as a Trustee in the processional at the Spring Convention. Welfare work was paramount in the Junior Membership Outline.

It was during Helen Adams' Presidency that the New York World's Fair was held at Flushing Meadows, Long Island in 1939 and 1940. Many clubwomen served as hostesses at the Fair and, on New Jersey State Federation Day, a newly-organized chorus of 202 members sang. The Garden and Conservation Department held many exhibits at the Fair, including "Gardens on Parade" and a floral map which was an exquisite example of needlework.

The first Nellie Wright Allen Art Exhibit , sponsored by the Ninth District Clubs, was held at the Jersey City Woman's Club. More than 3,000 visitors attended the annual exhibit of creative work by New Jersey clubwomen at the Trenton State Museum.

Clubs undertook the study of Pan-American Art, as a background for the Good Will tour during which a delegation of clubwomen from New Jersey went to South America. They took with them portfolios from the Art, American Home, Music and Garden Departments. These portfolios were given to Mexico as a good will offering from the Federation.

The good neighbor project which was carried on during this administration had particular significance because it was an inter-departmental venture. It began as a two-way scholarship with Latin America and grew to include some gesture on the part of every department which could develop a plan of participation. The Latin American Exchange Scholarship, a project of the International Relations Department, was suggested by the Chairman, Louie C. Francisco, and approved at the May 17, 1939 Board meeting. It became a reality in 1940 when Senorita Marina Orellana, a resident of Chile, was the first Latin American Exchange Scholar to attend the New Jersey College for Women. This recipient so distinguished herself that Smith College awarded her a scholarship for the following year and the Agnes Wilson Osborne Foundation gave her a scholarship to the International Summer School. In 1992, this first recipient of the scholarship contributed funds in the amount of $50,000 to NJSFWC which made possible the publication of this book and added to the completion of the Library at NJSFWC Headquarters. While Senorita Orellana was studying at the New Jersey College for Women, Elinor Dillon of Westfield —

a member of the class of 1932 at New Jersey College for Women — was sponsored by the Federation and sent to the University in Chile.

As a result of the success of New Jersey's Pan-American Scholarship (later renamed the Louie C. Francisco Pan American Exchange Scholarship in honor of the Chairman of this project), six other State Federations set up similar programs and others followed. Again, NJSFWC led the way.

The ever-active Civics Department continued its interest in Federal Housing, billboard control, Safety Education in Schools, better enforcement of traffic laws and the establishment of playgrounds and recreation programs. In cooperation with the Finer Film Federation of New Jersey, motion picture study and appreciation were fostered in the schools. Clubs formed study groups in consumer education and Home Safety Institutes were held throughout the state. With the Extension Service of the New Jersey College of Agriculture the Federation was helpful in formulation of parent/teacher programs.

New army encampments were being set up in New Jersey and the migration of labor from malaria-infested areas created the menace of the malaria-carrying mosquito. A pamphlet, "Companion to Mosquito Study", prepared by the Civics Chairman, was accepted by the State Board of Education and the State Board of Mosquito Control. Major LePrince, Sanitary Engineer under General Gorgas at Havana and Panama, asked for several copies and stated, "I feel that it will have a surprisingly practical influence in the friendly countries to the south of us through the Pan-American Sanitary Bureau."

The Education Chairman had an interesting experience by serving on the nine member Minimum Wage Bureau for Needleworkers and Allied Industries. She was one of three representatives of the general public. This Bureau sent to the State Commissioner of Labor a report which was accepted and became a law by act of the New Jersey Legislature. A Resolution opposing any law whereby the federal government offers financial assistance to education was presented and adopted at the NJSFWC Convention. Apparently, it was felt that education should remain under local and state control. The 50th anniversary of the New Jersey Library Association was observed with a special exhibit at Convention. Thousands of books and magazines were collected for use by men in military camps.

The Legislative and Citizenship Department still kept clubs informed of pending bills through the "Clip Sheet". A Resolution opposing the amending of the State Constitution to legalize race track betting was passed overwhelmingly by the Federation. Fortunately or unfortunately, this was to no avail since race tracks eventually were established. A Resolution favoring another State Constitutional revision proposed at that time was adopted.

Still showing creative spirit, 226 articles were entered in Creative Writing Contests. Twenty-four entries were sent on to General Federation by the Literature and Drama Departments. Thirty-two clubs entered the Little Theater Tournament and the first inter-state Drama Festival was held with the Connecticut Federation of Women's Clubs. This was a history-making event since these were the first two states to try this type of exchange in presenting plays. By this time many clubs were separating the Literature and Drama Departments within their organizations.

154

Much interest was shown in state and national programs for the reduction of maternal and child deaths. Venereal diseases, cancer, tuberculosis and mental hygiene problems were being studied. Attention was given to the elimination of marijuana, crime and delinquency. Sixty-nine clubs participated in a Welfare Achievement Contest with an award presented to the Minerva Club of Jersey City, a group of 26 business women. Cooperation with the Commission for the Blind resulted in increased sales of articles made by the blind and continued interest in the Vineland Research Fund resulted in a larger contribution.

The New Jersey College for Women and the College Committee of the Federation joined in participating in radio broadcasts over station WOR. This program, the Club Women's Hour, commemorated the 20th anniversary of the New Jersey College for Women. "Pilgrimages" to the college were promoted and several hundred availed themselves of this opportunity to see "their college." In 1941 the WOR Women's Club of the Air program was discontinued.

With the reactivation of the Fort Dix Army installation, a Chairman was appointed to assist the Federation in affiliating with a group of well-known organizations. This group became known as the Fort Dix Community Service. The voluntary endeavor undertaken by the New Jersey clubs was the remodeling and renovating of space in the building rented by this group for use as a study or library.

In 1939 the General Federation of Women's Clubs had accepted the NJSFWC's invitation to hold the 1941 Triennial Convention in Atlantic City. Three hundred and fifty New Jersey clubwomen served as committee members to organize this event. The Convention was attended by 7,000 members, the largest attendance in General Federation history. To present the story of New Jersey to the many visitors, 10,000 copies of the "New Jersey Club Woman" were printed. Birthday gifts from each District were presented to the General Federation Foundation Fund as voluntary contributions from the clubs (received at birthday parties held during Spring Conferences). Each District honored its pioneer women. Three State Pioneers were chosen, according to rules set by GFWC. They were Charlotte Emerson Brown (deceased), Ada B. Nafew and Cecilia Gaines Holland. New Jersey "did itself proud" in hosting this national event.

Mrs. Adams' administration closed after the General Federation Convention with admirable goals attained during a very challenging and decidedly progressive three years in club work.

A view of the auditorium stage at the GFWC Golden Jubilee Convention in Atlantic City, New Jersey in 1941.

Elizabeth Middleton Maddock
(Mrs. Charles S. Maddock, Jr.)
1941 to 1944

On December 7, 1941 when the Japanese bombed Pearl Harbor 130,000,000 Americans were plunged into World War II. By this time, Elizabeth Middleton Maddock of the Contemporary Club of Trenton had been President of NJSFWC for a scant seven months. With the Vice Presidents Sylvia Stackhouse and Louie C. Francisco, she was to lead the Federation during the major part of World War II. Remembering the advice of an earlier President, Edith Hubbard, Mrs. Maddock had chosen as her administration theme "Whatsoever your hand findeth to do, do it with your might". Indeed, much "might" would be required of the entire Federation.

An Emergency Committee on National Defense was established and later became known as the Committee on War Service. The heads of existing departments served on this Committee, and as special work came in it was assigned to the area best fitted to accomplish it Another committee established was for New Jersey Service Units which became the Committee for Recreational Work with the Armed Forces.

The President represented NJSFWC on the State Salvage Committee, the Committee for Women's Participation under the Office of Civilian Defense, the War Service Committee, the Constitution Foundation, the Committee for Consumer Information and two special committees formed to study labor situations in New Jersey. Two clubwomen were sent to Amherst College to the Training School for Civilian Defense.

Since Americans were fond of eating and the war changed much in this field, the American Home Department was kept busy at all times. Classes were sponsored in consumer and marketing problems in New Jersey. Food preservation, canning, freezing, and dehydration with proper instructions for storage of such food was a large part of the work of this Department. Canning Centers were set up, equipment checked and methods taught through the assistance of Public Service Gas and Electric Company and the County Extension Services. The clubs cooperated with American Red Cross in all phases of its program. Clothing exchanges for children and adults were established in many areas, and club houses were readied for emergency use.

The Civics Department concerned itself with war-time developments in community areas. Service was rendered on house registration, rent control and local Housing Authority Boards. Mosquito control became a wartime measure and it was feared that there would be a shortage of quinine for control of malaria. The Education Department cooperated with a radio council for the State of New Jersey. Ten thousand books were contributed by clubwomen who cleaned them, repaired them and distributed them among workers and soldiers in defense areas.

Garden and Conservation Departments were busy learning

about soil conservation and the growing and care of vegetables and flowers. The goal of 250,000 Victory Gardens was surpassed by 60 percent. Contributions were made to British War Relief for the purchase of seeds. The first project brought to the Committee for Recreational Work with the Armed Forces was the need of furnishing Company Day Rooms at Fort Dix. One hundred and thirty Day Rooms were furnished in six months at this Army facility. At a meeting of the Morale Officers of 145 camps in the United States it was disclosed that only Fort Dix had a comprehensive organized effort to furnish enough Company Day Rooms to meet the needs of the Camp.

The collection of furniture, recreational equipment, radios and pianos for Army posts along with washing machines and fur coats for Merchant Seamen, victrolas and musical instruments for the military continued for the duration of the war. One thousand Buddy Bags were sent to the Battleship New Jersey. Two thousand three hundred filled bedside bags were sent to Tilton General Hospital at Fort Dix and bedside radios were installed and kept in repair at the Thomas England General Hospital in Atlantic City.

The Committee on War Bonds and Stamps reported a stupendous amount sold by both Junior and Senior Clubs. Bonds were allocated to buy six ambulance planes. The first was named "New Jersey State Federation of Women's Clubs"; the second one was named "New Jersey—Sixth District" in honor of the District having the best record and the third was named for the newest club, "Woman's Club of Wood-Ridge", which allocated more than enough funds for a plane. The fourth ambulance plane was named "Perth Amboy Woman's Club" which also allocated more than enough bonds for a plane. The fifth was named "Spirit of Unity" (taken from the

State's seal) and the sixth became "Golden Year" honoring the Federation's coming 50th Anniversary.

The Junior Department geared its work to war service but continued to support its regular state projects and to participate in community services. The Juniors realized more than $22,000 for their emergency wartime project which was the purchase of army field ambulances. Fifteen ambulances were presented to the Army as the Juniors' gift and ten more were given by individual clubs. The Juniors also supported the Federation in furnishing the Day Rooms at Army installations and were the first to furnish a Day Room at Fort Hancock. They provided entertainment and hospitality for the men and women in the service and took an active part in all branches of the American Red Cross.

Through the Drama Department plays were promoted to sell War Bonds. One group presented an original play eleven times, selling over $570,000 in War Stamps and Bonds. The annual Drama Festivals were canceled due to wartime travel restrictions.

NJSFWC won second prize for American Art Week competing with all states and United States possessions. The Nellie Wright Allen Traveling Memorial, "Scarlet Cactus", was exhibited in all ten districts before being placed permanently in the Jersey City Woman's Club. This painting was awarded to the club in the memory of Mrs. Allen who had been a member of that club and founder of the Penny Art Fund. Club Art Departments contributed generously toward the purchase of supplies for service personnel in camps and hospitals. The first Art Seminar was held in New Brunswick.

The clubs continued to generously support the Pan-American Exchange Scholarship Fund, and local international groups undertook raising funds for war relief. They also worked for United States' participation in World Government.

The Drama and Literature Departments originated a campaign to eliminate "horror" magazines. In spite of all the wartime activities, 194 entries were submitted to the Creative Writing Contest. Sixteen plays had entered the Little Theater Tournament and thousands of books were contributed to the Victory Book Campaign. Drama became a separate Department in 1942, and the Literature Department studied the works of allied nations while supporting the Council on Books in Wartime.

The Music Department studied the music of United Nations. The State Federation Chorus (under the guidance of Past State President, Jessie Alexander Ropes) presented a program as part of the State Convention. Gena Branscombe conducted the Jubilee Chorus of 950 women from all over the United States with the New Jersey State Chorus as a nucleus. Several Meta Thorne Waters Music Scholarships were awarded during this administration.

Supporting the General Federation of Women's Clubs, the Public Welfare Department raised several thousand dollars for nursing scholarships. An award for meritorious war service in sponsoring recruitment, scholarship, nurses' aides and home nursing programs was received from the General Federation and given to the Woman's Club of Leonia.

The publicity committee participated in compiling a record of the war activities performed by 301 clubs. A news writing contest was opened by the General Federation and New Jersey won third place.

In cooperation with the state's dental health program, a dental trailer which served 123 communities in 16 counties was provided. 100 percent of the clubs contributed to the Vineland Research Fund. The mental tests formulated by the laboratory there were used by all branches of the armed services. There was still active participation in the sale of articles made by the blind.

Several citations were received from the United States War Department in recognition of services provided by NJSFWC.

An important event of this administration was that the Evening Membership Committee became a Department of the Federation. The prime interests of these club women were welfare work and support of all Federation projects.

Community work was not neglected despite heavy involvement in war activities. The establishment of a number of community centers started a campaign to combat juvenile delinquency. Public interest in the revision of New Jersey's State Constitution was aroused, and the Legislative and Citizenship Department worked for civic and social betterment through forums and panel discussions. Generous support by clubs to the Legislative Fund made possible the assembly and dissemination of information.

In 1944 NJSFWC celebrated its Golden Jubilee. A special gift in honor of this 50th birthday was given to the Library Fund of the New Jersey College for Women.

The Golden Jubilee Convention was held in the Grand

Ballroom of the Hotel New Yorker in New York City. The Convention theme came from Proverbs 29:18 — "Where there is no vision the people perish". By pantomime, tableaus and music the audience relived Federation history. In its resume of outstanding accomplishments this pageant renewed faith in the value of effective leadership, sustained effort and good will. Elizabeth Maddock had indeed proven to be an effective leader for these troubled times.

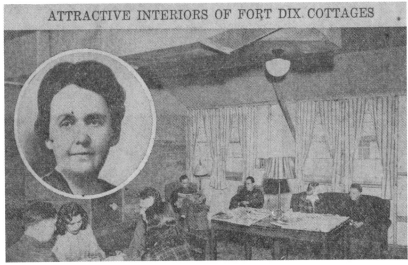

ATTRACTIVE INTERIORS OF FORT DIX COTTAGES

Louie C. Francisco
(Mrs. Stephen J. Francisco)
1944 to 1947

Louie C. Francisco of the Woman's Club of Little Falls, the first former Chairman of the Junior Membership Department to hold this office, became the Federation's 21st President while World War II was in its third year. Marie Catlin served as Northern Vice President and Grace Y. Christian was the Southern Vice President. This team of officers with the other members of the Board of Directors were destined to take NJSFWC into the atomic age.

All Departments were still geared to war service and the American Home Department created a theme, "Guarding the Home Front". At this time there were 193 American Home Departments throughout the State. Institutes pertaining to consumer information were held in cooperation with the New Jersey Division of the American Association of University Women, the New Jersey League of Women Voters, the New Jersey Extension Service, the New Jersey Home Economics Association and the New Jersey Council of Jewish Women. Support of the Governor's anti-inflation program and the work for price control was continued.

All War Service Department Projects went over the top. Sixteen thousand Christmas and Hanukkah gifts were distributed to camps and hospitals and gifts for the nurses at Tilton General Hospital were delivered. The Federation completely furnished a Non-commissioned Officers' club at Fort Dix, including kitchen and recreational equipment. Day Rooms for the WAC (Women's Army Corp) and new curtains for established Day Rooms were other projects. Two hundred clubs participated in the USO Scrapbook Service and Mrs. Catlin received a special Citation for her work in this project. She was the only women in New Jersey so honored.

The quota for the drive for the Air Armada of the Navy was $1,000,000. The amount credited to the Federation was $1,169,338. This entitled the Federation to name 11 Hellcat Fighter planes. The planes carried decals which identified them as "belonging" to the Contemporary Club of Englewood, Woman's Club of Montclair and the Woman's Club of Upper Montclair, Woman's Club of Maplewood, Woman's Club of Orange, Woman's Club of Wood-Ridge, the Fifth District NJSFWC and the Sixth District NJSFWC. The other four planes were all named New Jersey State Federation of Women's Clubs.

Solicitations for the Soldier Art Fund were later discontinued and a recommendation to establish an Art Scholarship Fund was considered. The "Help Youth Program" was met by insisting on public school art instruction and by raising funds for art materials and student aid. Two hundred dollars in Art Scholarships were awarded to two students in a high school contest and an Art Scholarship was given to the most deserving student at the New Jersey College for Women.

New Jersey was honored as the top state in the nation for quality and quantity of its Art Week Celebrations.

For the first and, so far, only time the Federation's Spring Convention in 1945 was cancelled and elections were held by mail. A convention-by-mail issue of the "New Jersey Club Woman" was utilized and the Chairman of Elections reported that 491 votes had been cast by mail.

Following Victory in Europe, and later in the Pacific, the thoughts and energies of the clubwomen turned to the reconstruction period that came with peace. Study was given to the problems of veterans' housing, rehabilitation and recreation centers. The Chairman of Civics was commended by the General Federation for support of recreational activities for veterans. Dogwood trees were planted along the Blue Star Drive as a memorial to the men and women serving in the armed forces. This was a project of the New Jersey Federation of Garden Clubs with which NJSFWC cooperated. Four hundred dollars was collected for seeds and chickens for the Philippine Friendly Fund. Cooperation with the New Jersey Roadside Council assisted in the passage of the Freeways and Parkways Bill, one of the first important steps in the beautification of the highways of New Jersey. The Victory Gardens supplied food for millions because clubwomen had been active in canning and freezing activities.

Two hundred clubwomen served as radio listeners for the radio networks and 35 clubwomen served on the Evaluation Committee for the New Jersey Radio Council's Guide to Good Listening. Books and magazines for county institutions were secured through a library book project. The Education Department held forums on the current world problems and arranged classes in Adult Education. Clubs established student loan projects and several sponsored extension courses. Two circulating libraries had been established in defense industry areas.

NJSFWC was honored by the New York Rotary as the first state group to include Canada in its study outline for the purpose of promoting better international relations with our northern neighbors. The International Relations theme was "Building for World Peace" and the department promoted the study of the Dunbarton Oaks Proposals. Large delegations of clubwomen attended United Nations sessions at Lake Success and received special mention in United Nations' publicity. Legislation to assist in the problems of displaced persons and refugees was supported, and the General Federation's call for aid to Greece brought (within two weeks) a response of $1,083.50 along with nine thousand yards of cloth and other supplies.

Through "Save the Children Federation", five schools abroad were adopted and individual children were sponsored at a cost of $95 per child. Substantial sums of money were sent to the Emergency Food Fund and the Friends Service Committee. Food and blanket packages were sent through CARE .

The Chairman of International Relations was appointed to serve as correspondent to carry out in New Jersey a General Federation project of contacting a foreign club. New Jersey was asked to communicate with the Community Club of Hastings, New Zealand. A yearly subscription to the "New Jersey Club Woman" magazine was also sent to the New Zealand Club.

The Junior Membership Department, which had been

active during wartime, contributed another field ambulance to the United States Army before the end of the war. Juniors sent 3,000 packets of seeds to war-devastated countries and 35 families were adopted (with 2500 pounds of food and clothing being sent to them). Many members of the Junior Clubs had served in various branches of the Armed Services, and they were warmly welcomed home. The Junior project at that time was raising $10,000 for the Commission for the Blind to purchase a Mobile Eye Clinic. New Jersey was the first state to pioneer in the field of preventive services by reaching out to remote areas with this traveling clinic.

The Evening Membership Department reported on eighteen projects. The EMD had steadily increased in membership. A Fellowship Fund was sponsored to send, without regard to race or creed, a woman to a professional school. The award was given to a black student studying nursery education at Columbia University, New York City. Another $900 was given to a student in the field of Social Service. The EMD furnished a room at the New Jersey College for Women to be used by a foreign student, and also a room in a hospital. These clubwomen continued to support all other Federation activities.

A conference on Public Affairs was held in Newark with eight Districts participating. The study of Constitutional Revision, Labor Legislation and the merger of our Armed Forces, as well as panel discussions on the present and post-war problems relating to compulsory military training, composed the day's agenda. The returning veteran and the GI Bill of Rights were also of vital interest to clubwomen.

Travel restrictions during the war had forced the cancellation of District Drama Festivals. A Creative Writing

Contest which was to have been sponsored by the Drama Department was omitted due to a lack of entries. Play-lending libraries and five original plays were entered in a contest sponsored by GFWC.

The aim of the Literature Department was "under-standing". They wanted to understand problems everywhere and to study people of the enemy and allied nations. They read books about America for the democratic traditions and about other countries for information. Three prize poems were sent to GFWC for its Anthology. Thirty-three entries on the topic "The Modern Woman's Place in the Home" were submitted in an Essay Contest conducted by the Atlantic Monthly Magazine. The clubs responded generously to the plea of veterans hospital libraries for microfilm projectors.

During the War "Singing Our Way to Victory" was a pattern for the Music Department. Sunday Supper Musicals emphasizing current events in the world of music were inaugurated. The Federation Vocal Ensemble still functioned and several Meta Thorne Waters Scholarships were awarded at New Jersey College for Women. CARE packages were sent to a needy musician in Europe.

During the war years, District College Teas or College Nights were held in place of College Days. When War restrictions were lifted, College Day was resumed with the first one being attended only by clubwomen.

Largely as a result of pressure from clubwomen in New Jersey, a Department of Health Education and a Bureau of Cancer Control were established by the New Jersey Department of Health. Following a Public Health Institute, held at the New Jersey College for Women, many more were held in several Districts. In Woodbury, a Mental Health Clinic was held. The microfilm projector project, begun under the War Service Department, was continued and was over-subscribed, reaching a sum well over $10,000. In addition to all veterans' hospitals, other hospitals in the New Jersey area were supplied with this equipment. This fund was closed and a Veterans' Service Fund was established in its place.

Due to increased costs of publication, the subscription rate to the "New Jersey Club Woman" was raised to $1 a year. An International Highlights page and a special section for the Evening Membership Department were added to the magazine. Other State Federations sent letters congratulating New Jersey on the magazine, which they claimed provided them with inspiration and guidance. News coverage in the newspapers in the state grew from 40 papers in 1945 to 77 papers in 1947.

In June of 1947, the Youth Conservation Chairman arranged the first Citizenship Institute for Girls. It was held at Montclair Teachers' College for two days. This became an annual event later known as Girls' Citizenship Institute (GCI) and still later as Girls' Career Institute. One hundred girls sponsored by clubs were chosen from the high schools in the ten Districts. The cost was $5.25 per delegate for the two days. There was increasing interest in programs for youth conservation. The Pitman Woman's Club gave land (which they had planned to use for a club house) to their town for a Youth Center, and The Woman's Community Club of Cape May established the first complete youth hostel.

The 1946 Convention had again been held in New York City. For the 53rd Convention in 1947 the Federation happily returned to Haddon Hall in Atlantic City. During the war,

170

Haddon Hall had been known as the Thomas England General Hospital and devoted to the treatment of the wounded.

Despite the hardships of wartime, the Federation had continued the Pan-American Scholarship Exchange program. Mrs. Francisco was justifiably pleased that it had continued during her term as President of NJSFWC. This project had originated when she was Chairman of International Relations.

This administration truly demonstrated "citizenship in action as a stepping stone to peace" with Federation members serving valiantly in time of war and gladly returning to peacetime activities.

Alice L. Cornelison
(Mrs. Robert W. Cornelison)
1947 to 1950

As a theme during her three years in office, Alice L. Cornelison of the Civic League of Somerville chose "Modern Woman" — with emphasize on the life phases, "Her Role in this Problem World", "Her Education for Leadership", and "Her Vision for the Future". With Marion S. Spain and Mildred Bayer as Vice Presidents this was indeed a major assignment and a great challenge for all clubwomen. Judging by the projects undertaken and accomplished, the purpose of this leader was clearly understood. The addition of 13 General and 20 Junior Clubs greatly increased the opportunity for enthusiastic action during this administration.

Representing the clubwomen of New Jersey, as their liaison with other organizations and state officials, Mrs. Cornelison served on the Committee for State Aid for Schools, the Committee for Adequate Welfare and Educational Buildings, the Citizens' Committee for a $75,000,000 Bond Issue for Schools, Institutions and Agencies and the Governor's Conservation Committee. Her calendar was certainly a full one.

172

Interest was not only along state lines but spread to many national issues. Some of the most important were "Renewal of the Reciprocal Trade Agreements Act", "Federal Aid for Education", "Hoover Report", "Reaffirmation of Faith in the United Nations", "The Marshall Plan", and "The Displaced Persons Bill".

The welfare of the New Jersey College for Women still held a very important place in the planned projects of the clubs. By virtue of office, the President served as a member of the Board of Trustees of Rutgers University. She was able to learn of the many problems that might affect the autonomy of the Women's College. These she thought could best be interpreted and explained by a Policy Committee which she established in the Federation. At this time a Past President of the Federation, Elizabeth Middleton Maddock, was elected a Charter Trustee of the University and the Cecilia Gaines Holland award was bestowed upon Dean Margaret T. Corwin of the College. To help promote better understanding of Rutgers University and its needs, a plan suggested by its President to have the Federation Board visit the campus twice a year was adopted. The Federation and the College were linked in other ways such as the renewal of College Day when club members accompanied interested high school students to the College as well as the project of raising funds for a Student Center. This was the most pressing need at the time.

The fine work done by various departments in previous years was continued with many "firsts" added. Midwinter Conferences of Club Presidents were initiated to afford the opportunity of learning a wide variety of techniques in all departments.

For the first time "certificates of commendation" were given to selected personnel of New Jersey institutions. These brought to light the wonderful work being done by humble and conservative employees. This, and the plan to humanize our institutions, highlighted the many important projects of the Public Welfare Department.

Another "first" was the sponsoring of teenage corners in public libraries through the work of the Education Department. Under the guidance of the Youth Conservation Chairman a two-day Citizenship Institute was held for 100 high school girls at the Montclair State Teachers' College. NJSFWC had been the first to develop such a program and was invited to have the Youth Conservation Chairman speak about this project at the General Federation Convention.

During this administration clubs became more aware of the need to express and disseminate opinions on current issues. For the first time a Public Relations Chairman was appointed to keep the President and the Board of Directors informed of the views of the club members and also to interpret to the clubs the plans and development of Federation policies. As a means of keeping the public aware of the activities and the influence of Women's Clubs in various fields of endeavor more than 70 newspapers covered Federation news.

Since the departments of NJSFWC closely paralleled those of GFWC, three New Jersey clubwomen were able to serve on the General Federation Board as Chairmen of Penny Art, Welfare, and Consultant for International Relations. As a result, there was closer cooperation in the worthy project of purchasing paintings done by American artists with funds donated to the Penny Art Fund. The promotion of clean waters for America and the special appeals of the United

Nations for the children of the world were also better supported. Requests for help in providing Youth Centers in Greece did not go unheeded. Numerous packages were sent through Cooperative for American Remittance to Europe (CARE) and thousands of packages of seeds found their way to the Philippines through the generosity of the clubs.

There were many varied and novel programs held by the clubs during this period of time. Projects of special interests to certain communities, safety workshops, interest in roadside improvement, continued study of mosquito control and an alertness to the quality of motion pictures were evidence of vital civic interests. Creative Writing Contests and Drama Festivals provided an outlet for many members who were especially gifted along those lines. An intensive study of the Navajo Indian (for the purpose of revealing means of improving their status), a Rutgers Workshop (for discussing ways of learning to live in better harmony with one's fellow man) and a two-day conference on Civil Rights provided the stimulus so necessary for club growth. The Sixth District held a Women's Club Show for two days at which the work of all Departments throughout the District was demonstrated. This same District, for reasons of efficiency and expediency, was divided into two Districts making a total of 11 Districts in the state.

For some time there had been growing recognition of the need for complete cooperation among the Senior, Junior, and Evening Department groups. Drawing together these categories of clubwomen resulted in significant growth toward full partnership.

The Juniors were commended for their foresight in contributing $10,450 to establish a Curative Workshop for the

New Jersey Chapter of the National Society for Crippled Children and Adults, and the Evening Membership Department netted $1,580.70 for its project — the "G.I. Babies in the Philippines". Sensing the need for more time to obtain working knowledge of all phases of Federation, the Evening Membership Department held its first Full Day State Conference.

In reviewing the record of Alice Cornelison's administration we not only obtain information about the accomplishments of inspired clubwomen but also detect the underlying interest in the future so aptly expressed in the words of this leader, "Imagination and vision, like a sense of humor, are an incalculable aid in projecting the future".

Marion S. Spain
(Mrs. Batt L. Spain)
1950 to 1953

The Woman's Club of Maplewood again provided the NJSFWC with a President when Marian S. Spain took office. Eleanor Colville and Frances Gaskill served as Northern and Southern Vice Presidents respectively. During these three years, reports showed that most of the former projects had been maintained and new interest trends arose.

The Korean Conflict emerged at this time and clubwomen found themselves with husbands, sons, and brothers again serving overseas. There were members of the clubs also serving in the military, primarily in the field of nursing. "CARE" for Korea was an important project as New Jersey clubwomen faced their world involved in yet another war.

People had become aware that a new concept of human rights and responsibilities was emerging all over the world, and the Federation was a means of developing the potential powers of the women in that world. The President so aptly expressed her views when she said, "Clubwomen should consider it a privilege to be part of an organization devoted to the betterment of mankind and strive to make our influence count in the march of history".

The influence of the Federation was used in many directions by supplying a working knowledge in fields of endeavor that needed the special attention of all. On the international level, the "Crusade for Freedom" with over 4,000,000 signatures and generous contributions took a prominent position. The "General Clay Fund" for German youth assistance and the many packages sent to Arab refugee camps through CARE were some of the other endeavors that helped to promote international good will and to develop an informed public opinion on world affairs.

The Federation did its share in supporting a "Bond a Month Campaign" and the Civil Defense Program. Wonderful work, both physical and educational, was done for the Cancer Society. The "Get out the Vote Campaign" netted the largest vote on record in New Jersey and helped the General Federation to win the prize of the Foundation's Award Committee. It was a masterpiece of Americana by the celebrated illuminator, Arthur Szyk.

Ever mindful that young people are the future and the nation's most valuable asset — although often in need of guidance — much emphasis was placed on youth. Girls Citizenship Institute (GCI) was held each year at New Jersey College for Women. The "Fifth White House Conference on Youth" found 500 students discussing mental, emotional and spiritual qualities necessary to individual happiness and responsible citizenship. The Conference was attended by a New Jersey student. The "National Allied Youth Conference", held at Buck Hill Falls in Pennsylvania, gave young people an opportunity to learn the facts about alcohol and the problems of drinking. The contest, "Build Freedom with Youth", conceived by the General Federation and launched with the cooperation of Kroger Baking Company, (in which prizes were given for adult-youth participation in community planning and community affairs) proved how interested the Federation was in providing good investments for the future through youth.

By 1951, local activities of the various clubs were being publicized by 185 newspapers and by many radio and television programs. These revealed that the objective of every woman's club was two-fold: to develop the individual to become a more useful member of society and to provide an effective medium through which women could make their influence felt in ever-widening circles. More women were recognized by their communities to serve on Boards of Education, Library Boards, Defense Councils and many other important posts of service.

There were many services of information available to help women improve their programs. The Newark News Speakers Bureau, newspaper forums, banking forums with the cooperation of the New Jersey Bankers' Association, all-day Northern and Southern Presidents' Councils, Public Speaking Luncheons, Councils on Local Health and Civil Defense and workshops introduced at the Fall Conferences proved to be of great assistance to clubs.

The Historian of GFWC asked for a summary of New Jersey Federation activities from May 1912 to May 1950. This was sent to Washington, and General Federation announced that Anniversary Scrolls would be presented to clubs which had been organized twenty-five, fifty, sixty and seventy-five years. That first year there were 97 New Jersey Clubs who became proud possessors of these scrolls. The only club in the state to receive a 75 Year scroll was the Kalomathia Club of Hightstown, although this was not the oldest club in New Jersey. The Woman's Club of Orange had completed 81 years of active service.

Although the Federation maintained a large number of scholarships, new ones were added during this administration. The Home Economics Scholarship, which would assist students majoring in that subject at New Jersey College for Women, was established. The Drama Scholarship was born and named in honor of a Past State President, Jessie Alexander Ropes. The New Jersey Scholarship Fund also was initiated, allowing clubs which were not able to give a full scholarship to contribute to this broader program. The Pan American Scholarship Exchange Fund and the Margaret Yardley Fund were continued.

The clubs provided generous contributions to support the Walt Whitman Library in the Walt Whitman Home located in Camden. Many clubwomen toured this facility.

There were many gatherings of federated clubwomen such as Conventions, Conferences, Club Woman Day at Hahne and Company, Hurley Day in Camden, College Day at New Brunswick, Music Festivals, Art Symposia and Drama Festivals. These supplied opportunities to promote the activities of the Federation and to develop friendship and understanding among clubs while providing the means of sharing opinions and ideas.

To further emphasize their determination, and to have their opinions recorded, the Federation endorsed many important

Resolutions during these three years. Those pertaining to world situations were to have members call upon their leaders to maintain bipartisan policy in foreign affairs; to promote economic stability in the world by establishing "Free Channels for World Trade". Especially important was a Resolution on "Narcotics" which urged all to consider the seriousness of the evils involved in drug use and to adopt measures to cope with this situation.

Some Resolutions of national interest which were adopted included: "Top priority, after military needs, should be for Education"; "Oppose, in principle, Governmental Crop Controls and Subsidies that create artificial scarcities" and "Inflation" whereby clubwomen would pledge themselves to avoid black market prices, urge further Hoover Report reforms and avoid waste.

The clubs were mindful of conditions which would interest the State Legislature when they urged that laws should be enacted to control the sale of lurid literature, continued interest in roadside planting and the endorsement of a "Program for Exploration of the Crime Situation in New Jersey". The latter was a protest against a situation in which the state found itself as a result of the Kefauver Crime Hearings.

In addition to helping with Federation projects, the Junior Membership Department and the Evening Membership Department raised large sums of money for their own special projects. The Evening Membership Department contributed generously to the appeal of the Vineland School and also sur-passed expectations when they raised $11,891.38 to furnish the needed equipment for the speech and physical therapy departments of the Kessler Institute for Rehabilitation.

The Junior Clubs were becoming fantastic fund-raisers with their donations too numerous to mention here; however, they continued their wonderful support of projects for the blind and raised $1,650 to provide a full year scholarship for a student from the Philippines to study at New Jersey College for Women. The Mobile Cancer Unit which they presented to the New Jersey Division of the American Cancer Society was a unique special project during this administration. The Mobile Unit toured the entire state, dispensing information about the causes and treatment of cancer. This provided much-needed education on this subject to many people who might not have been reached otherwise.

The years during which Marion Spain led NJSFWC introduced the clubwomen to a new decade — "the fabulous fifties". They became aware of the problems confronting everyone and tried valiantly to do their share to alleviate them.

Grace Y. Christian
(Mrs. Wilson Y. Christian)
1953 to 1956

When the movement for Women's Clubs began it was primarily a literary or cultural movement. Over the years it had become a great civic force. By the time Grace Y. Christian from the Women's Research Club of Ocean City became NJSFWC President in 1953, many well-known organizations had seen the value of cooperation with the Federation and were united in the ultimate goal to build a better world for everyone. One of the administration themes was "So they strengthened their hands for this good work". Supporting this theme with Mrs. Christian were Southern Vice President, Rose Stratton, and Northern Vice President, Ruth P. Sanborn, (now Mrs. Charles M. Burrill).

The influence of the Federation was further established when the President served in an advisory capacity on many committees. Some of these were the New Jersey Division of the American Cancer Society, New Jersey Welfare Council, the New Jersey State Committee to Employ the Physically Handicapped, the New Jersey Chapter of the National Society for Crippled Children and Adults, along with many others. Serving in these capacities, as well as being a guest of many other organizations, Mrs. Christian was able to understand and communicate the factors considered of vital importance to women and the status of women. This enabled her to direct the clubs of New Jersey into many fields of worthy endeavor.

There were definite changes taking place in the Federation's New Jersey College for Women. Aware of the special trust to keep alive the interests of the college, which was a trust so carefully maintained by her predecessors, the President attended Board meetings of the Trustees of Rutgers University and accepted membership on the Advisory Committee for the selection of a new Dean for the college. In 1955, Dean Margaret Corwin announced her plan to retire and Dr. Mary I. Bunting assumed the duties of Dean. A change which was much discussed by club members was that of changing the name of the college. On April 16, 1956 the New Jersey College for Women became Douglass College. This was a tribute to the clubwomen, who with Dean Douglass, had helped to establish the college and given enthusiastic support throughout its 37 years of existence.

With pleasure, clubwomen attended the formal opening of a beautiful Student Center Building for which they had contributed $28,901.52. This special dedication ceremony reminded the club members of former visits to the campus to dedicate Federation Hall and the Music Building for which the Federation had also been responsible. The many other gifts and scholarships presented to Douglass College through NJSFWC since 1918 had given positive proof of continued interest in the facility. All of these events were instrumental in closely binding the college to the Federation.

184

In 1955, the Girls Citizenship Institute Scholarship at Douglass College was established. This was used to assist a student who had been a delegate to Girls' Citizenship Institute (GCI). This yearly gathering of high school girls was now in its 10th year and reached a new high of 260 attendees. Continued interest in supporting work for youth and guiding young people to the role of good citizenship was recognized when Mrs. Christian attended the White House Conference on Education and became a member of the newly-formed New Jersey Citizens for Public Education.

Memories of World War II and the Korean War were part of the background of NJSFWC, and they aroused the interest of everyone concerning the sufferings of those most affected. When appeals were made to support the projects of the United Nations in helping to provide food for the world's hungry, (especially children), for clothing for refugees and many other good-will projects, the women of New Jersey displayed what collective action could do.

There was a need for Community Centers in the Philippines. The response was generous and a pinnacle of achievement in international good will was reached when contributions totaled $14,936.83 (raised from the sale of New Jersey Historical Place Mats). This project was based on the social concept of helping people to help themselves. It guaranteed that (after natives of the Philippines donated the land, construction material and labor), the contributions of the clubs (through CARE) would provide audio-visual equipment necessary for conducting an extensive educational and demonstration program at each center. The funds collected provided for the cost of two centers at $5,500 each, and the remaining money was used to purchase revenue-producing equipment to be used in the centers.

Reports of the Junior Membership Department revealed that the younger members of the Federation were doing inspiring things. In addition to their continued help for the blind and their many other civic projects, a special project raised $31,043.27 for the "Upper Extremity Amputee Fund". GFWC had recognized the outstanding work done by Juniors throughout the nation by selecting Juniors as Co-Chairmen of each of its Departments.

The steady growth in membership of the Evening Membership Department and the increase in its interest in the Federation were most pleasing to President Christian. She realized that all forms of cooperation tended to strengthen the main body. Since it was anticipated that the majority of the Junior and Evening Membership women would eventually become members of General Clubs, the transition from one group to another became easier and more pleasant when there was mutual understanding of the problems and aspirations of all. The Evening Department had achieved much through the support of local charities, Federation Funds and special services. The outstanding accomplishment was the presentation of a check for $25,368.21 for the equipment of a laboratory for the Totowa Nursery.

A national project in 1956 was the restoration of Independence Hall sponsored by the GFWC and its President, Mildred Ahlgren. The project was in keeping with the theme of the GFWC Convention, "Preservation of our American Heritage". Grace Christian was proud to present New Jersey's check for $13,320, the second highest contribution from the State Federations. Clubwomen remember urging local school children to bring their pennies to school to help in the restoration of Independence Hall, and the Junior Membership Department held its Fall Conference in Philadelphia during an early winter snow storm.

The General Federation was still sponsoring the Community Achievement Contest which later developed into the present Community Improvement Program (CIP). Fifty-one clubs from New Jersey entered and reported.

A valid means of expressing and recording opinions about state, national and world affairs was the presentation and adoption of Resolutions where there was evidence that changes were desired. During this administration, the Federation reaffirmed the support of the program of the United Nations and favored the holding of a "Review Conference on the UN Charter". The latter would permit a re-examination of the Charter in the light of a decade of experience and world change so that amendments, if any, could enable the United Nations to be a more effective instrument to preserve peace. The Federation also went on record as opposing the authorization of television stations to transmit programs paid for directly on a subscription basis. (Obviously, "Cable TV" was on the horizon). Also, in the field of television, a Resolution was passed urging sufficient state legislative appropriations to be sought which would provide for the erection and maintenance of a TV station in New Brunswick. Other Resolutions urged the Legislature of New Jersey to take appropriate action to meet the need of expanding park and forest areas (Green Acres); the recommendation for more severe sentences, including the enforcement of mandatory prison terms, for those convicted of selling drugs; and action to establish a medical and dental college in New Jersey.

Just as the machinery of any important plant must be adjusted periodically to maintain peak production so, too, must the working parts of the Federation be carefully inspected and changed when the need arises. After careful study, the Federation was redistricted to take effect in May, 1957. The Bylaws were also revised to comply with needed changes and requests. One such change was the term of office for the President to two years. Grace Christian was the last NJSFWC President to serve a three-year term.

The "New Jersey Club Woman" marked the challenge of change by growing into a larger magazine and paid advertising returned to its pages. It had developed into a high quality publication of interest to all clubwomen.

Grace Christian by her intelligence, personality and demeanor was an impressive President of NJSFWC. Under her direction and guidance, the Federation accomplished many successful endeavors which were a tribute to her stimulating and challenging leadership. She went on to a meritorious career with the Office of Civil Defense and was Executive Secretary of the General Federation of Women's Clubs, handling the administrative duties of the Headquarters in Washington, DC, for several years. She also continued her interest in NJSFWC and was a welcome guest at many of its events until her death in 1991.

Ruth P. Sanborn Burrill
(Mrs. C. Howard Sanborn -
    later Mrs. Charles M. Burrill)
1956 to 1958

Unity, Membership and Service were the three goals that President Ruth Parlin Sanborn, of the Woman's Club of Glen Ridge, used to implement the theme of her administration — "Not to be served, but to serve". Sharing these goals were the Northern Vice President, Elizabeth Drew and the Southern Vice President, Elizabeth B. Alton. Convinced of the actual power of women who worked together, and realizing that the success of an organization lies in the definite understanding of each member as to her part in the whole, the President planned to strengthen the links in the Federation chain. She encouraged the growth and individual interest of the membership in her efforts to direct the clubs toward diversified departmental activities and community service.

In accomplishing these goals the long hours of service and many club activities were recorded in the "New Jersey Club Woman," which was the visible symbol of the Federation's progress toward unity. For the first time, the magazine combined to serve not only needs of the General Clubs but

189

those of the Junior Membership Department and the Evening Membership Department. As a further means of communication, a pamphlet entitled "Protocol for Club and District Meetings" was prepared by the Executive Committee and made available to all clubs.

For the first time, NJSFWC cooperated with the New Jersey Broadcasters' Association in a state-wide Register-and-Vote Campaign, on daily programs for two months preceding the election. Twenty-six affiliated radio stations carried spot announcements prepared by the Radio and Television Chairman of the Federation. The story of Federation activities was also carried to this large outside audience by means of personal appearances on television.

In order to stimulate interest in a field that was fast becoming important to women, Banking Seminars were made available through the New Jersey Bankers' Association. Groups of clubwomen went to their local banks to study wills, estate planning and the current money market. The seminars, in addition to continued Finance Forums and tours of the Financial District of New York, provided information necessary to women who wanted to understand their own financial situations.

An excise tax had been required on club dues and clubwomen sought a release from this burden. After Mrs. Sanborn's presentation of facts to the Bureau of Internal Revenue in Washington, D.C., applications from clubs requesting exemption from the excise tax were approved. This not only lifted a heavy burden of taxation from the clubs, but gave national recognition to Women's Clubs as philanthropic and charitable organizations rather than purely social clubs.

Interests in civic development had been a major concern since the Federation began. Such interest continued to be felt in Education and College Forums, Civil Defense Organizations, Mosquito Control, air pollution, etc. Alertness to civic responsibility was shown in participation and cooperation with other local organizations in various appeals for service. It was now reasonable to consider the fact that enactment by the New Jersey Legislature of many policies favored by the Federation was the result of combined efforts of individual clubs for cleaner towns; better playgrounds; more libraries, schools and colleges; strengthened safety programs; stronger means to combat the menace of narcotics and the removal of obscene literature from the news stands.

Tremendous time, effort and money were spent in the field of education. Realizing the enormous importance and great interest of everyone in present-day education, special study of the situation gave not only suggestions for improvement but also the means to aid those who needed help. For the third consecutive year, the Margaret Yardley Fellowship was granted to the same person to enable her to continue her studies toward a medical degree. The support and generosity of clubs netted thousands of dollars for scholarships.

The Education Department Fund for Fellowship Aid was established. This provided graduate study in the United States for a foreign woman who had been active in public service in her own country. The first such Fellowship was given to Attorney Josefina Phodaca Ambrosio of the Republic of the Philippines. She was known as the "Moral Crusader" who was appointed by her government as the Official Observer to the eleventh session of the United Nations Commission on the Status of Women. This worthy endeavor helped to forge a chain of friendship which bound together clubwomen from opposite sides of the world.

NJSFWC continued to maintain a close relationship with GFWC. In recognition of this cooperation New Jersey received citations for its excellent work in public health, finance forums and civil defense. Some of the other appeals to which the State Federation responded were the Community Achievement Contest, the Vogue Pattern Sewing Contest, attendance at General Federation Conventions and to the special request for the Maintenance Fund for GFWC Headquarters in Washington, DC .

Rutgers University was undergoing reorganization. At the final meeting of the Board of Trustees prior to reorganization, a motion was passed giving NJSFWC the opportunity to suggest a candidate whenever a vacancy occurred among the women Trustees. A soon as such a vacancy did occur, the Federation presented the name of Mildred Bayer and she was duly sworn as a member of the Board of Trustees. Although the President of NJSFWC was no longer a member of the Rutgers Board of Trustees, Douglass College still remained of great interest to club members. Many students at Douglass received Federation scholarships and other aid, and the Federation enjoyed the hospitality of the college when it held many of its important events on the campus. Some of these were State Fall Conferences, Art Symposia, College Days and Girls Citizenship Institute (GCI). The many programs of the college to which the Federation was invited gave strong evidence of the mutual helpfulness existing between the two groups.

The Youth Conservation Programs were extended to meet the existing challenges of the times — the interest of the welfare of young people. GCI had continued to provide new avenues of interest with nearly 300 participants. Valuable information was gained from attendance at the National Conference on Citizenship held in Washington, DC and at the International Conferences of Allied Youth at Buck Hill Falls, Pennsylvania.

The first Allied Youth Post in New Jersey was chartered in Somerville High School and closely followed by another one in Collingswood High School. Allied Youth taught teenagers the facts about the consumption of alcoholic beverages with the organization's basic function to teach young people that "fun" was not dependent upon drinking.

As the world seemed to move faster and people became more tense and wary, there was a need for periods of relaxation. In surroundings made as attractive as possible, opportunities for the exercise of skills and for wholesome recreation were the objectives of those Departments dedicated to building happier homes. Efficient and happy homemaking was a part of the Federation's earliest history and the need was still apparent. The American Home Department held Forums and sponsored a Miniature Room Contest which gave the clubwomen a chance to "play with doll houses" again. This competition was of architectual and creative value.

The satisfaction of self-expression was evident in the many responses to art interests, including the contest to design a cover for the "New Jersey Club Woman" magazine. An Art Symposium was held, Music Festivals were enjoyed and there were numerous entries in the Creative Writing Contests, including many original plays. The variety and number of activities in these fields continued to increase, showing an ever-growing interest along cultural lines.

Health was an essential phase of "real club work". Realizing that there were many things that public and private institutions and agencies could not do, other than supply essential needs, clubwomen assisted by rendering their services. Contributions to Vineland School and cooperation and combined services with other civic groups were some of the ways they responded to President Sanborn's theme.

Continuing the Federation policy of preserving precious evidence of early America, clubwomen contributed voluntarily to restore one of the buildings of Allaire as a museum. The slogan "Virginia has Williamsburg; New Jersey has Allaire" caught on effectively.

The concrete accomplishments of the young members of the Federation — the Juniors and Sub-Juniors — were reviewed with great pride. Sub-Junior clubs for girls ages 14 to 18 had been formed as a "lifeline" to the Junior Membership Department. The Sub-Junior Spree, held in December 1957, was their first State Conference. Growth in numbers and the outstanding record of financial assistance to their many projects proved that the word "understanding" was the touchstone of real accomplishment. The continued efforts to raise funds for the Upper Extremity Amputee Fund met with success. The 100 percent participation in the Community Achievement Contest of the General Federation by the JMD assured community betterment throughout New Jersey.

The broader horizons of the Evening Membership Department proved that these clubwomen performed a great service to the Federation and to those whose welfare was of deep concern to them. They had a workshop for the first time at Convention to better acquaint them with Federation purposes and to give them a clearer picture as to how they could best participate. They generously supported the designated funds of the Federation along with many national fund drives, and also set out to reach their major objective. They raised $10,000 for New Jersey Boys Town. This sum provided needed renovations and recreational facilities. This accomplishment proved that they subscribed to the theory, "It is easier to build boys than to mend men".

The work of federated clubwomen is done without thought of reward, just for the knowledge and satisfaction of attainment through united effort. Ruth Sanborn is the epitome of a dedicated clubwoman and is devoted to her family. Her three sons and their families gathered closely around her when she became a widow in 1973.

Ruth continued her active interests in NJSFWC and ever-widening interest in many other organizations. One of the loves of her life is activity with UNICEF which she served on many levels. Now Dean of Past State Presidents, she is warmly welcomed at every Federation event.

In June 1986 Ruth Parlin Sanborn married Charles M. Burrill and welcomed the members of his family into her own family. This extended group now refers to itself as the "Sanborn-Burrill Clan". Some fortunate clubwomen still receive holiday cards from Ruth. They feature pictures of her family and original poems describing important events in her unusual and active life — they are truly "collectors' gems" which help to tell the story of this most remarkable woman who has served the Federation so well.

Elizabeth B. Alton
(Mrs. John M. Alton)
1958 to 1960

When Elizabeth B. Alton of the Woman's Club of Atlantic City became NJSFWC's 26th President she had already been involved in Federation for 35 years. She states that she became an "involuntary member" of the Federation in 1923 when the Woman's Research Club of Atlantic City organized a Junior Club. Her aunt, who was its President, simply included her name in the Charter Membership. At that time she was a sophomore at Atlantic City High School. After completing a term as President of her Club, she had not considered seeking state office; however, Alice Cornelison appointed her as Second District Vice President to fill a one year vacancy. She was then elected to a full term in this office. She was later prevailed upon to run for Recording Secretary in order to increase representation from southern New Jersey on the Federation's Executive Committee. This led to being Southern Vice President prior to being elected President of NJSFWC.

196

The theme of this administration was "We may make these times better if we bestir ourselves", taken from the writings of Benjamin Franklin. Serving as Southern and Northern Vice Presidents were Peg Atkinson and Lora Starkweather.

The years of Mrs. Alton's presidency were clouded by the Cold War with the U.S.S.R. and the threat of nuclear bombs reaching our country. People were urged to provide Fall Out Shelters for safety in case of attack. The space age was developing, and the Federation had to meet the challenges that came with it.

Early in this term of office a problem arose when Rutgers University "invited" the Federation to leave its long-established Headquarters in the YWCA in Newark because they needed the space for University Extension classes. The Headquarters was relocated to a commercial building nearby.

Keywords in Elizabeth Alton's Presidency were "Leadership" and "Know How". Three Leadership Institutes were originated with the help of College Presidents at Montclair State College, Douglass College and the College of South Jersey in Camden. To provide the "Know How" Mrs. Alton prepared a booklet entitled "How to Conduct a Club Meeting" for club presidents and reviewed Federation Funds for clarification to benefit club Treasurers. In order to make better known the policies of the Federation, all of the Resolutions which had been adopted since 1898 were reviewed by the Resolutions Committee for the first time. At the following Convention, only the Resolutions establishing current policies were maintained. The remainder were placed in the historical file. Bylaws were amended so that Resolutions would be reviewed every three years for timeliness.

Among the many projects undertaken by this administration, the first was the selection of a design for a new Federation pin identifying club presidents. This pin in the shape of a square was made available at the Fall Conference. The pin, purchased by the club, is worn by the club president while in office and then passed on to her successor.

As a result of an inspection tour by invitation of the Women's Prison at Clinton, a committee was formed to study rehabilitation at the two women's correctional institutions in New Jersey. Funds were raised for a much-needed delivery table for the infirmary at Clinton, which would be small enough for eleven and twelve year olds as well as teenagers delivering babies. Clubs supplied residents at the State Home for Girls with needed personal items, recreational programs and other gifts. They established appropriate personal contacts designed for positive influence with the residents of the home. The Juniors raised funds for an athletic field there.

Fund-raising campaigns were undertaken on behalf of US Savings Bonds and the Crusade for Freedom, then known as Radio Free Europe and now called the Voice of America.

The "woman power" of the Federation was asked for help by Rutgers University in regard to the passage of the sixty-five million dollar Bond Issue for Higher Education in 1959. It was passed, providing the University with significant funds for new buildings and expansion of facilities.

The Federation also supported a state-wide drive to pass the Water Referendum Bond Issue for conservation and preservation of Island Beach in its natural style, the Wharton Tract and Goose Pond. An outbreak of encephalitis throughout New Jersey stimulated a project to establish Mosquito

Control Commissioners in the three counties which were without such Commissions. A Forum was held in Camden for Mayors, Freeholders and government officials of Camden, Gloucester and Salem Counties to urge action.

The annual Conventions held in Atlantic City featured notable speakers such as GFWC President, Chloe Gifford; GFWC Chairman of Legislation, Sally Butler; Governor Robert B. Meyner who accepted questions from the audience and Pauline Fredericks, NBC-UN Correspondent. John W. Tramburg, Commissioner of Institutions and Agencies for New Jersey, was also a featured speaker. Neil Rankin, Eastern Vice President of Sears Roebuck and Company spoke at another Convention since this firm was providing monetary awards for the Commmunity Improvement Program (CIP) sponsored through the General Federation of Women's Clubs.

Mattie Eastlack Driscoll, a Past State President of NJSFWC, had passed away during this administration and a memorial service was held.

Many excellent projects during Mrs. Alton's Presidency brought national and state awards along with recognition from GFWC. Notable was the Fall Out Shelter Project which built shelters in nearly every county — 17 in all — with 30 more in the planning stages. One was built on Steel Pier, in Atlantic City in time for exhibition at the Convention. Florence Walsh, Chairman of Civil Defense and Disaster Control, was invited to speak at a conference in Massachusetts on "The New Jersey Plan". Her expenses were paid by the New Jersey Department of Civil Defense and Mr. Dignan, Acting Director, wrote GFWC about the outstanding success of the project.   Mrs. J. Raymond Hays, Coordinator of Women's Activities of the New Jersey Department of Civil

Defense and Disaster Control, presented Command Awards to Mrs. Walsh and Mrs. Alton. This was the highest award given to civilians. Grace Y. Christian, Past State President NJSFWC, was Director of Women's Activities of the Office of Civil Defense Mobilization, Region I via appointment by President Eisenhower. She also presented national awards at this time.

The Day in Court project under Catherine Lindelow stimulated unusual interest in clubwomen visiting juvenile courts. It won national recognition. The GFWC Chairman invited Mrs. Lindelow to speak at its Convention about the project which was considered most outstanding in the country.

For the first time NJSFWC achieved 100 percent participation in the Community Improvement Project (CIP) of the General Federation and Sears Roebuck Foundation. A plaque and $500 were awarded at the General Federation Convention. The money was used to purchase furniture and equipment for the new Headquarters in Newark.

The Federation also placed first in the country for participation in American Art Week. The first American Home Day was held at the Newark Museum and Governor Robert B. Meyner issued a proclamation announcing American Home Week. Strong clubwomen opposition succeeded in removing Farm Markets and road signs from the Garden State Parkway.

Among the organizations which presented awards at the Convention were the New Jersey Division of the American Cancer Society for support of cancer programs; CARE for contributions, including 25 sewing machines, medical kits, garden tools, clothing and farm animals; Crusade for Freedom; New Jersey Safety Council for supportive campaigns against traffic speeders and Meals for Millions which presented a plaque and gold bar for each year this organization had been supported by the Federation.

During Mrs. Alton's administration the Federation passed Resolutions which included opposition of the circulation and sale of pornographic material; simplification of language on election ballots; the establishment of a Foreign Service Academy and safety devices in cars. Another Resolution generated a review of Child Labor Laws.

Indeed, during this period of time NJSFWC did "bestir" itself to extend its influence and reputation far and wide through outstanding leadership of its Board of Directors and club members. The Federation continued to grow in stature as a powerful influence for good in New Jersey.

Five of Mrs. Alton's Board Members eventually became State Presidents. They were Margaret Wagner, Lucille Dangremond, Geraldine Brown Sentell, Dorothy McGlade and Lavenia Taylor.

Elizabeth Alton has long been a force for good in her community, and is active in many things in addition to her work for the Federation. She has maintained her affiliations and friendships throughout the years. She is noted for being an excellent speaker who can articulately discuss many subjects and maintain the interest of her audience. Her writing skills are also exceptional.

John M. Alton passed away in 1992, following several years of ill health. The sympathy and concern of her many Federation friends were warmly expressed to Mrs. Alton at that time, and many Federation officers and members were able to attend the services to express their loyalty.

"Liz" Alton is revered by the Federation and all who served with her during and after her term as President of NJSFWC.

Lucille M. Dangremond
(Mrs. Harley L. Dangremond)
1960 to 1962

As the New Jersey State Federation of Women's Clubs began its 67th year, Lucille M. Dangremond from the Woman's Club of Bogota became its 27th President. Serving with her as Northern Vice President was Mariamne Bowen. The Southern Vice President was Mrs. Arne E. Bernard.

The new President observed that the challenges of world communist growth centered in Russia. The rise of new powers in Asia, emerging cultures in Africa and revolutions in Latin America all contributed to make a changing world which was both frightening and exciting. Quoting from Matthew 17:20, she focused her administration on the theme, "If ye have faith . . . . nothing shall be impossible unto you."

During the first year of this administration, NJSFWC undertook and completed the massive project of reviewing all Federation Minutes dating back to 1894, along with revising and collating Federation policies. To promote club leadership, a uniform agenda of basic information was compiled for use at the District Presidents' Councils.

This era marked a very close presidential election during which John F. Kennedy defeated Richard M. Nixon. The Federation participated actively in the elections by effective involvement in the Get-Out-the-Vote campaign. As always, the Federation was non-partisan, but actively involved in making sure that all citizens took advantage of their right to vote.

New Jersey members of the GFWC Board of Directors participated in the first International Conference held in Montreal, Canada, September 28 to October 1. This was an historic event, since it was the first time that the official Board of Directors of GFWC had met outside the continental limits of the United States, and also the first time that the General Federation had met with the National Council of Women of Canada.

Further interest at the international level was stressed through CARE, Meals for Millions, and the Pan-American Exchange Scholarship which had been in effect for 21 years. Cooperating with the American Friends of the Middle East, the Ninth District supported a Muslim student at Fairleigh Dickinson University for the school year.

Supporting libraries, schools and scholarships had always been a major interest of the Federation. By this time the Federation's scholarship programs amounted to approximately $100,000 annually and were given in many fields of study to various colleges. The Federation gave $10,000 in scholarships to Douglass College alone. As part of a state education project started two years earlier, the Federation presented the Library-Study Center at Douglass College with a check for $11,377.92.

Through the program of Youth Conservation, clubs increased their support to Girls' Citizenship Institute (GCI) and sent more than 350 delegates from nearly every club in the state.

NJSFWC membership continued to grow with the addition of 11 new clubs. New Jersey was now tied with the Florida Federation for having the largest number of clubs with a membership of 500 or more. Total New Jersey state Federation of Women's Club membership was 46,486.

The strength of purpose increased in the Junior Membership Department as it adopted an "Invitation to Initiative" project, the purpose of which was to devote more time to service than to financial pursuits. Working closely with the auditors and the Finance Committee of the Federation, the Junior Finance Committee set up a financial statement patterned after the one used by the Federation. Another example of the close cooperation between the Federation and its Junior Membership Department was exhibited by this move.

An outstanding humanitarian project was adopted by the Evening Membership Department. More than $10,000 was raised for research and development for the protection of birth abnormalities in Babies Hospital in Newark. Increased membership and interest in activities contributed to a stronger and ever-growing Evening Membership Department.

Increased participation in Federation activities and general education of clubwomen were fostered by such events as an Art Symposium at Douglass College, an Art and American

Home Departments' Day at Newark Museum and a financial aid project on mental retardation in support of the Vineland Training School.

Upon her retirement, Mrs. Dangremond noted that the achievement and successes during her administration belonged to the dedicated clubwomen of New Jersey. Under her leadership, the Federation grew, prospered and met its obligations to the citizens of the state.

Lucille Dangremond went on to serve the General Federation of Women's Clubs following her NJSFWC presidency. After her death, the Ninth District clubs held a Memorial Service at Headquarters during which the old flag was burned in a proper ceremony. A new American Flag was flown and the flagpole area was permanently illuminated in her honor.

Margaret D. Wagner
(Mrs. Douglas G. Wagner)
1962 to 1964

As the first NJSFWC State President who graduated from the New Jersey College for Women (now Douglass College), Margaret D. Wagner was from the Woman's Club of Rutherford. Alice Thurnall was the Northern Vice President and Lavenia Taylor was the Southern Vice President during this administration.

"Seek and Ye Shall Find" was the administration theme carried to the 478 clubs and State Organizations in a Federation comprised of 44,851 clubwomen during these two years. The Federation showed growth, strength, leadership and several "Firsts" at this time, and there was increasing cooperation with the General Federation of Women's Clubs evidenced.

During the entire two years of Mrs. Wagner's regime the demanding work of NJSFWC was greatly increased by preparation and planning for two important events to occur in 1964. The State of New Jersey celebrated its Tercentenary in 1964 with clubs throughout the state heavily involved in special events and programs connected with it. NJSFWC again hosted the Convention of the General Federation of Women's Clubs in Atlantic City in June 1964.

Nearly every New Jersey club held a Tercentenary Program or participated in local celebrations. Many clubs planted Red Oak trees, the official tree of the State of New Jersey, as part of this observance. President Wagner and members of her Board of Directors (which at this time consisted of 31 elected Trustees, 24 Standing and two Special Committee Chairmen) visited clubs throughout the state, aiding them with their club projects, programs and philanthropies. Visits by these leaders stimulated clubs by providing them with knowledge of the State and General Federations and the history of New Jersey for use in Tercentenary activities. NJSFWC promoted continuing preservation of the Palisades which had been "saved" by NJSFWC at the dawn of its history.

At the 1963 Annual Convention of NJSFWC a motion was adopted to establish a special fund to be used in underwriting the expenses which would be incurred as host organization for the GFWC Convention and to assist in programs to observe the New Jersey Tercentenary. This was a voluntary fund with the hope expressed that each member of the Federation would contribute twenty-five cents. Clubs in the Southern Districts planned and executed a Federation Day at Strawbridge and Clothier in the Cherry Hill Mall. The management of Strawbridge and Clothier presented a check for $1,000 to the Federation based on attendance of clubwomen at this event. The special fund proved to be most successful and a total of $10,410.38 was raised by 1964.

In spite of the additional work generated by the 1964 special events, the regular projects and activities of NJSFWC were continued and plans were well-executed.

The growth, strength and great philanthropic influence of the New Jersey Federation is shown by a study of the Treasurer's reports in the Yearbooks published during this administration. At the first Annual Convention in 1895 the NJSFWC Treasurer reported a balance on hand of $21.97, and at the 70th Annual Convention in 1964, the Treasurer reported: Total disbursements of budgeted and restricted funds of $115,541.23. The balance on hand of general and restricted accounts was $175,000.31. Although never "wealthy" and always seeking funds to be used for its many charitable endeavors, NJSFWC had become "big business" in the financial sense.

A few of the large contributions reported during Mrs. Wagner's tenure were: $29,648.76 given by the Evening Membership Department to the South Jersey Medical Research Foundation for Cancer; $7,634.23 to the Vineland Training School for research in mental retardation; a $1,000 bequest from Mrs. Cornelison presented to Allaire for a gazebo as a Tercentenary gift and $21,154.68 given by the Junior Membership Department to the Children's Aid and Adoption Society. The largest contribution from any State Federation was given by NJSFWC to Meals for Millions that provided over 90,000 multiple meals. All of this was accomplished in addition to the many scholarships given to Douglass College, the Margaret Yardley Fellowship and the Pan-American Exchange Scholarship.

A conference of the Middle Atlantic Region (MAR) consisting of Federations from New York, Pennsylvania,

Delaware, Maryland, Washington, DC and New Jersey held its conference at the Savoy-Hilton Hotel in New York City. Two hundred and seventy-one clubwomen from New Jersey attended this event. A workshop for Home Life was conducted by Mrs. Wagner and Lucille Dangremond, the immediate Past President of NJSFWC. At the general session of the Conference Mrs. Dexter O. Arnold, President of GFWC, was the speaker.

A two-day Community Improvement Seminar was held in Boston for the State Federations located on the eastern seaboard. This was sponsored by the Sears Roebuck Foundation, Land Grant Colleges and the General Federation of Women's Clubs. It was followed by a one-day seminar held at Douglass College to initiate the plans established in Boston.

Among other "firsts" of Margaret Wagner's administration was the procedure that the Historian or Historical Chairman for each President's term would write a condensed history of the regime to have on file at Headquarters. This additional documentation, along with published reports etc. in state Yearbooks and Minutes of Federation Board Meetings would become part of the Federation's archives and a valuable research tool for preparing subsequent Federation histories.

In 1963 the Evening Membership Department celebrated its 25th birthday with a gala dinner at the Annual Convention. A representative from the Evening Membership Department was appointed to the NJSFWC Board of Directors as a liaison.

The Junior Clubs planned, organized and promoted a "Feeling Exhibit for the Blind" at the Newark Museum and provided transportation to those wishing to view the exhibit.

The Federation Bylaws were amended to permit the re-election of the Treasurer for an additional two-year term, making it possible for her to serve for four consecutive years as Treasurer, if elected.

A rule was established that each District Vice President would have a Leadership Institute once during her term of office. Such Leadership Institutes, conducted by officers and other members of the Board of Directors, have become important additions to the education of clubwomen throughout the state.

During this administration 18 new clubs were welcomed into the Federation. These organizations covered the entire state and included eight Women's Clubs, one Evening Membership Department, four Junior Clubs, four Sub-Junior Clubs and one State Organization — The Filipino Ladies Circle. Three new club houses were dedicated while Margaret Wagner was in office. These were in Freehold, Matawan and Stone Harbor. Stone Harbor had replaced, within two years, a club house which had been washed out to sea in the severe storm of 1961.

The wide interests of the Federation were summarized in the Resolutions presented by clubs and adopted at State Conventions. Copies were sent to all appropriate authorities related to the Resolutions. In 1963, Resolutions urged a revision in national election laws which would permit mobile citizens to vote in presidential elections; urged more stringent regulations covering advertising and distribution of motion picture films which were licentious in nature; appealed to the State of New Jersey and to other State Federations of Women's Clubs to continue urging the State of New York to raise the age limit for the legal consumption of alcoholic beverages; urged improved street lighting to combat juvenile delinquency; sought state laws which would hold parents responsible financially for vandalism committed by their children and favored more stringent laws and heavier mandatory sentences for illegal narcotic peddling to juveniles.

In 1964 the Federation went on record with Resolutions seeking state and federal laws regarding the sale, purchase and distribution of firearms; urged the declaration of Bluff Point in the Palisades area as an historic site; requested state laws to protect innocent persons involved in child abuse cases and to punish the guilty; urged clarification through popular media of the United States Supreme Court's decision on prayer in schools and urged more stringent regulations on control of air pollution.

Margaret Wagner's guidance during these vital two years of Federation activity proved that women's clubs were increasing in number, vigorous in their efforts, thriving on hard work and most actively supporting the objectives of GFWC and NJSFWC — "The promotion of higher social and moral conditions, and the improvement of members by the study of civic and social problems". Her later death left a void in the fabric of the Federation, and she has been greatly missed.

Lavenia S. Taylor
(Mrs. S. Herbert Taylor)
1964 to 1966

When installed as President of NJSFWC on May 15, 1964 Lavenia S. Taylor of the Woman's Club of Merchantville announced the theme for the first year of her administration would be "'Tis the Mind that Makes the Body Rich" taken from Shakespeare's The Taming of the Shrew. In the second year of her administration, the theme was "Life, Liberty and the Pursuit of Happiness" from the Declaration of Independence. Serving during this administration as Southern Vice President was Geraldine V. Brown. Mildred Hollenbeck was the Northern Vice President.

In her acceptance speech, Mrs. Taylor said that her number one project would be the establishment of a new, permanent Federation Headquarters. In June 1964 a Headquarters Committee chaired by Mrs. Hollenbeck presented its recommendations to the Executive Committee.

Events from this time to the completion of the NJSFWC Headquarters in New Brunswick provide a tale of achievement worthy of being told. It is detailed in a special section of this volume (see Headquarters). This major accomplishment of NJSFWC was entirely due to the phenomenal cooperation and hard work of the clubwomen of New Jersey, their families and friends — spurred to action by Lavenia Taylor's dream.

Just one month after her election as President, Lavenia Taylor acted as official hostess to the General Federation of Women's Clubs at their Convention in Atlantic City. In October 1964, NJSFWC was hostess for the Middle Atlantic Region (MAR) Conference held at Cherry Hill Inn. The night before the beginning of the Conference Mrs. Taylor held a dinner with the General Federation President, Mrs. William Hasebrouck, the Presidents of Pennsylvania, New York, Delaware, and Washington DC Federations and all of the Past New Jersey State Presidents as guests of honor.

Later she attended the General Federation Study Mission, held in Athens, Greece. Mrs. Taylor returned with the message that clubwomen must be concerned about world conditions. After she had completed her term of office, Lavenia Taylor served the GFWC as its Convention Chairman.

This administration's association with Rutgers University and Douglass College was especially close because of the Headquarters project. A new type of College Day was held at Douglass College with special emphasis on academic excellence. It provided information about four broad fields of study in the Humanities which included Science and Mathematics, Social Studies and Professional/Pre-Professional courses. Mrs. Taylor's speech gained state-wide press attention with a plea to students for more appropriate dress in public. The 1964 State Fall Conference was held on the Douglass campus with 26 workshops, a joint session in the Voorhees Chapel and an overall theme of "Accent on Leadership".

A new idea was the teaching of a course in Parliamentary Procedure conducted by Grace Schongar. Forty-three club-women took this course, many of whom became members of the National Association of Parliamentarians upon its completion. Mrs. Taylor also wrote a booklet, "A New Dimension in Leadership", as a guide to clubs.

Federated Art Days were held at the Montclair Art Museum, Trenton State Museum and the Newark Museum.. Roebling-Boehm Scholarships were awarded to high school students. An Art Symposium was held at Fairleigh Dickinson University in Madison, and ten Music Festivals were held throughout the state. There were special essay contests on the subject of "This is New Jersey" held to celebrate the New Jersey Tercentenary, and essay contests were also held to observe the 400th anniversary of Shakespeare's birth.

This State President was concerned that New Jersey must be kept beautiful despite the fact that there were many new homes, public buildings, schools, highways and recreation areas developed throughout the state. She urged support of the Green Acres program which was geared to keeping the beauty of New Jersey intact. Senator Clifford P. Case spoke on the conservation of our natural resources at the 1965 Annual Convention in Atlantic City. A contribution was made to the Palisades Park Commission to be used for the construction of a wooden footbridge over the sphagnum bog in the Greenbrook Sanctuary that would allow visitors to observe and study this natural habitat.

215

Aware of the dangers of narcotics addiction, the Woman's Club of Morristown produced a pamphlet to be distributed to high school students, warning about drug abuse. As a result, a member of that club was appointed to Governor Hughes' Narcotics Advisory Council. Speaking at the Junior Women's Club convention, Mrs. Taylor emphasized her great concern about crimes against women in New Jersey, and asked that members make an in-depth study of this severe problem.

The largest contribution ever, $4,500, was made to the Vineland Training School when a record crowd of 1,000 attended Vineland Day.

Legislative Day in Trenton (an event putting clubwomen in touch with state government) had its highest attendance in four years in 1964. Governor Richard Hughes spoke at the morning session. Attending a meeting of the New Jersey Legislature, Mrs. Taylor was given the privilege of the floor and invited to speak to the General Assembly and Senate. She was presented with an American Flag by this legislative body.

An accomplished actress, Lavenia Taylor was particularly pleased with "Drama Firsts" in the Federation during her administration. There were nine Drama Festivals held, the Drama Scholarships were doubled and thirteen plays were written by clubwomen. An historical pantomime, "No Summer Soldiers These", which consisted of scenes by five different club Drama Departments was presented at Convention instead of the usual keynote speaker. The pantomime was later presented at the Fine Arts Conference of the General Federation Convention in June.

Mrs. Taylor was concerned about the problem of high

school dropouts, the plight of migrant workers, and the condition of the American Indian. She urged the members to become involved in solutions to these situations. One club raised over $1400 to provide a house and housemothers for refugee Tibetan children in India. Contributions to UNICEF amounted to more than $13,000, and New Jersey was highest in the nation in its contributions to Meals for Millions. At a Convention workshop, a Past State President spoke in support of PBS Channel 13, and about the need to stimulate educational and cultural programs on television.

"Vin" Taylor, who was a vibrant titian-haired woman of many talents, will always be remembered by the Federation for the realization of her dream of a Headquarters for NJSFWC. This building has become a central core of activities for the Federation, and Mrs. Taylor is memorialized in many ways within the structure. She passed away in 1975.

Geraldine V. Brown Sentell
(Mrs. Douglas P. Sentell)
1966 to 1968

The second former Chairman of the Junior Membership Department to become President of NJSFWC, "Gerry" Brown, was nominated by the Woman's Club of Matawan. She is also a member of the Woman's Club of Keyport, and was the founder and first President of The P.M. Club which is a State Organization. Miss Brown was a "career woman" prior to assuming the Presidency. Having been a teacher and the editor of two weekly newspapers (The Matawan Journal and The Keyport Weekly), she had served the Federation Board in many capacities prior to her election. Dorothy B. McGlade served as Southern Vice President during this administration and Annette Brickmann was the Northern Vice President.

Miss Brown chose as one theme of her administration a quote from Thomas Paine, "The world is my country, all mankind are my brethren, and to do good is my religion". Later, she announced a spiritual theme taken from A Collect for Club Women, "Let Us Take Time for All Things". The clubwomen worked diligently to make both of these themes realities.

As the Federation settled into its newly-built Headquarters, it became an important part of the President's job to see to the full operation of the building. Like any new "home" it needed furnishing. She led the search to obtain funding for the furnishings in a variety of ways. Personal letters were sent to the clubs of all the Past State Presidents and to many friends of the Federation. A notepaper project and sale of tiles and coasters was held to provide a Maintenance Fund. Miss Brown appointed a committee of Past State Presidents to approve the furnishings and to request contributions.

To honor the use of trading stamps in financing the building of Headquarters, the Trading Stamp Institute of America, Inc. gave the Federation 1,000,000 trading stamps which were used to purchase a magnificent Sarouk carpet for the foyer. Many lovely gifts have been received as Honors and Memorials through the years, giving evidence of generosity, interest and pride shown by the donors. By the end of Miss Brown's term of office, the building was completely furnished, all debts were paid, and a balance of $10,000 was left in the Headquarters Fund.

Gerry Brown felt that NJSFWC should be tax- exempt, and campaigned to receive such a tax exemption for the Federation and its individual clubs throughout the state. She circulated information on the procedure for filing for state tax exemption to all of the clubs. This effort was not immediately successful, and was continued for many years until it became a reality.

The September 1966 Fall Conference chaired by Shirley Foulks was held in New Brunswick and featured five seminars with Past State Presidents as moderators. Ruth P.

219

Sanborn (now Burrill) conducted a Seminar on Public Affairs; Levenia S. Taylor led the Program on Fine Arts; Elizabeth B. Alton presided at the Seminar on Education; Leadership was the topic of the Program led by Margaret D. Wagner; and Lucille M. Dangremond moderated a Seminar on Home and Conservation. The keynote speaker for this Conference was Dr. Charles R. Smyth, headmaster of the Pennington School, who spoke on "Find Time: Find Time for God, Find Time for Others, and Find Time for Yourselves".

The next Fall Conference was held at the Military Park Hotel in Newark and attended by over 800 women. It followed a similar format with Seminars entitled Public Affairs I, Public Affairs II, Federation Extension, Fine Arts and Home and Conservation. The moderators were Mrs. Alton, Mrs. Wagner, Louie C. Francisco, Mrs. Taylor and Mrs. Dangremond respectively.

This President was honored to represent NJSFWC at the Bicentennial Convocation of Rutgers University, when Vice President Hubert Humphrey was the speaker. Miss Brown addressed the audience at the 50th Convocation of Douglass College. Accompanied by more than 100 New Jersey club-women, she attended a luncheon at the Plaza Hotel in New York which celebrated the issuance of a commemorative postage stamp honoring the 75th Anniversary of the General Federation of Women's Clubs. At the GFWC Diamond Jubilee held in Chicago, NJSFWC received awards for increased membership and for outstanding work in drama and literature.

There were many innovations during this administration. One of these was the promotion of a trip to Jamaica which included a one-day meeting with the Jamaica Woman's Club in Kingston. There were subsequent Federation trips to Hawaii and to St. Thomas in the Virgin Islands. The registration fees were contributed to the Pan-American Scholarship Fund.

Other "firsts" during this term of office included two theater-fashion show parties held at the Paper Mill Playhouse in Millburn with proceeds going to Federation scholarships at Douglass; award-winning entries for two years in the New Jersey Flower and Garden Show at Morristown Armory; a certificate awarded by Radio Free Europe which was the first ever received in New Jersey; five classes in public speaking added to the course in Parliamentary Procedure conducted by Grace Schongar; a collection of all available State Yearbooks filed at Headquarters and an award from UNICEF for fourth place in contributions throughout the United states.

A three-day Conference was held at GFWC Headquarters in Washington, DC which included the World Affairs Conference at the state Department. It ended with tea at the White House where participants were greeted by Mrs. Lyndon B. Johnson, the First Lady of the United states.

A "legend in her own time" with the New Jersey Juniors, Gerry Brown has always considered young women a vital part of the Federation. She worked hard during her administration to maintain the "lifeline", encouraging Juniors to continue their connection with the Federation by becoming part of the Evening Membership Department or a General Club. She has continued her interest in the Juniors and will always be an Honorary Junior. She is an Honorary Member of the Junior Ex Club, composed of former Junior State Board members, and the State Ex Club.

At the 1967 Girls' Citizenship Institute (GCI) Miss Brown addressed the group on the topic "The Rest is Up to You". Mrs. Taylor spoke on "Know Thyself" and Mary Roebling sponsored an essay contest on "The Ideal Form of Government for New Jersey". The delegates published a newsletter for the first time called "A Time to Remember". The following GCI had a record attendance and Governor Richard Hughes was the first Governor to attend in many years.

The first NJSFWC Craft Workshop was held at Headquarters. The Federation doubled its contribution to the Walt Whitman project. Most of the Federation scholarships were increased, and Vineland Day featured the authors, James Michener and Pearl S. Buck, to commemorate the 36th year of Federation involvement with the Training School. The first Federation picnic at Batsto was held to acquaint members with this unspoiled pinelands site.

The New Jersey Cottage at the MacDowell Colony received continued support from the Federation during this administration. It was reported that Sheila Burnford, author of "Incredible Journey", occupied it.

The 1967 Annual Convention held in Atlantic City included a "Status of Women" luncheon, with emphasis on housing for elderly women and the Governor's report on women's status. Addresses were given on "Trouble Spots in Focus" by Willem Oltmans, and "Opportunity Unlimited" by Dr. Carl S. Winters, as well as "The Changing Enemy" by Dr. Donald Barnhouse. Among the musical presentations was one by the Villa Victoria Academy Choir.

Speakers at the 1968 Annual Convention featured Dr. Margery Somers Foster, Dean of Douglass College, who discussed, "In this 50th Year of Educational Participation" and the Vice President of GFWC, Mrs. Earl A. Brown, on "Madame President — Your World Unlimited". A popular speaker at this Convention was the former Miss America, Marilyn Van Derber, who told the clubwomen about "Your Mental Horizons". As had become the custom at Convention, musical selections were presented by Meta Thorne Waters Scholarship students from Douglass College.

The sudden death of Executive Secretary Mrs. W. Hughes White (Peg) in 1967 saddened the entire Federation. In order to keep the busy Headquarters office open and running, volunteers from many clubs came to the rescue. Mrs. Earl Emerson (Grace) took over as Secretary until the permanent appointment of Mrs. Constantine Mackaronis (Olga) was finalized. This really was a "permanent" appointment since Olga celebrated her 25th anniversary as Executive Secretary in 1992.

The extraordinary accomplishments listed here are only a selection of Geraldine V. Brown's dynamic efforts. At the conclusion of her administration she said, "These have been the two most rewarding, richest and happiest years in my life and I would not have traded this experience for anything else in the world."

On September 4, 1972 Gerry Brown married Douglas P. Sentell, a former journalist. Although she has since been widowed and experienced several severe illnesses, she has maintained her loyalty to the Federation and provided much valuable insight and advice to those she mentored as they followed her in office. An accomplished writer and effective speaker, Gerry Brown Sentell is much admired and warmly welcomed when she is able to attend Federation events.

Dorothy B. McGlade
(Mrs. Thomas H. McGlade)
1968 to 1970

A member of the Haddon Fortnightly of Haddonfield, one of NJSFWC's Charter Clubs, Dorothy B. McGlade was President during the year in which the Federation celebrated its 75th Anniversary. Mary R. Bixby served as Southern Vice President and Dorothy T. Weinheimer was the Northern Vice President during this administration.

With the forthcoming special anniversary in mind, Mrs. McGlade chose as her administration theme "Seventy-five Years of Service and Educational Milestones".

Dorothy McGlade had long been involved in the building and furnishing of Headquarters, and this interest continued during her term of office. The sale of placemats and note-paper provided funding as did the proceeds of shopping days at Strawbridge and Clothier, sale of the booklet "Procedure, Policy and Protocol" by Grace Schongar and trips to Hawaii and Mallorca which were sponsored by the Federation. All of these projects added to the Headquarters Fund and helped to

224

purchase modern office equipment.

A well-known New Jersey artist, Michael Lenson, was commissioned to paint a mural depicting Federation interests and projects. This project was handled by the Art Department in celebration of the 75th Anniversary, and a tea was held at Headquarters for the dedication of the mural.

The 1968 Fall Conference chaired by Shirley Goettel was held at Military Park Hotel in Newark and featured five seminars moderated by Past State Presidents. Geraldine V. Brown spoke on Education; Elizabeth B. Alton conducted the Seminar on Federation Guidelines for Presidents; Fine Arts was moderated by Lavenia S. Taylor; Lucille M. Dangremond led the Seminar on Home and Conservation and Ruth P. Sanborn (Burrill) was in charge of the Seminar on Public Affairs. The keynote speaker, historian John J. Cunningham, received a standing ovation for his talk, "From Gadfly Female to Federation Woman" which detailed the accomplishments of women's clubs in New Jersey over the years.

The importance of education for youth was stressed at the assemblage of 400 high school juniors who had been selected to attend Girls' Citizenship Institute (GCI) at Douglass College. Over 1,000 high school girls visited the campus for College Day which included campus orientation and tours. By this time, the Federation was noted for having annually contributed over $12,000 in scholarships and financially maintained twelve rooms for foreign students at Douglass College. Scholarships were supported by Federated Art Day at the Montclair Art Museum and a benefit performance at Paper Mill Playhouse in Millburn which added to the Meta Thorne Waters Music scholarships.

Publications were important to Dorothy McGlade. "The New Jersey Club Woman" had continued to expand and a plaque was presented to Hahne and Company for 35 years of service and contributions to the magazine. Diamond Harvest, a booklet containing writings by New Jersey clubwomen throughout the years, and the "Anniversary Almanac" were all published during this period. Federation Milestones, a Seventy-Five year history of the accomplishments of NJSFWC, was published in paperback and presented at the 75th Annual Convention in 1969 by the Historical Chairman, Grace Mathis Williams.

The "Diamond Jubilee" Convention which was chaired by Eleanor MacCord, celebrated the 75th anniversary of the founding of NJSFWC and was held in Atlantic City in May 1969. It began with the presentation of the key to the city by Mayor Richard Jackson to President McGlade. The cast from the Miss America Pageant and Miss America of 1969, Judith Anne Ford, presented an exciting musical show entitled "Diamond Jubilee". A special anniversary luncheon was held with the curent Presidents of all of the Charter Clubs still in existence seated at the head table. Elizabeth Alton, Past State President, presented certificates to the 21 active clubs which

226

had been established for 75 years or more. In the evening a fashion show, "Fashion Glimpses of the Past", was presented. Convention speakers included the Chancellor of the Department of Higher Education, Ralph A. Dungan, who discussed "The Future for Higher Education: What Next?"; Dr. Donald B. Stewart, Superintendent of Palisades Interstate Park Commission, whose topic was "The Preservation of the Palisades, Then and Now"; and the actor/producer Robert Montgomery on "Communications".

Other special events of this Diamond Jubilee Year included the establishment of a state Music Library at Headquarters and the planting of trees in honor of the anniversary by 90 percent of the clubs in New Jersey. The top conservation award was won by the Federation at the Third Annual New Jersey State Flower and Garden Show, and an Art Symposium was held at Headquarters with critique by artist Joseph Rossi. There was outstanding support of the research program at Vineland's American Institute of Mental Studies (AIMS) which was the first of its kind in the United States. This facility was the former Vineland Training School. The Alumnae Association of Douglass College presented a silver tray to the Federation in recognition of the part that NJSFWC had played in the founding of the college and its sustained interest. Six Past State Presidents and President McGlade were granted honorary membership in the Associate Alumnae of Douglass College.

Governor and Mrs. William T. Cahill congratulated a capacity crowd at the Legislative Luncheon held in Trenton and President McGlade spoke before the New Jersey Assembly and the Senate.

In September 1969, three Regional Fall Conferences were

held — one at the Brunswick Inn in East Brunswick, another at the Governor Morris Inn in Morristown, and the third at the Smithville Inn in Smithville. The identical theme for each conference was "Accent on Education, Service and Understanding". Four Seminars were held concentrating on "Involvement" — in Learning, in Federation, in Living, and in the Community. Various Board members and Past State Presidents served as moderators, and recorders gave accounts of the panels so that all could benefit from the discussions. Speakers were the Mayor of New Brunswick, the Honorable Patricia Q. Sheehan, who discussed Involvement in the Community; the Reverend David Fernandez who spoke on his life in Cuba and Involvement in International Affairs, and the Reverend David L. Bailey, Executive Director of Ranch Hope for Boys, who gave an inspirational talk on Involvement with Youth. Ranch Hope for Boys, a home for pre-delinquent boys, was the first project for boys which involved the Evening and Junior Membership Departments along with the Youth Conservation Department of NJSFWC.

Mrs. McGlade, after judging essays for the "Ability Counts" contest which was sponsored by the Governor's Committee to Employ the Handicapped, promoted the General Federation project of Fashions for the Handicapped as part of the American Home Department activities. The first statewide Author's Day was held in Paramus. The theme for College Day was "The Value of a Liberal Arts Education".

A highlight of the 76th Annual Convention in Atlantic City in 1970 was the presentation of the Cecilia Gaines Holland award by Dorothy McGlade to the woman she credited with the vision to build the Headquarters, Past State President Lavenia S. Taylor.

Speakers at this Convention were Edward C. Harsch, correspondent for The Christian Science Monitor; star athlete Jesse Owens who received a standing ovation when he spoke on "Changing Times"; Dr. Margery Somers Foster, Dean of Douglass College who discussed "Aims and Effectiveness"; Commissioner Edmund T. Hume on "The Role of Community Agencies in Community Affairs"; James H. Gillie of the Advertising and Sales Executive Clubs on "The Role of the Volunteer"; and anthropologist Dr. Ethel J. Alpenfels on "Changing Values in American Society". Musical performances included Meta Thorne Waters Scholarship students and "Musical Moonbeams", under direction of Florence Scudder, State Music Chairman.

Mrs. McGlade was honored by a scholarship given in her name at Rutgers University in Camden. Upon completion of her term of officer she served as Chairman of Urban and Rural Planning for the General Federation, and she continued to be very active in all Federation affairs.

Dorothy McGlade is still pleased that Headquarters is in constant use and is very proud of the continuing achievements and involvement of New Jersey clubwomen. Her message for future clubwomen is "Keep high standards in all you do". A diminutive, auburn-haired woman with a great deal of energy and enthusiasm, "Dot" McGlade did just that throughout her Federation career. She is proof of the adage "the best things come in small packages" and, although she is not up to traveling as much these days as she did at one time, she attends Federation events whenever possible and continues to bring with her the spark of inspiration.

Dorothy T. Weinheimer
(Mrs. George F. Weinheimer, Jr.)
1970 to 1972

Dorothy T. Weinheimer's administration theme was "Let us be large in thought, in word, in deed" from A Collect for Club Women. Although this phrase is repeated by clubwomen throughout the state at their individual club meetings and at all Federation functions, concentration on it provided a thoughtful challenge to the members of NJSFWC.

Mrs. Weinheimer was nominated for office by the Rahway Woman's Club and was also a member of The Woman's Club of Westfield. Serving as First Vice President during this administration was Bernadine Rock. The Second Vice President was Marjory W. Bonynge (later Fielding) and Mary R. Bixby was the Third Vice President. The change from a Northern and a Southern Vice President to three Vice Presidents with specifically outlined duties was implemented during this Presidency as a result of a Bylaw Revision previously approved by NJSFWC members.

Special State Projects since the 1962-1964 administration

230

had been devoted to the construction and furnishing of the Headquarters Building. With the Headquarters a full reality, Mrs. Weinheimer chose a new project, the establishment of support for the Volunteer Program at the New Jersey Training School for Boys at Skillman. The dedication of a playground plaza with fifteen eight-foot picnic tables and benches, six outdoor grills, a large community style barbecue, carpeting for a dormitory, books, games, magazine subscriptions, contributions toward programs, craft supplies, tickets to concerts, clothing and monthly birthday cakes were just some of the many gifts donated through the efforts of the clubs. The motto was "Help that boy today — to find his way". It was a heart-warming project chaired by Marijane Singer, and support for Skillman continued in the future.

Three Regional Fall Conferences chaired by Jean Pollard were held in September of 1970 at the same locations used by the 1969 conferences. Each conference featured four "Panels in Environment Perception". They dealt with improving Learning Environment, Federation Environment, Living Environment and Community Environment. At the East Brunswick conference, Arne Gubrud spoke on "Air and Water Pollution" and Joseph Hamlen spoke on the same topic at Morristown and Smithville.

In 1971 the united Fall Conference returned to the Douglass College Campus and was held on a Saturday. The theme was "A Better Environment for Women". Workshops were conducted by the Chairmen of all of the Departments and Committees of NJSFWC. The afternoon session held in Voorhees Chapel featured an organ recital by Dr. Gladys Grindeland, a welcome by Dr. Margery Somers Foster, Dean of Douglass College, and a talk by Dr. Edward J. Bloustein, the new President of Rutgers University. Dr. Bloustein told of his dream of building a great State University for New Jersey. Katherine Elkus White, a former United States Ambassador to Denmark and Mayor of Red Bank as well as a member of the Board of Governors of Rutgers, spoke on "Women's Responsibilities in Public Affairs".

Eight new clubs were welcomed at the 77th Annual Convention in May 1971. Guests bringing greetings included Major William Casey, the Deputy Mayor of Atlantic City, and Mrs. Earl Lockwood, President of the New Jersey State Federation of Colored Women's Clubs. Grace Y. Christian, a Past State NJSFWC President and the Executive Secretary to the GFWC spoke on "Yesterday — Today — Tomorrow". The keynote address was given by Patricia Reilly Hitt, Assistant Secretary of Health, Education and Welfare, whose topic was "Partners in Progress".

An Awards Luncheon featured a fashion show by clubwomen and a presentation by Vogue Patterns. The State Ex Club dinner was followed by a program, "Our Time for Music", given by the Music Department of the Federation. There were so many women to be placed on the Honor Roll at this Convention that it was done in two parts. There were three performances of Drama Festival prize-winning plays. The New Jersey Boys' School Chorus, under the direction of Mrs. James McCarthy, and the Meta Thorne Waters Scholarship winners provided musical interludes.

The next Convention, also held at Haddon Hall in Atlantic City in May 1972, found four new clubs being welcomed into the Federation. Mrs. Constantine Mackaronis, NJSFWC's Executive Secretary, was honored with the Cecilia Gaines Holland Award for her many civic activities. Archbishop Fulton J. Sheen held the audience spellbound with his talk,

"The Three Forms of Love (Eros, Philia, Agape)", and was accorded a standing ovation by the attendees.

Also at this Convention Dr. Margery Somers Foster, Dean of Douglass College, spoke on "Douglass as a College for Women". Grace Y. Christian, Dean of Past State Presidents and Executive Secretary of GFWC discussed "No Man is an Island". The Superintendent of the New Jersey Training School for Boys at Skillman, Dr. Alfred E. Vuccolo, expressed his appreciation for the Federation's interest and generous support. The Awards Luncheon featured fashion designs for the handicapped and awards from UNICEF, Shell Oil Co., and The GFWC - Sears Roebuck Community Improvement Program. The State Ex Club dinner was followed by "A Century of Music 1872 to 1972" produced by the State Music Chairman, Bessie S. Boland, with performances by clubwomen assembled from Music Festivals and Achievement Days throughout the state.

A Prayer Breakfast was held for the first time at this Convention . The hotel management had said that it could not be held for less than fifty — as it turned out 300 women attended. The event featured the Reverend Edwin G. Mulder, Pastor of the Second Reformed Church of Hackensack, who gave the Invocation and his wife, Luella Mulder, who gave a talk entitled, "It Works, it Really Does!" An evening program featured comedienne-author Irene Kampen with "Of Cabbages and Kings and Other Things". Final speakers at this Convention were Joan Buchanan, GFWC Director of Junior Clubs (a former New Jersey Junior Director) and Dorothy Sarnoff who discussed "Speech and Your Total Image".

There were many "milestones" in Dorothy Weinheimer's

administration. "The Gifts", a film on water pollution was purchased for use by the clubs. It was viewed at the January 1971 Board meeting and later shown by over 140 clubs.

At the request of GFWC, the Federation investigated the Croly Family plot in the Evergreen Cemetery at Lakewood, New Jersey. This led to a project for perpetual care for the grave of Jennie June Croly, who is called "The Mother of the Women's Club Movement". Sufficient funds were raised to accomplish this task.

In 1971 and 1972 the Federation published a post-convention "Almanac". The pamphlet "Conducting a Club Meeting" was revised and updated as well as other publications called "Protocol for Club and Federation Meetings" and "Policies for Board Meetings". A series of new covers were designed by the Art Chairman, Jeanne Colson, for use on the "New Jersey Club Woman" magazine.

To foster closer relationships with the Junior Membership Department, members of the Federation Board of Directors attended a meeting of the Junior Executive Board and hosted a luncheon for the Juniors following their attendance at an adjourned meeting of the Board of Directors.

A Lecture Pavilion was dedicated at the May 1972 picnic at Batsto. Clubwomen sent individual letters to 120 Senators and Assembymen to arouse their interest in conditions at children's shelters and detention homes and to encourage updating of the 50-year old statutes regarding these facilities.

Books were shipped to former recipients of the Pan-American Scholarship to help them teach English in their native countries. This project, in coordination with Douglass, was called KIT (Keep in Touch). Pan-American Scholarship winners received copies of Federation Histories and all recipients of Federation scholarships at Douglass were given copies of "Federation Facts." College Day format was changed to become more timely by giving the attendees a choice of seminars and replacing many faculty speakers with Douglass College students. In 1972 an attendance of 1633 clubwomen was recorded for Club Woman Day at Hahne's in Newark, and the fashion shows connected with this event were presented at the Robert Treat Hotel for the first time. Unfortunately, Strawbridge and Clothier regretted that they could no longer sponsor Federation Day at their Cherry Hill Store. NJSFWC won a silver bowl for its exhibit at the 5th Annual State Flower Show.

The Federation-sponsored trips had been continued and a substantial amount was added to the Federation treasury. A fine time was had by the attending club women, their families and friends. Mrs. Weinheimer participated in the London Trip in August 1971.

A change was made in the method for presenting resumes of candidates for the Cecilia Gaines Holland Award and for voting on the recipient. This promoted a new secret and suspenseful procedure which was in use until 1993 when it was revised for the 1994 recipient's selection.

Matters concerning Civics and Legislation have always been dear to the hearts of NJSFWC clubwomen. In 1970-71 the Federation received a Commendation from Governor Cahill for its part in the passage of the Wetlands Act. The Legislative Luncheon held on March 22, 1971 at the Holiday Inn in Trenton found more than 600 clubwomen listening to Governor Cahill and eight legislators speak on pending legislation and interests of New Jersey. Later, the clubwomen occupied reserved seats in the State House and saw the Legislature in session. President Weinheimer was presented in both the Senate and the Assembly.

Over $1700 was contributed during this administration to support the Deserted Village of Allaire, and Mrs. Weinheimer presented a check for this amount on September 8, 1971 at the Allaire Picnic. Senator Robert E. Kay was the main speaker at the Civics and Legislation Seminar held at the 77th Annual Convention. Governor and Mrs. William T. Cahill were guests of honor at the March 20, 1972 Legislative Luncheon held in Trenton with over 500 women in attendance. At the 78th Annual Convention, Senator Wynona M. Lipman spoke on Bill S-662, for Child Care Centers. Assemblywoman Millicent Fenwick spoke on juvenile justice in New Jersey at this same Convention.

Dorothy Weinheimer is a revered Past State President who truly taught the clubwomen of New Jersey to be large in their thoughts, in their words, and in their deeds. In her valedictory address, Mrs. Weinheimer said, "The presidency is indeed a reflection of the scope and diversity of Federation activities, but it is more than that. Above all, it is a challenging, stimulating, broadening, exciting experience." She continued with her activities by serving as Chairman of Constitution and Bylaws for GFWC and becoming President of New Jersey State Association of Parliamentarians from 1975 to 1977. Her advice is sought and valued by the clubwomen of New Jersey, and she is greeted with enthusiasm whenever she is able to attend Federation events.

Mary R. Bixby
(Mrs. Donald T. Bixby)
1972 to 1974

"Dedication, Inspiration and Communication" was the theme chosen by Mary Ross Bixby of the Ewing Woman's Club as she became the 33rd President of NJSFWC. As she reviewed her administration, Mrs. Bixby felt that this was a good choice for a theme because it was a time during which promises were made and kept, friendships were made and reinforced, records were made and goals set higher and achieved — years in which memories were made and treasured forever. She states that it was an administration abundant with "dedication, inspiration and communication".

Serving with Mary Bixby as First Vice President was Marjory W. Bonynge (who later became Mrs. Robert W. Fielding), Virginia E. Zanetich as Second Vice President and Gloria Meyer as Third Vice President.

During this term of office there were two General Clubs, one Evening Membership Department, six Junior Clubs and two Sub-Junior Clubs added to the Federation for a total membership of 41,242 by 1974.

Members of NJSFWC Board of Directors visited the General Federation of Women's Clubs Headquarters in Washington, DC — the first time many of them had been there. During this trip they enjoyed a tour of the White House, visited Arlington National Cemetery and toured many other points of interest.

In September 1972, the Federation decided it would contribute $100,000 to the Arts Center at Douglass College in an all out effort to aid the college, founded by the Federation many years before. With Edna Chase heading the project, three major trading stamp companies were contacted and agreement was received for a Stamp Redemption Program which raised $5,257 towards the goal. A trip called "A Chance of a Lifetime" raised $31,801. The Junior Membership Department contributed $8,054.10 and the Evening Membership Department donated $3,148. Interest on Federation investments netted over $500 and the remainder was raised by contributions from clubs and clubwomen, including generous amounts from individuals. The goal of $100,000 was exceeded by $64 . . . a dream come true.

At the Federation's 79th Annual Convention in Atlantic City one of the new clubs welcomed was the Bergen Pines Woman's Club. This club was unique in that the membership consisted of patients with physical infirmities residing at the Bergen Pines Hospital. The Club's President, Miss Agnes Martin, was brought to the Convention in a hospital bed and greeted by Mrs. Bixby and the GFWC President, Mrs. Kermit Haugan, who was the guest speaker at this Convention.

Many memorable photographs had been taken at this Convention; however, by autumn it became apparent that there was a problem in regard to these 1973 pictures. They had been paid for by the clubwomen, but never delivered. During the next few months, Mrs. Bixby made inquiries about the best method of resolving this situation. After all data had been compiled to the satisfaction of the Atlantic City Prosecutor, legal action was established to recover more that $14,000 owed to the defrauded clubwomen. The matter went to the Grand Jury. On a personal trip, three years later, Mrs. Bixby learned of the whereabouts of the photographer. Thanks to the efforts of the Atlantic City Prosecutor's office, all members eventually received their photographs.

Vineland Day at the American Institute for Mental Studies was continued as a special Federation event. Members gathered there at a luncheon to present a check in support of the facility's work. Outstanding speakers were Julie Nixon Eisenhower and Pearl S. Buck who told of their interest in mentally-challenged children and commended the clubwomen for their financial aid and personal assistance to the school.

Julie Eisenhower, Dr. Walter Jacob, Mary Bixby, Pearl S. Buck

The first Status of Women Luncheon was an innovation at this time, and was an outstanding success. A new format for the NJSFWC 1973 Fall Conference was tried. Instead of workshops, seminars on Leadership, Parliamentary Procedure, Public Speaking, and Federation Involvement were held. The success of this change in programming caused it to be continued for later Fall Conferences.

During 1973, an energy crisis arose. Several of the District Days, Vineland Day and the Status of Women Luncheon were cancelled in a patriotic move to help conserve vital energy sources. Despite travel restrictions, clubwomen chartered buses for the 40th anniversary of Club Woman Day at Hahne's in Newark. It was a tremendous success and confirmed the ability of clubwomen to cope with crisis and to overcome problems.

At the 1973 Annual Convention, Governor William T. Cahill presented an address which emphasized the fact that women were being given more job opportunities throughout New Jersey than at any previous time. Also at this Convention, a Resolution was passed urging every club and all clubwomen to support the national campaign for "Justice for Juveniles".

At the 1974 Annual Convention, NJSFWC passed a Resolution on alcohol and highway safety which urged the state legislature to reduce blood alcohol levels from .15 to .10 as a definition of intoxication. This later became law.

Mrs. Bixby felt that representing NJSFWC at General Federation Board Meetings held in Washington, DC and Scottsdale, Arizona were learning experiences. During her administration she represented New Jersey at two Good

Fellowship Banquets of the New Jersey School Board Association, the annual dinner of the National State Bank honoring presidents of women's organizations and the launching of the New Jersey Talent Bank for Women. She also attended two annual dinners of the Women's Press Club of New York, the Gimbel Award Luncheon, two banquets of the New Jersey State Federation of Colored Women's Clubs, and the National Prayer Breakfast with President Nixon as the guest speaker. Brendan Byrne had been elected Governor of New Jersey and Mrs. Bixby was entertained for tea at Morven by Mrs. Byrne. Mary Bixby climaxed her administration by being a guest of New York City's Mayor, Abe Beame, and Mrs. Beame at the 1974 Woman of the Year Awards to honor outstanding achievers in the fields of creative arts, sports, communications, public affairs, businesses and professions, scientific research, human rights and community service.

Two special memories described by Mrs. Bixby were when the Junior Membership Department named her an Honorary Member at their Convention and when the Fourth District and Mary Roebling presented a Boehm porcelain to the New Jersey State Federation Headquarters in her honor. A statuesque blond, Mary Bixby is an avid golfer wherever she travels. She especially enjoys wintering in Florida.

Mary Bixby states that the administration was one of unity in diversity, of hope, of joy, of challenge, of dedication, inspiration and communication. Because of the enthusiasm and talent of thousands of New Jersey clubwomen, it was an administration of fulfillment and achievement.

Mrs. Bixby later was elected Treasurer of GFWC, joining a distinguished group of NJSFWC women who served as officers of this international organization.

241

Marjory W. Bonynge Fielding
(Mrs. Winfield Bonynge, Jr. - later
 Mrs. Robert Winton Fielding)
1974 to 1976

When Marjory W. Bonynge from the Woman's Club of West Orange became President of NJSFWC the United states of America was preparing to celebrate its Bicentennial which culminated in 1976. Mrs. Bonynge chose as her theme, "America the Beautiful". Virginia E. Zanetich served as First Vice President, Marijane Singer was the Second Vice President and Edna C. Chase was the Third Vice President during this administration.

The 81st Annual Convention was held in May, 1975 at Haddon Hall in Atlantic City. The total registration for this event was 1754 clubwomen. The 1976 Convention recorded a total attendance of 1812. Three new clubs were presented at the 1975 Convention and six new clubs at the 1976 Convention.

Louise Scott from the First District was honored as the Cecilia Gaines Holland Award recipient in 1975, and this award was presented to Lucille M. Dangremond — a Past State President, 1960 to 1962 — at the 1976 Convention.

Also in 1975 a Memorial Service was held at Convention for Past State President, Lavenia S. Taylor who had passed away shortly after serving as Coordinator of the Middle Atlantic Region Conference which was again hosted by New Jersey in Cherry Hill.

Two important Bylaw changes which affected the structure of NJSFWC were made during this administration. The Third Vice President had Membership added to her duties, and the Junior Membership Chairman and Evening Membership Department Chairman became members of the Executive Committee. There was also a change in the wording of the Federation's Certificate of Incorporation in order to continue the process of obtaining Tax Exempt Status. This move was still in progress at the end of Mrs. Bonynge's term of office.

Three Regional Fall Conferences, chaired by Jean Passaro, were held each year with five Seminars being held in the morning sessions and general meetings in the afternoons. Clubwomen from the southern part of New Jersey gathered in Smithville each year while those from the central portion of the state met in Clark. In 1974 the members from the northern area of the state met in Morristown, and in 1975 their meeting was held in Hasbrouck Heights. Total attendance of the 1974 Conferences numbered 1140 registrants and the 1975 Conference grew to 1557 attendees. A Legislative Brunch held on March 3, 1975 attracted 340 clubwomen for a program of speakers related to this important area of concern. On October 24, 1975 a celebration of the forthcoming United

States Bicentennial was held in Liberty Village, Flemington with 770 in attendance. Margaret Howarth served as NJSFWC's Bicentennial Chairman.

Although there was no special state project during Marjory Bonynge's administration, the clubs continued to contribute heavily to all of the existing funds along with the many local community projects they supported. Cultural activities were not neglected and there were Art Symposia held on October 25, 1974 and October 29, 1975. An attendance of 314 interested clubwomen was recorded for these events. College Day at Douglass College was held each year and 750 young women attended the day-long programs which gave them a "taste of college life."

The Federation continued to sponsor Girls' Citizenship Institute (GCI) in June of each year. Four hundred high school juniors attended these week-long events during which they lived on campus at Douglass College and participated in interesting programs that would prepare them for the future.

Other important Federation events included Cornwallis Day on April 21, 1975, Vineland Day on May 8, 1975 and Americana Day on November 7, 1975. A Southern Program Preview was held on April 9, 1976 to provide "cameos" of interesting programs available for club meetings.

Club Woman Days at Hahne's in Newark were held with 1759 in attendance at the 1975 event. It raised $1862.70 for the publication of the "New Jersey Club Woman." The 1976 Club Woman Day — 42nd to be held — provided the Federation with $1757.40. There were only 1586 in attendance that year due to a bus strike which was in progress on March 18, 1976. Frances Girardi was Chairman of these successful events

244

which raised funds for the magazine that was then being edited by Marilyn Tonneson.

Representing NJSFWC on the GFWC Board of Directors, Mrs. Bonynge attended the General Federation Board Meeting in Washington, DC where Mrs. Gerald Ford hosted a tea and reception in the White House. The 1975 GFWC Convention was held in Washington, DC also. Another GFWC Board Meeting was held in White Sulfur Springs, Virginia and the 1976 General Federation Convention was held in Philadelphia, Pennsylvania. Since this site was "just across the river" from New Jersey it was possible for many NJSFWC clubwomen to attend all or part of the Convention. Philadelphia, as the "Cradle of Liberty", was an ideal location for all clubwomen to observe the Bicentennial Celebration.

Marjory Bonynge was an attractive, vibrant woman who led the Federation with enthusiasm and warmth. She was widowed shortly after her administration was completed. She later remarried and became Mrs. Robert Winton Fielding. At the May, 1984 Convention a Memorial Service was held for Mrs. Fielding during which the clubwomen sincerely mourned her death. A gift of $10,000 was made to NJSFWC from her estate, and this bequest is commemorated with a plaque in the foyer at Headquarters.

Virginia E. Zanetich
(Mrs. Anthony T. Zanetich)
1976 to 1978

Following her installation as the 35th President of NJSFWC Virginia Zanetich, of the Contemporary Woman's Club of Washington Township in the Ninth District, was able to be a part of the General Federation Convention in Philadelphia, Pennsylvania. Marijane Singer, Edna Chase and Emily Strakosch were the First, Second and Third Vice Presidents during this administration.

Mrs. Zanetich chose as her theme "Rise - and Be Counted". With Marion Graham Arnao as Chairman, a Special State Project to benefit the Eye Institute of New Jersey resulted in $54,547.25 being collected during a two-year period. The State President served as a member of the Board of Directors for the Eye Institute during her term of office.

At the Annual Convention in May, 1976 delegates had adopted a Bylaw change eliminating the designation of Sub-Junior Clubs. During the Junior Membership Department

Convention which immediately followed the Federation Convention, the Junior delegates expressed displeasure at not having had input to this action. At the Junior Business Session Mrs. Zanetich promised that she would try to hold a Special Federation Meeting to rescind the action. This meeting was held on July 20, 1976 at Voorhees Chapel, Douglass College. The 366 clubwomen who attended this Special Meeting rescinded the action, and the Sub-Junior Clubs were reinstated with continuous membership in NJSFWC. The elected Junior Membership Chairman, Delores Thierfelder, later resigned and Dorothy Lowe Greene, Southern Vice Chairman of Juniors, served as Junior Chairman until 1978.

The autumn months were busy ones for New Jersey clubwomen. The number of Regional Fall Conferences was increased from three to four in 1976 and 1977. In 1976 gatherings were held in Edison, Morristown, Hasbrouk Heights and Smithville with attendees totaling 1540. In 1977 the sites remained the same with the exception of the fourth conference being held in Hickman Hall at Douglass College. Attendance in 1977 at the Fall Conferences totaled 1332. The format of holding Seminars in the morning and a general meeting in the afternoon was continued. Ruth W. Supp chaired these events.

The 44th and 45th College Days were held during this administration with approximately 800 girls spending the day at Douglass College. Art Symposia were also held in October of each year and a special United Nations Seminar took place on November 3, 1976. Americana Day was held in November of 1976 and again in 1977. On March 28, 1976 a "Women in Action" Luncheon was held, and a Legislative Luncheon occurred on April 3, 1978.

Girls' Citizenship Institute continued to attract 400 young women in June of each year. GCI had become an even more important event with the number of attendees limited by available space at Douglass College. Clubs learned to submit their delegates' applications early, in order to meet the "first come, first served" registration restrictions.

The 1977 Annual Convention held in Atlantic City welcomed four new clubs and the total registration was 1795 clubwomen. The keynote speaker for this event was Mercedes McCambridge who discussed "Courage and Chemicals". Her address dealt with alcohol abuse which was becoming more prevalent among women in the United States.

In May 1978 the Federation held its Annual Convention (84th) at Resorts International. This was the former Haddon Hall which was about to become Atlantic City's first casino. The 1735 clubwomen attending the Convention welcomed three new clubs and heard Virginia Graham, a TV personality, as the speaker at the Tuesday night banquet. Since casino gambling would not begin until the end of May, 1978, the Convention attendees were "entertained" by watching the new casino employees practicing their skills in what had once been the Pennsylvania Room. Since it had been decided to move the Convention to another area due to increased hotel costs, etc., many of the women who had attended Conventions in Atlantic City for many years bid a fond farewell to the beloved Haddon Hall era, which included memories of the famous "March of the Waiters" bearing flaming Baked Alaska!

Dorothy B. McGlade, who had served as NJSFWC President 1968 to 1970 received the Cecilia Gaines Holland Award in 1977. The 1978 recipient was Ellen Shiplee. Both of these honorees were from the Third District.

Club Woman Day was held on November 10, 1977 at Bambergers in Eatontown instead of Hahne and Co. in Newark. Although the attendance dropped to 1227 club-women, an amount of $2,000 was received by the Federation to support the publication of the magazine.

As with all NJSFWC state Presidents, Mrs. Zanetich's schedule was extremely busy. She was one of 38 women to serve on a Committee for the International Woman's Year Conference during which she filled the post of Nominations Chairman. She attended a "Hands Up" Seminar held in Philadelphia and a GFWC Board Meeting held in Washington, DC. The 1977 General Federation Convention was held in Seattle, Washington and the 1978 Convention was held in Phoenix, Arizona. Also in 1978 the General Federation of Women's Clubs Board Meeting was held in Hawaii with a tea at the Governor's Mansion hosted by the First Lady of Hawaii. The GFWC Board of Directors was entertained lavishly by the Women's Clubs of Maui during this event.

During Virginia Zanetich's administration the General Federation presented NJSFWC with a Charter to the Epsilon Sigma Omicron (ESO) Reading program. Fifty-one New Jersey women received awards in this program during the first year it was activated in New Jersey. Reading lists for ESO are distributed to interested clubwomen who wish to participate. As they complete their reading of various books in several categories, they prepare a brief report for submission to the program. Awards in various levels are given, based on the number of books read and reported upon. This program has continued to grow and to interest more and more clubwomen in New Jersey.

Participation in a pilot program called "ARTribution" sponsored by GFWC resulted in $3325.55 being sent to the General Federation from the New Jersey Federation. The money was raised by holding a state-wide formal evening in connection with affiliated artists. The President of GFWC and her husband attended this event.

The NJSFWC Headquarters building in New Brunswick continued to be enhanced with a movable door added to the Board Room so that it could be divided when it was necessary to hold two meetings at the same time. As with any dwelling place, the Federation's "Home" continued to require maintenance and improvement. Clubs and individual clubwomen have continued to support the building with contributions and other gifts over the years.

Every club in NJSFWC entered the Community Improvement Program (CIP), as a result of efforts made by Joan M. Hunt, who served as state CIP Chairman. This marked the achievement of a goal which is still one the Federation strives to attain on a continuing basis.

On May 4, 1978 — at the completion of Virginia Zanetich's administration — New Jersey State Federation of Women's Clubs finally received its Tax Exemption Status. This was the culmination of many years of effort!

A striking brunette with classic features, Virginia Zanetich led NJSFWC with verve and aplomb, during an active administration. She continued her club work by serving on the GFWC Board as Chairman of International Hospitality.

Marijane Singer
(Mrs. Frederick D. Singer)
1978 - 1980

"The Future Is Today", the theme adopted by Marijane Singer of The Valley Contemporary Woman's Club in Park Ridge for her administration, signaled New Jersey clubwomen that the coming two years would be oriented toward action and accomplishment. Building on a foundation deeply rooted in the traditions of the Federation and reinforced by the unified diversity of New Jersey clubwomen, the new President focused the strengths and resources of the Federation on current and future needs of the state and its communities. The First, Second, and Third Vice Presidents were Emily Strakosch, Gloria Malasky and Dorothy Constants respectively.

Bringing the Federation's concern for children together with its historic ties to Douglass College, Mrs. Singer selected support of the Douglass Developmental Disability Center as the Special State Project with Betty P. Loizeaux as chairman. The Douglass Developmental Disability Center was established to provide special education for autistic children while offering practical field work to more than 100 Douglass College undergraduates annually. The school was housed in a trailer, and a new building was to be constructed on campus. Furnishings and materials were also required, and "The Teddy-Bear Project", as it came to be called, was committed to making a major contribution. Clubwomen throughout the state joined in the program to raise the necessary funds, and more than 7,000 proudly wore teddy-bear stick pins next to their Federation pins, displaying their active individual participation in the project. The success of the Special State Project was evidenced by raising over $126,000 for the school.

Following her installation in office, the first administrative problem facing Mrs. Singer was the location for the 85th Annual Convention to be held the following year. Casino gambling had become legal in New Jersey, and traditional accommodations in Atlantic City were no longer available to the Federation. Traveling extensively throughout New Jersey and two adjoining states, the President and Convention Chairman, Dorothea Kinney, identified the Playboy Resort and Country Club at Great Gorge in McAfee, New Jersey as a suitable and accessible site for the 85th Annual Convention. The new location and exciting convention programs drew record attendance to the Convention and to the Junior Membership Department Convention as well.

To commemorate the Federation's 85th Anniversary, a paper-bound book, From the Beginning - A Page of History was compiled and published. Each Woman's Club, EMD and JMD was invited to submit its history for inclusion in the book. Over 300 clubs responded to the delight of the Editor, Ginger Secunda!

Support and promotion of Federation Headquarters was a top priority of Marijane Singer. Built through the donations of clubwomen, it is the only state Headquarters on a university campus. Symbolizing the strength of the Federation, an artistic rendition of Headquarters became a part of all stationery, note paper, calendar datebooks, and the cover of the "New Jersey Club Woman" magazine. Headquarters and its valuable contents were professionally appraised, and an insurance contract was approved which adequately insured the value of Federation property at Headquarters. It also provided for federated clubs to participate in coverage under the master contract. A structural engineer from Rutgers University surveyed Headquarters and reviewed basic problems, recommending corrective action. Specifications for better security and fire detection were drawn by Rutgers, and the new systems installed. New azalea bushes were planted at the building entrance and a new roof and partial heating system were installed.

Federation Bylaws underwent a detailed review and audit, and were amended to conform with the General Federation of Women's Clubs' Bylaws. The two organizations could now coordinate and function more effectively and efficiently with their joint programs. A new "Club Manual" was written, published and presented at the 85th Convention.

The traditional ties of the Federation to Douglass College and Rutgers University were recognized and strengthened on June 20, 1979 when the Board of Trustees of Rutgers University elected Mrs. Singer their Chairman, making her the first woman to hold this post in the history of this 213 year-old university.

The President led the Federation in active support of the General Federation of Women's Clubs "Free" project. Meetings were conducted in clubs and at regional conferences to educate clubwomen in the functioning of the traditional American free enterprise economy, and in the techniques of influencing legislative action. Educational materials and seminars were furnished to secondary schools throughout the state.

The administration actively supported programs for Continuing Education for Women, the Training School at Skillman, Girls' Citizenship Institute, strengthening of the Evening Membership 'and Junior Membership Departments and the many scholarship funds of the Federation.

Throughout her administration, Marijane Singer advocated and emphasized the traditional volunteerism of the Federation. Through the late 1960's and early 1970's, the growing feminist movement in the United states tended to demean the volunteer worker and the value of volunteerism in American society. The accomplishments of the Federation and its clubwomen during this administration, and the focus of Federation leadership on the value of volunteers, proved the efficacy of the Federation's purpose. The goals of the administration were met and surpassed, building the strength and confidence today, which would be required to meet tomorrow's challenges.

IN DEEPEST APPRECIATION

TO THE MEMBERS OF THE

NEW JERSEY STATE
FEDERATION OF WOMEN'S CLUBS

WHO HELPED BUILD THIS CENTER FOR CHILDREN

DOUGLASS DEVELOPMENTAL DISABILITIES CENTER,
RUTGERS UNIVERSITY

APRIL 1990

MARIJANE SINGER, PRESIDENT, NJSFWC
BETTY LOIZEAUX, STATE PROJECT CHAIRMAN, NJSFWC

Emily Strakosch
(Mrs. George T. Strakosch)
1980 to 1982

Nominated by the Woman's Club of Franklin Lakes, but also a member of the Woman's Club of Wyckoff, Emily Strakosch took office as the 37th President of NJSFWC. Her theme was "Meet the Challenge" which proved to be prophetic with many challenges being met during this administration. Gloria Malasky served as First Vice President, Dorothy Constants was the Second Vice President and Betty Loizeaux served as Third Vice President during this era. JoAnn Rivard, JMD Chairman, resigned on September 2, 1980 when she moved out of the area. Barbara Spillane assumed the office on September 27, 1980 and was elected to fill the unexpired term at the May, 1981 Convention. The elected Treasurer, Evelyn Lester, resigned during the winter of 1980-81 and Fran Girardi became Treasurer until the May, 1981 Convention when she was elected. Even with these unexpected changes, the administration proceeded smoothly with the continuity of the Federation intact.

Since two previous administrations had raised large sums of money for Special State Projects, Mrs. Strakosch wisely decided that her two years as President would have the clubs devoting special attention to work in their respective communities. This proved to be a popular idea, and many communities throughout New Jersey benefited from the efforts made by the clubwomen. Awards were given to the clubs for community services. Even though the clubs concentrated on work for their own towns, they continued to generously support the various funds of the Federation.

Two Regional Conferences, chaired by Margaret Hickey, were held in October of each year during this administration. The Northern Conferences were held in Saddlebrook and the Southern Conferences in Cherry Hill for 1980 and Point Pleasant for 1981. Attendance totaled 683 clubwomen in 1980 and 602 in 1981. The format of seminars in the morning sessions and a general meeting in the afternoon sessions was continued. The meetings of the Middle Atlantic Region (MAR) affiliation of State Federations continued to gain in popularity with 44 New Jersey clubwomen attending the 1980 Conference in Lancaster, Pennsylvania and 36 attending the Conference held in Wilmington, Delaware in 1981.

The Federation continued to hold College Day at Douglass College each fall, and Founders Day was celebrated at the college on April 15, 1981. At this time the President of NJSFWC was accepted as an honorary member of the Associate Alumnae. The 1980 Art Symposium was held on October 23, 1980 at Lake Mohawk Country Club and the Contemporary Club of Trenton hosted the Symposium on October 1, 1981. Americana Day held on November 6, 1980 was in North Brunswick. On November 5, 1981 it was held in Clark. The Legislative Luncheon was held on March 29, 1982 and the first "Recognition Day for Women" was held during that same year. This event was co-sponsored by Douglass College and NJSFWC. It marked the beginning of the New Jersey Women of Achievement Award program which is now conducted annually. Congresswoman Millicent Fenwick was the recipient of the award and featured as the Keynote Speaker.

87th Annual Convention
Joyce Farnham, Emily Strakosch, Helen Sparacio, Katie Henn

A total registration of 1518 was recorded for the 87th Annual Convention held in 1981 at the Playboy Resort and Country Club at Great Gorge located in McAfee, New Jersey. Helen Sparacio, a former state Chairman of EMD, was Convention Chairman. Kitty Carlisle was the Keynote Speaker on Tuesday evening and two new clubs (Shadow Lake Village Woman's Club and the Fifth District EMD Past Chairmen's Club) were welcomed into the Federation. Dorothy Virginia Wescoat was the 37th recipient of the Cecilia Gaines Holland Award presented at this Convention. The May 1982 Annual Convention was held at the same site in

McAfee; however, the name had been changed to Americana's Great Gorge Resort. This conclave drew a total registration of 1600, and two new clubs were received into Federation membership. Mary E. Volz of Runnemede in the First District was the Cecilia Gaines Holland honoree. The Tuesday evening program featured Celeste Holm as the speaker.

Emily Strakosch did her share of traveling, beginning with the 1980 GFWC Convention held in St. Louis, Missouri. At this Convention, the New Jersey Public Affairs Department was the recipient of the First Place Award for Best Overall Program in the country. The 1981 General Federation Convention found the New Jersey President in Cedar Rapids, Iowa. She also attended the GFWC Convention in June of 1982 in Bismarck, North Dakota when 13 clubwomen attended from New Jersey.

A General Federation Board Meeting was held in Arlington, Virginia during which the Board members went to the Capitol to meet with members of Congress and were received in the White House by Mrs. James Carter, the First Lady. Another GFWC Board Meeting was held in Vail, Colorado during this administration.

Other GFWC activities included the Shell Oil Conservation Seminar held in Washington, DC where New Jersey was one of nine State Federations selected for the pilot program. Marijane Singer, a Past President of NJSFWC, chaired a two-day "FREE" Workshop for the General Federation during this administration. GFWC also initiated a "Red Badge of Courage" program which was adopted by New Jersey in 1981. Clubwomen in the state and throughout the country wore and displayed red ribbons for those missing in action in

258

Vietnam.

On the "homefront" in 1980 the New Jersey Federation began its participation in the RKI group insurance plan which has proven to be very helpful to the clubs throughout the state. Increased awareness of liability and increases in the number of law suits brought against organizations had made the need for protective insurance essential to clubs.

Boys from Skillman came to Headquarters during the Christmas holidays to put up a tree and decorate it with ornaments they had made. Skillman (now known as the Lloyd McCorkle School) had long been supported by the Federation.

During this administration Mrs. Strakosch was honored to have Dorothy T. Weinheimer as Parliamentary Consultant to the Board of Directors. Mrs. Weinheimer was kept busy in this post as there were many Bylaw changes enacted at this time.

"Leadership" was added to the duties of the Third Vice President, and she became Consultant to the Headquarters Committee instead of being its Chairman. The position of Headquarters Chairman was added to the Board. A Yearbook Committee with a Chairman was formed, and this group of women took on the office duties involved in publishing the "Federation's Bible". The number of clubs needed to call a Special Meeting of the Federation was increased from 20 to 25 clubs.

Another change was the increase of Federation dues from $1 to $1.50 per member. The Honor Roll Committee was changed to Honor Roll/Honors and Memorials Committee which provided clubs the opportunity of honoring deceased, as well as living, members. Department and Committee Outlines were sent out for a two year period instead of a one-year period.

Another major change was in the procedure for Nominations and Endorsements. Instead of a single deadline date for both functions, which had been March 1, the revision made Nominations due by January 1 and Endorsements by February 1 each year.

At the 1981 Annual Convention it was not possible for the members of the State Ex Club to hold their usual banquet nor to process during the Wednesday night session. The custom was resumed as often as possible during subsequent Conventions. Recognizing the members of this special state organization, composed of women who have served in many capacities on the Board of Directors, is an important tradition.

Emily Strakosch is a friendly and enthusiastic woman who exhibited a great deal of executive ability and maintained composure while leading the Federation through many important structural changes. Although she now lives in Florida, she maintains her contacts with the New Jersey clubwomen. Florida's gain is definitely New Jersey's loss. Emily is warmly welcomed whenever she finds it possible to "come North"

Gloria Malasky
Mrs. Lee J. Malasky
1982 to 1984

New Jersey clubwomen were urged to "Care, Dare, Share" when Gloria Malasky of the Woman's Club of Runnemede in First District took the helm of the New Jersey State Federation of Women's Clubs as its 38th President. A most attractive brunette, with sparkling eyes and a brilliant smile, it was soon evident that Gloria was a President who would "Care" — was ready to "Dare" — and would willingly "Share" her organizational expertise to bring further progress to NJSFWC.

Dorothy Constants, Betty Loizeaux, and Shirley Goettel were First, Second and Third Vice Presidents respectively during this administration.

The goal for a Special State Project, chaired by Jody Joel, was to equip two classrooms for the most severely handicapped children at St. John of God School for Special Children located in Westville Grove, New Jersey. The work being done at this unique facility touched the hearts of the clubwomen throughout the state, and over $93,000 was raised within two years. The two classrooms are realities with a plaque showing that NJSFWC provided them. In addition to raising funds, coupons, labels and other items were sent to St. John of God School which has become a continuing project of the Federation.

Not content with one major goal, Mrs. Malasky also dreamed of setting up a Headquarters' Foundation Fund which would be used to maintain Headquarters without the necessity of continuously raising dues. This was begun in May of 1982. Although there was some opposition, the continued support of thousands of clubwomen made the dream come true at the May 1984 Convention when a Bylaw change set this fund in motion. At that time, it was announced that, through the determined efforts of Chairman Joan M. Hunt, over $59,000 had been raised to start the fund. The Headquarters' Foundation Fund continues with the receipts being used to keep the Federation's "home" in good repair.

At the 65th Founder's Day held at Douglass College, Mrs. Malasky was inducted into the Associate Alumnae of the college. College Days were held here in 1982 and in 1983, and were well attended by high school students. Girls' Citizenship Institute (GCI) was held during both years of the administration with a full complement of high school juniors enjoying a week on the Douglass campus.

Americana Day and the Art Symposium held on November 4, 1982 at Lyons Veterans' Medical Center found 261 clubwomen in attendance. This event was held again in November of 1983. The Legislative Luncheon held March 28, 1983 at Battleground Country Club drew 409 attendees to hear United States Senator Bill Bradley as the main speaker.

This event was billed as a Public Affairs Luncheon.

NJSFWC in coordination with Douglass College had initiated New Jersey Women of Achievement Awards in 1981. The first luncheon was held in 1982 with six women being honored. In 1983 the event honored five more women in recognition of their accomplishments. This has been continued as an annual event.

Two Regional Fall Conferences, chaired by Doris Malle, were held in October 1982 at Quail Hill Inn, Smithville, and Wayne Manor, Wayne. Four Seminars were held in the mornings and a general meeting was conducted in the afternoons. The total attendance of 831 was recorded for the two conferences. At the one held at Quail Hill Inn, President Malasky was surprised to find her only daughter and her youngest grandson modeling during the luncheon fashion show. Her husband and her mother were also surprise guests. In 1983 two Regional Fall Conferences were held at the same locations with 808 clubwomen enjoying the day.

Americana's Great Gorge Resort in McAfee was again the scene of the Annual Convention in May, 1983. A total registration of 1390 women was announced. Governor Thomas Kean attended the Convention and was a speaker. This marked the first time since 1973 that a New Jersey Governor had been among the participants. The Keynote Speaker at the Tuesday Banquet honoring Club Presidents was Peg Bracken, noted author and speaker. Phyllis E. Cable, a member of the New Milford Woman's Club was the 39th recipient of the Cecilia Gaines Holland Award. Especially important to the members of the State Ex Club was the reinstatement of their processional on Wednesday evening at this Convention.

Americana's Great Gorge Resort was once more the site of the Federation's 90th Convention in 1984. A special fashion show was held and a "first" was a reception for all club presidents which was held on Wednesday by Mrs. Malasky. Although unable to attend, Governor Kean sent a telegram of congratulations to the assembled body. Linda Rissel, a Dover Township Junior, received the Cecilia Gaines Holland Award and Suzette Charles who was then Miss New Jersey and later Miss America, performed for the Tuesday night program. This Convention was attended by 1592 clubwomen.

On October 27, 1983 the first "Leadership Seminar" was held with the three Vice Presidents conducting the session. This type of program was helpful to the clubwomen, and was incorporated into Federation activities for the future.

The Middle Atlantic Region (MAR) encompassing the Federations of Pennsylvania, Delaware, New York and New Jersey was gaining in popularity with the NJSFWC members.

Middle Atlantic Region Conferences held in Suffern, New York in October 1982 and in New Brunswick in 1983 were attended by contingents from New Jersey. The 1983 Conference was hosted by the New Jersey Federation.

Travel for the State Presidents had become a trend, and Gloria Malasky "went on the road" in June, 1982 when she attended the GFWC Convention in North Dakota along with her immediate predecessor and 11 other New Jersey clubwomen. The post-convention meeting of the GFWC Board of Directors marked Gloria's first official duty. That summer she attended a General Federation Conservation Symposium in Washington, DC. and went to "the hill" to meet with Senator Bradley of New Jersey. September, 1982 found five New Jersey officers, including the President, attending a General Federation Board Meeting and Leadership Institute held in Raleigh, North Carolina. It was off to Orlando, Florida in late May of 1983 when the President and 28 New Jersey clubwomen attended that General Federation Convention. In the meantime, Gloria Malasky had attended the GFWC Board Meeting held in Toronto, Canada.

Mrs. Malasky joined other State Federation Presidents at a GFWC meeting held at the White House in Washington, DC, and attended Exxon's "Grass Roots Energy Seminar". She also attended the Convention of the Pennsylvania Federation during her administration. In addition to traveling the length and breadth of New Jersey, Gloria Malasky completed her official duties at the 1984 General Federation Convention in Las Vagas, Nevada with a delegation of 30 women from New Jersey.

Mrs. Malasky was selected by Governor Kean to serve on a committee devoted to the public responsibility for education success. She attended many meetings of this group including one held at Dr. Bloustein's home and another at Drumthwacket with the Governor in attendance.

This administration marked several changes in structure and organization, beginning with the reduction of the number of women required to start a new club from 20 to 15 members. State Organization dues were increased from $15 to $30 per year, and the quorum needed for the Executive Committee's meetings went from seven down to six members.

Prior to this a club had to have a membership of 300 in

order to nominate more than one candidate for offices on the NJSFWC Board of Directors. A Bylaw change was adopted which lowered this requirement to 150 members. Clubs with less than 150 members could still only nominate one candidate. In 1984 a Bylaw change provided that a Junior Club member who joined the club between the ages of 18 and 35 could remain on Junior status until she reached the age of 40.

Some of these changes reflected the fact that membership had "leveled off" to slower growth due to fewer woman having time to become active in the Federation. More younger women were headed for college, followed by intensive careers etc. which reduced time available to them for club work. Families had become more mobile with children and young people being active in many school activities requiring transportation and other types of parental support. Also, more mature women, who had completed their responsibilities of child raising, were entering the workforce and taking full or part-time positions outside of the home. All of these circumstances contributed to a decrease in membership. By 1984 total membership was listed as 28,816.

In 1984, the General Federation of Women's Clubs had increased national dues from $1 to $2 per member, and this generated a less popular Bylaw change to increase New Jersey's dues accordingly.

Gloria Malasky initiated the custom of having "grace" said prior to luncheon at Federation Board Meetings. This met with favor and is still being done. Another activity which was undertaken was a complete review and revision of the Manual for Board Members. This is still being done every two years in order to keep this informative material current.

With a highly successful term of office completed, Gloria Malasky has continued to be very active in Federation activities. Mrs. Malasky served as GFWC International Affairs Chairman. She has been a "mentor" to many of the State Presidents who have succeeded her, and served as Parliamentary Consultant to the Board of Directors for the 1992-1994 administration. She was also MAR representative to GFWC Legislative Committee. Gloria is gracious and always appreciative of courtesies shown to her as a Past State President — this, among many other things, makes her a welcome guest at any event.

New Jersey State Federation of Women's Clubs

1894-1984
90th
ANNIVERSARY
YEAR BOOK
1983-1984

Dorothy M. Constants
Mrs. Alfred C. Constants, Jr.
1984 to 1986

When Dorothy M. Constants of the Woman's Club of Oakland took over the reins of NJSFWC, the country was in the throes of a great feeling of Americanism and the restoration of the Statue of Liberty was being undertaken. What greater way to unite over 28,000 clubwomen to bring about involvement, commitment and strength than to ask them to be supportive of a project such as this? Mrs. Constants felt that the women wanted to be stimulated and to have renewed faith in the organization and what it could accomplish. With this in mind, she chose as the administration theme "Together All Hands — Make it Happen". The First Vice President for this administration was Betty Loizeaux; the Second Vice President was Shirley Goettel and the Third Vice President was Marion Graham Arnao. All three of these officers later became Presidents of NJSFWC.

Right from the beginning, the decision was made to be part of the Restoration of the Statue of Liberty — Ellis Island

Foundation Incorporated. Chaired by Marilyn Tonnesen, this was considered the Special State Project for 1984-1986; and affectionately called "The Lady of Liberty". Essays and poems were written, songs were sung and programs were arranged as a new spirit of patriotism and pride in our country was seen.

Historical knowledge was enhanced by the Board of Directors' visit to the Statue of Liberty where the restoration was under way. They also traveled to the Governor of New Jersey's homes, Drumthwacket and Morven, which are now operated by the New Jersey Historical Society. The Morristown Flower Show provided the setting for the Federation's spectacular exhibit of "The Lady of Liberty" (made completely from recycled material), and a great deal of attention was drawn to the Federation by this wonderful display. A commemorative cruise and luncheon gave 300 people the opportunity to travel the harbor waters surrounding Liberty Park and the Statue of Liberty. Special shopping nights were held at Hahne and Company in Newark with 10 percent of the proceeds devoted to the project. A "Lady" pin, a plate and a mug were made available to the clubwomen and this gave the project added dimension. The overwhelming support of the New Jersey clubwomen resulted in the unprecedented amount of $172,217 being raised for the Special State Project.

Mrs. Constants traveled to Houston, Texas and Cincinnati, Ohio for General Federation Conventions. In attending an Environmental Seminar sponsored by GFWC, she was confronted with the fact that New Jersey had the dubious distinction of being #1 — in hazardous waste! Out of this knowledge came the Federation's first Environmental and Conservation Day.

The clubs became highly involved with the New Jersey Highway Safety Department by adopting S.O.B.E.R (Slow on the Bottle, Enjoy the Ride). The support of this activity developed a public awareness program on drunk driving and drug abuse. The Federation received the Governor's first Highway Safety Award for its activities.

The President represented the Federation on various New Jersey task forces involving women, alcohol, and health-related issues. Several Board members sat on local community committees dealing with these subjects.

Of special concern to Dorothy Constants was the fact that, in accordance with the NJSFWC Bylaws, the Department and Committee Chairmen were to have two-year Outlines; however, somehow it was not working properly. By making some adjustments in the schedule and giving the State Chairmen additional time to incorporate GFWC information, it was found that the outlines which were to carry the activities of this administration were more complete. To make sure that each and every club received the outlines in adequate time to use them efficiently, they were mailed to the clubs instead of being distributed at Convention. In this manner, there was no hesitancy as to the Federation's activities for a new administration. With the close of the first year, "The Supplement" was added by the Departments and Committees. These were included in the Club Presidents' Convention packets. Mrs. Constants felt that the Federation had moved forward in its organization and now had the ability to inform clubs effectively.

"The real world" was brought to the attention of the Federation's officers as the Headquarters Building approached its 25th anniversary. Having just completed a 10-

year period, the value of the property rented to the Federation by Rutgers University was reassessed. The Board of Directors was totally dismayed when a 700 percent increase in rent was proposed by Rutgers University! After several months, with a presentation of the Headquarters background, our association with Douglass College and how the Federation dispensed its money in contributions and scholarships, the annual rental was agreed upon. While the total amount over the 10-year period was cut in half from the original proposal, there was an increase that brought about an amendment to the Bylaws increasing Federation dues.

In order to work more closely with GFWC, it was agreed to elect all Executive Officers, District Vice Presidents, and Department Chairmen in the even-numbered years. This change would take place in subsequent administrations.

A Grants Chairman was added to the Board of Directors in an effort to obtain additional revenue. Raphael Sorbello was named to this position. The Foundation Fund was kept in mind as a luncheon-fashion show at the Hyatt Regency in Princeton was held, jewelry was sold, trips were sponsored to the Bahamas and a bequest was received from the Estate of Past State President, Marjory Bonynge Fielding.

Governor Thomas H. Kean signed a Proclamation declaring April 24, 1985 as General Federation Day in New Jersey.

Conventions for 1985 and 1986 were held at the Americana-Great Gorge Resort in McAfee with over 1,000 delegates attending each year. The General Federation speakers at these Conventions included Alice C. Donahue, First Vice President GFWC, and Phyllis Roberts, GFWC President Elect. An afternoon reception for the club presidents was part of the activities and an Inspirational Breakfast closed the week. In 1986 the Juniors were honored for their 60th year as a Department. An Emergency Resolution was brought by the Ukrainian National Women's League of America, a State Organization, on the nuclear disaster at Chernoybl.

The Federation's relationship with Douglass College, now under the direction of Dean Mary Hartman, remained strong as over 350 high school juniors attended Girls' Citizenship Institute each year. The clubwomen's support of the scholarships in Political Science, Art, Drama, Home Economics, Literature, Continuing Education, Music and the Margaret Yardley Fellowship was consistent.

The New Jersey Women of Achievement presentations were held in conjunction with the Annual College Day at Douglass College. In 1985, Ruth Sanborn Burrill, a Past State President 1956 to 1958, was so honored. The previously separate Americana Day and Art Symposium Day became the Creative Arts Seminar. An "Anthology of Poetry" was compiled by the Literature Chairman, Gloria Andriulo. The clubs contributed to the Ethiopia Famine Relief Fund. The "New Jersey Club Woman" and the "Almanac" continued to be the means of communication to all of the clubs.

During this administration, Spina Bifida, (with Deen Meloro as Chairman) was the Juniors' State Project. Their involvement with the "Brown Paper Bag" went on to the national level. Jeanne Bakelar, a Sparta Junior, chaired this project. The Evening Membership Department supported the Valerie Fund for Cancer and Blood Disorders by raising over $52,000 with Carol Vivona as Chairman.

During Mrs. Constants' administration it was a challenge

for the clubwomen to become "part of the action" and to move from the status quo. She wanted them to realize how important it was to be involved as women of today's world — concerned about present day issues. She also wanted the membership to survive and the Federation to move ahead. It was an exciting time for this President, and she hopes that it was as exciting for the clubwomen. It was a chance for proving that "Together All Hands — Make it Happen".

Betty P. Loizeaux
Mrs. Jerry B. Loizeaux
1986 to 1988

For Betty P. Loizeaux, of the North Plainfield Woman's Club, the culmination of her 30 years of Federation service (which began when she was a Junior Clubwoman) came on May 16, 1986 when she was installed as the Federation's 40th President. She fondly recalls that Dorothy T. Weinheimer, a Past State President, was the Installing Officer. Shirley G. Goettel, Marion Graham Arnao, and Joan M. Hunt served as First, Second and Third Vice Presidents during this administration.

NJSFWC listed over 27,000 members when Mrs. Loizeaux took office, and she knew that it was important that the tremendous accomplishments of the organization become much better known to the public. With this in mind, the theme "Let Our Voice Be Heard" became the top priority. Media Workshop Seminars were held each year with representation from the largest newspapers in the area. These editors advised members how to obtain coverage in all of the news media. This was most enlightening and well-received.

274

Concern for children and their place in the world brought about the Special State Project, The People Care Center in Finderne. With Ora Kokol as Chairman, it specialized in the interaction between children and adults through day care. The Hunger Project, the Association for Retarded Citizens, Home Sharing, American Cancer Society, and Vision of Peace were among the many agencies housed under one roof. Education played an important part in the project with the District Chairmen disseminating information throughout the state. Funds were raised, tours were conducted, a special birthday party was held at the Center, toys were created and clown pins with the project's logo were sold. Throughout the Districts of the Federation many unique fund raisers were held which won awards at the end of the two years. Millicent Fenwick, former Congresswoman and United States Ambassador to the United Nations, later became the Honorary Chairman for raising funds for the Center. Another vital phase of the project was that of being a role model for all communities in the state. The Thursday Morning Club of Madison, after hearing Mrs. Loizeaux speak about the Center, planned and opened their own Adult Day/Respite Care Center held in the Madison Community House. Other Centers were opened at a later time.

Through the many programs undertaken during this administration, a voice _was_ heard. With detailed planning Dean Mary Hartman of Douglass College and the President gave new meaning to the joint venture of the Women of Achievement Awards by holding a special luncheon to honor the recipients. In 1987, Dorothy B. McGlade, a Past State President, was one of seven women so honored. Marie Alberian, a member of the Woman's Club of North Hudson and an outstanding volunteer, was a 1988 recipient. The President presented Dean Hartman with a plaque for her dedication and devotion to the Federation plus the effort she had made to contribute to this outstanding event. A highlight of Betty Loizeaux's administration was being made an honorary member of the Associate Alumnae of Douglass College on Founders' Day.

A Tenth Anniversary Tea was held to honor ESO. Education thrived through Department Chairman, Celestine Filipkowski, and her committee. Two programs, College Day and Girls' Citizenship Institute continued to benefit students.

A special committee called "New Image" was created as yet another up-to-date form of communication. The Chairman, Anne M. Wolff, spoke throughout the state urging members to "keep up with the times" and to make whatever changes had to be made to improve their clubs and activities.

Fall Conferences dealt with issues concerning women and families. New locations were chosen by the Conference Chairman, Betty Schubert, to promote interest. Speakers were experts on topics of the day. Members received a collector's issue of Woman's Day Magazine from its Director. These Conferences were well attended, and the subjects were of great importance to the members.

Public Affairs made Highway Safety a continued effort, working for S.O.B.E.R., marking evergreens against holiday drinking and distributing a tremendous amount of safety material. The Chairman, Enid Bernabe, received recognition as the NJSFWC and MAR recipient of the Outstanding Clubwoman Leadership Volunteer Award and the "Just Say No" Award. The People's Choice Award was received by the Federation at the 1988 Governor's Luncheon. Public Affairs had become the important department it should be to interest today's clubwoman. Even the "Brown Paper Bag" was promoted over the use of plastic bags, a program initiated by Jeanne Bakelar who was a Junior clubwoman. This later became a General Federation program. Bumper stickers on clubwomen's cars proclaimed "Paper Bags Have Sacks Appeal."

The environment was a vital concern of the Conservation and Garden Department and its Chairman, Betsy Davis Foster. The Hackensack Meadowlands Environmental Center gave the Federation a silver bowl for its fine display at the New Jersey Garden and Flower Show. The Pine Lands display was honored in the same way the following year.

The Evening Membership and Junior Membership Departments continued to play vital roles in the Federation, a fact that Mrs. Loizeaux especially recognized. The EMD and JMD Chairmen brought valuable expertise to the Executive Committee. Each of these segments of NJSFWC chose special projects which reflected their dedication to helping people. The EMD with Jean Hudson as project Chairman brought attention to the Children's Seashore House by raising funds and educating the public as to its needs. The Juniors chose Tourette Syndrome Association to benefit from many hours of hard work so that everyone could better understand this behavioral disorder. This project was chaired by Linda Caputo. A backdrop at the Annual Convention displayed a picture portraying a united group of women working together as one entity.

Membership took a giant step forward when the Third Vice President, Joan M. Hunt, initiated the first statewide Recognition/Membership Day which brought much attention to the Federation. She received an award at the

GFWC Convention for her fine efforts regarding membership. Betty Loizeaux realized, as did all Federation Presidents, that there is no future without members.

There were many changes made at Headquarters during this administration, and one of the most moving was the dedication of a U.S. Flag and its illumination in memory of Past State President, Lucille M. Dangremond. Many other gifts were given in honor of clubs, members and districts. "Quarters for Headquarters" was a way of supporting the Headquarters Foundation Fund, and a trip to Baltimore Harbor as well as a luncheon/fashion show added to this vital fund. A festive party was arranged by Cathy Southwick and her committee for the Board of Directors' meeting in December so that everyone could enjoy the beauty of Headquarters at holiday time.

Two important issues came to the floor of the Annual Conventions. One was to decide whether or not the Federation wanted to change the structure of its officers by creating an office of President-Elect. After much discussion, this was defeated. The other Bylaw change recognized the current structure of the Junior Membership by striking out the word, "Department". This was adopted and the Junior Membership is now in alignment with GFWC, with its leader titled "Director" instead of Chairman.

Important Resolutions adopted during these two years were on issues concerning environment, recycling, safety and human rights plus many others. In 1987 the issue was about GFWC raising its dues. Delegates attending the GFWC Convention in San Diego were instructed to oppose this increase, and President Loizeaux did this in speaking for all of the New Jersey delegates.

Each of the Departments, with dedicated efforts made by each Chairman, gave importance to the work of the Federation. As always, the work of the Departments had to continue to generate the interest of the membership. This was made possible with the outstanding help from the District Chairmen, who were sometimes "unsung heroines".

A Ways and Means Project, the selling of Innisbrook wrapping paper products, shared its profits with the clubs. It became a most successful venture which has become a continued source of income. This has gone on to GFWC as one of its most beneficial fund- raisers. In addition to the Innisbrook sales, crystal was sold and Federation decals were among the ideas of an innovative Ways and Means Chairman, Jane D. Collins.

Scholarships remained a vital way of supporting students of all ages. The need for granting Fellowships became apparent when 875 applications were received for the Margaret Yardley Fellowship during these two years. Fourteen graduate students received aid through this fund.

When it was New Jersey's turn to host the Middle Atlantic Region Conference, Princeton was chosen as the ideal location. Much work was done in preparation for this meeting by the Third District Vice President and her Committee. The GFWC Board of Directors and Officers made this a most outstanding Conference. Members conducted a "country store" with their many beautiful crafts, and this project supported the MAR treasury.

Each Annual Convention was a highlight for Betty Loizeaux, and she felt they were ways to show the members her deep appreciation for all that they had done. The Board of Directors held meetings, had a "Children's' Party" and reported the accomplishments of each year's work. The Conventions' agendas reflected the need to expedite procedures whenever possible. Punctuality was one way and a new voting system was another. The processionals were shortened and business meetings pertained strictly to business. In doing this, members were able to share their free time with friends and other members. The 93rd Annual Convention was again held in McAfee where attendees enjoyed the mountains. In 1988 it was back to Atlantic City and the seashore for the New Jersey clubwomen when Convention was held at Trump Plaza.

At the 1987 Convention, recognition was given to Olga Mackaronis for 20 years of dedicated service as Executive Secretary. Mrs. Mackaronis is responsibile for running the office at Headquarters. Also at this Convention, the State Chorus performed and a tribute was paid to Karen Edson, its Director. In 1988 Hugh Downs, Chairman of UNICEF, brought a vital message about the women in the Third World. A check for $21,291 was presented to Mr. Downs by the International Affairs Chairman, Marie Lemiska, bringing the total for two years to over $41,000. Seventy members were honored by having their names placed on the Honor Roll and there were many other awards and forms of recognition presented to the Federation during this administration.

The Cecilia Gaines Holland Awards were given to Betty R. Bransdorf and Carolyn Hartman (now Lunn) during Mrs. Loizeaux's term of office.

By 1988 the President's theme, "Let Our Voice Be Heard", had truly been carried out by all the members of New Jersey State Federation of Women's Clubs, including Shirley Kiefer and her EMD members and Roberta Dyrsten and her Junior members.

Betty Loizeaux has continued to be supportive of all NJSFWC goals, joining other Past State Presidents as honored guests whenever it is possible for her to attend Federation functions. In addition, she has made NJSFWC extremely proud by serving as the General Federation of Women's Clubs United Nations Non-Governmental Organization Observer, which now includes working with UNICEF. This position has taken her into the heart of the United Nations where she represents the General Federation and NJSFWC very well indeed!

Shirley G. Goettel
Mrs. Edward C. Goettel
1988 to 1990

Times were exciting in the Federation when Shirley G. Goettel from the Modern Muses Woman's Club of Tom's River took office. She would lead NJSFWC during the two final years of the decade and into the "'90's". Marion Graham Arnao was the First Vice President, Joan M. Hunt was the Second Vice President and Dorothy Lowe Greene had been elected Third Vice President. This team of officers would complete their respective terms at the GFWC Centennial Celebration in New York City in July 1990.

Reaching back to the past history of NJSFWC, relating it to the present and embracing it for the future, Mrs. Goettel chose as her administration theme, "Yesterday. Today, and Tomorrow."

Her State Project was the Headquarters Foundation Fund and $120,500 was raised to ensure that the interest income from this fund would be sufficient to maintain the beautiful Headquarters in New Brunswick. The capital of the fund was increased to well over $200,000 under the chairmanship of Marie Lemiska.

The People's Choice Award was a highlight of the fourth annual Governor's Highway Safety Awards Luncheon. It was presented to NJSFWC in October, 1988. The fantastic Public Affairs Department, chaired by Betsy Davis Foster, gave the Federation visibility in the state Highway Safety Department to warrant this award.

The Junior Past Presidents' Club of the Fifth District placed plantings and raised money for an engraved marker at the site of Jane Cunningham Croly's grave in Evergreen Cemetery, Lakewood, New Jersey. This was dedicated on June 30, 1990 with appropriate ceremonies during the GFWC Centennial Convention. The sponsoring club published an informative booklet on Mrs. Croly's history from research performed by Ann Quinn, a former Junior Director and NJSFWC Public Affairs Chairman in 1990. Officers of the General Federation traveled by bus from New York City to attend this event, and a luncheon followed in their honor at Woodlake Country Club in Lakewood. This was a most fitting prelude to the General Federation of Women's Clubs Convention since "Jenny June" was the woman responsible for beginning the Women's Club Movement!

The 1990 Centennial Celebration of GFWC began on July 1 with a meeting of the Board of Directors at Delmonico's, the site of the very first GFWC Board Meeting. The Convention climaxed with dinner on a Circle-line boat as it cruised New York harbor waiting for a spectacular display of fireworks on the evening of July 4, 1990. Seven NJSFWC Clubs which were 100 years old or older in 1990 were honored during the Convention.

Promoting an identity with the General Federation was a thrust of Mrs. Goettel's administration. Clubs in New Jersey were encouraged to use "GFWC" before their club name in media releases. The General Federation was putting forth a great public relations effort as part of its 100th birthday. The time was right for New Jersey to further identify with the largest volunteer service organization of women in the world.

Roberta Dyrsten, NJSFWC Director of Junior Clubs 1986 to 1988, was elected GFWC Junior Director Elect and went on to serve as GFWC Junior Director 1992 to 1994. Roberta is an outstanding leader of the Juniors who are the "Tomorrows" of the Federation, and New Jersey was honored and proud to have Roberta serve in this capacity.

Past State President, Dorothy Constants, had appointed a special committee to look into the feasibility of developing a Library at Headquarters. Phyllis Schneck had started the ball rolling by generating a computer listing of the books and other records, materials etc. available. The committee had been ongoing, but no other action took place until Gail C. Shast, a former First District Vice President, volunteered in 1989 to begin cataloging books, publications and other material in NJSFWC's possession. Mrs. Shast became the Librarian for NJSFWC in 1990. During this administration the clubs of the Fifth District presented a check for over $600 for library equipment in Mrs. Goettel's honor. The Library became a reality in 1991 when shelving was purchased and a room was designated to house the Library.

The State Ex-Club purchased a television for Headquarters in 1990 and the Ninth District purchased a VCR. These gifts were much needed additions to Headquarters and greatly appreciated. The Modern Muses Woman's Club honored Mrs. Goettel by giving a series of four GFWC Centennial figurines to Headquarters.

Increasing the capital of the Headquarters' Foundation Fund made it possible to purchase carpeting throughout the building along with new office equipment and necessary outside repair work on the structure. The clubwomen were lauded for their support of the President's project. Evelyn M. Barton chaired this effort.

Two Fall Conferences, chaired by Adelaide Matarazzo, were held each year — one in the northern and one in the southern areas of the state. Margaret Long Arnold, Honorary GFWC President, was the keynote speaker in the north and south in alternate years. Elizabeth B. Alton, a Past State President, was the keynote speaker at the Southern Conference in 1989 where she spoke first hand of her knowledge of the Headquarters Building. Mrs. Alton put her recollections into writing which made a very important addition to the Library.

The 1989 and 1990 Annual Conventions, chaired by Doris Malle, were held at Bally's Park Place in Atlantic City. At this point in time there was no other facility available to accommodate the convention except in Atlantic City.

Two award recipients were very special to Mrs. Goettel. Mary Lou Sullivan, Junior Director, was the Cecilia Gaines Holland awardee and Linda Volker, the visually-impaired Sixth District EMD Chairman was named as a New Jersey Woman of Achievement. Hope Cooke, author and former wife of the Crown Prince of Sikkem, was the guest speaker at the Convention's opening banquet. GFWC International President, Alice Donahue, and GFWC President Elect, Phyllis Dudenhoffer, were honored guests at the 1990 Convention.

Something new at the Convention which appealed to many clubwomen was having some of the Workshops held in the morning prior to the Business Sessions. This enabled attendees to cover more Workshops.

A Resolution passed at the 1989 Convention stated that plans should be formulated for a special project or projects to culminate in 1994, NJSFWC's Centennial Year. Resolutions passed at the 1990 Convention stated that anyone charged with sexual assault should be denied bail and anyone convicted of sexual assault should be denied parole. NJSFWC urged adoption of mandatory sentencing for a rapist on his or her first offense.

Literacy became a project under the Literature Department in order to put more emphasis on this issue. Sally Lowden was Literature Chairman. Support for the newly-dedicated New Jersey Museum of Agriculture on the Cook College Campus in New Brunswick was added to the outline of the Conservation and Garden Department by Nancy Walling, Chairman. Mrs. Goettel was elected to the Board of Trustees of the Museum in 1989.

Legislation became a Standing Committee in 1988 due to a

Bylaw change, the rationale being that legislation warranted its own committee. In 1990 a Bylaw change was made combining Nominations and Elections as one Standing Committee. This was done to consolidate the committees and reduce expenditures since elections are held only in even-numbered years.

At the instigation of the President in April 1990, the Board of Directors adopted a recommendation of the Executive Committee as follows: "That a Special Committee be appointed to research and write a one-hundred year history of NJSFWC to be published for distribution at the 1994 Centennial Convention". Grace Mathis Williams was designated as the "Coordinator" for the four year period needed to complete this publication. The group which would begin work on this project met in June 1990 and members dubbed themselves "The First Centuryans"

Redistricting was considered and explored by a committee during this administration. The Board of Directors approved its recommendation, but it was later rescinded. Changes in Districts are not always popular with the clubs.

Shirley Goettel feels that her goals were met beyond expectation and that many important issues were addressed thanks to the expertise of the Executive Committee and the support of the Board of Directors. She stated that, "If it were not for the clubwomen throughout the state, no State President would be able to see her goals come to fruition. Their devotion to the Federation and its leaders is unsurpassed." The clubwomen of New Jersey feel that Shirley Goettel, a quiet and sincerely friendly woman, is also "unsurpassed"!

Marion Graham Arnao
Mrs. Edward C. Arnao
1990 to 1992

In May 1990 Marion Graham Arnao of the Woman's Club of Parsippany-Troy Hills was installed as President of NJSFWC. Serving with her as First, Second and Third Vice Presidents were Joan M. Hunt, Dorothy Lowe Greene and Cathy Southwick.

"A Legacy for the Future" was chosen by Mrs. Arnao as the theme of her administration.

Marion Graham Arnao's first official act following her installation was to announce that the State Project would be the New Jersey Children's Hospital AIDS Program (CHAP). Helping babies born with AIDS through no fault of their own touched the heartstrings of New Jersey clubwomen throughout the state. Fund-raising events were held all through New Jersey, and many of them were innovative. Clubwomen, along with their spouses, family members and friends, participated in card parties, garage sales, Chinese auctions, theater parties, raffles, boat trips, fashion shows and

288

the sale of holiday crafts, wrapping paper and baked goods. They sold T-shirts, baseball caps and other items as well as conducting Walk-A-Thons where they walked a number of miles for sponsors who had pledged amounts of money per mile.

Betsy Davis Foster, who headed the Special State Project Committee, received permission to sell small stuffed rabbits made of purple and white plush. This tied into the project because Dr. Jim Oleske who worked with Pediatric AIDS at Children's Hospital in Newark always carried a similar stuffed rabbit in his pocket when visiting the children in the hospital and in the clinics. The "bunnies" became a symbol for the CHAP project. $20,000 was raised by selling the plush bunnies, and the clubwomen made purple stuffed rabbits of various types which were used for centerpieces at the 1992 Convention. Following the Convention, the stuffed rabbits were distributed to clinics for children infected with AIDS throughout the state.

Betty Lou Mitchell
Dorothy Richards
Ginny Campion
with a few of the
1600 Bunnies made
by Clubwomen.

All of the fund-raising events for the State Project made it possible for Mrs. Arnao to present a check for $153,974 to Dr. Oleske at the 1992 Convention. In addition, the clubwomen had used this project as an educational tool to learn more about AIDS and to disseminate information so vital to those uninformed about the disease. More than 100,000 volunteer hours went into the CHAP project. A video tape called "A Gift of Time" was provided to the clubs and shown in many areas. Brochures were distributed, and the entire state of New Jersey learned a great deal about this threatening disease through the efforts of NJSFWC.

During this administration the Junior State Project was Lyme Disease, with Janice Bengivenea as Chairman. They raised $52,918 during the two-year period. The Evening Membership Department project was Deborah Heart and Lung Center, and they raised $64,178 for their project, with Evelyn Stoveken as Chairman.

State President Marion Graham Arnao suffered a brain hemmorhage after just three months in office; she underwent brain surgery. During the time she was recovering, First Vice President Joan M. Hunt assumed the President's responsibilities. Over 700 get well wishes and gifts were received by Mrs. Arnao from Federation members. She believes it hastened her recovery so she could return sooner to her duties.

Plans were instituted during Marion Graham Arnao's administration to celebrate the NJSFWC Centennial in 1994. Anita Rosen designed the Centennial Logo and the unusual Centennial Pin. A crackle glass pitcher was also designed and Wheaton Village of Millville, NJ was commissioned to produce it. All of these items were sold at the 1992 and 1993

Conventions. The Literature Department of the North Arlington Woman's Club was the winner of the Centennial Theme Contest with - A GLORIOUS PAST - A BRILLIANT FUTURE. The 1991 and 1992 Annual Conventions were held at the Parsippany Hilton Hotel and chaired by Betty J. Schubert.

The decision to place the Library, which would house the Federation's archives, in the small board room at Headquarters was made and serious work begun. Gail C. Shast continued on as NJSFWC Librarian and took on the demanding task of cataloging and setting up the Library. Work continued on the 100 year history of the Federation. Video taping of surviving Past State Presidents by NJSFWC Historian, Mary Lou Sullivan, was started with each one asked to recall interesting memories of her administration.

The Federation worked with the New Jersey Literary Hall of Fame to set up Seminars. The State Fall Conferences held during these years concerned subjects such as "Children - Our Legacy for the Future" and "Healthy Women, Our Legacy for the Future". Well over 800 women attended the two Fall Conferences, planned by the Chairman, Helen J. Sparacio.

The Persian Gulf War in January 1991 stimulated plans to support this action; fortunately the war was over quickly and the plans did not require implementation. The Federation and the individual club members did feel a surge of patriotism during this time. Several clubwomen saw active duty in the Gulf.

Legislative interests continued. The Federation actively pursued the passage of two Bills enabling New Jersey women to have coverage from their health insurance and Medicaid for annual mammograms. Third Vice President, Cathy Southwick, testified at hearings. President Arnao and other representatives from Federation were present at the signing of these Bills by New Jersey's Governor James Florio.

Resolutions Chairman, Mary Ellen Brock, presented a total of 23 timely Resolutions proposed by club members and NJSFWC Department Chairmen which were adopted by the delegates at the 1991 and 1992 Conventions. These Resolutions covered many areas of interest from Restricting Truck Size and Weight Limits to Testing for Drugs and Alcohol in Fatal Boating Accidents. Mrs. Brock also reviewed all Resolutions presented by NJSFWC since its beginning and prepared a notebook of them. This provided a valuable research tool to be stored in the Federation Library.

Mrs. Arnao decided it was time for NJSFWC to have a new Past State President's Pin to reflect our own Federation. Anita Rosen was asked to design the pin and the State Ex Club of NJSFWC paid $320 for the die used to produce the pins.

Marion Graham Arnao, a most attractive and energetic woman of many talents, thoroughly enjoys her club work and is devoted to her family. (Devoted to the extent that she is often found working in the "pit" at auto races in which her son participates.) As a woman of today, Mrs. Arnao has left "A Legacy for the Future".

JOAN MULLIGAN HUNT
(Mrs. John A. Hunt)
1992 - 1994

On May 15, 1992 Joan Mulligan Hunt, a member of the Contemporary Woman's Club of Washington Township, Ninth District, was installed by her close friend Gloria Malasky, Past State President 1982-1984. According to Joan, "I was projected into one of the most rewarding experiences of my life; and my administration was truly blessed". The support and cooperation she received, almost instantaneously, was the hallmark of this very active administration.

Mrs. Hunt was also a member of The Woman's Club of Ridgewood, Eleventh District, and Charter Member of the newly formed Centennial Club, the Middlesex Area Woman's Club, Fourth District. She began her Federation career as a Middlesex Junior. She is a Past President of the State Organization, the New Jersey Woman's Press Club.

Serving with her was an exceptional Board of Directors and a caring and dedicated Executive Committee: Dorothy Lowe Greene, First Vice President; Cathy Southwick, Second Vice President; Carol B. Hancock, Third Vice President; Ruth Supp,

Recording Secretary; Deen Meloro, Corresponding Secretary; Jane B. Fagundus, Treasurer; Mary Ellen Brock, Financial Secretary; Sandra Johnston, Director of Junior Clubs and Phyllis Schneck, Evening Membership Department Chairman. ALL decisions were made as a unit. Gloria Malasky served as the Parliamentary Consultant to the Board.

The Theme for her administration was quite fitting, TODAY'S WOMAN - FACING TOMORROW'S CHALLENGES.

With the cooperation and guidance of the two Headquarters Secretaries, Olga Mackaronis, Executive Secretary, and Carol Sas, Secretary, she quickly learned the workings of the office.

She threw herself into the job, working at Headquarters at least two or three times a week all summer long doing the necessary things for a full transition and also researching Federation's various financial problems. The furnace and air conditioning put in during the previous administration had to be paid for and to benefit from this necessary improvement, the building was insulated and the process of redoing the windows started.

With Federation's Centennial just around the corner, the entire building had to be looked over. Years had passed since any serious renovations had been done. Third Vice President, Carol B. Hancock, developed a long-range plan and work began. Realizing money played a major role in Federation's existence, Mrs. Hunt activated travel trips as an easy and profitable fund raiser. The first trip consisted of 84 satisfied travelers to England. Later, she took groups to Cancun, Ireland, Portugal and on a Cruise of the Caribbean.

One of the biggest problems facing Federation was financing this very book, A Century of Challenge; but she never doubted it would be funded. She persuaded Dean Edna M. Newby, formerly of Douglass College, to be a positive intermediary with Federation's first (1940) Pan-American Scholarship Winner, Senorita Orellana of Chile, who at the time was seriously thinking of making a donation either to Douglass College or Federation to show her appreciation for bringing her to this country, via the Scholarship. Senorita Orellana donated $50,000 for the purpose of completing the Library, to which Douglass students and faculty will have access, and documenting NJSFWC's first one hundred years. The book has been dedicated to this exceptional woman. It is the Board of Directors' hope that Senorita will be at the Centennial Convention so the first book can be presented to her. Dean Newby will be part of this celebration too. She made it possible.

President Hunt knew it was important that Federation be brought into the 21st Century as quickly as possible; a necessary collator was first on the list, closely followed by a sophisticated alarm system, an answering machine, FAX and finally the computer! New, innovative and cost-effective things could now be accomplished in this modern office.

In her acceptance speech, she announced four main goals: First, to develop PRIDE IN MEMBERSHIP in NJSFWC and GFWC; Second, emphasize Women's Issues; Third, as her Special State Project, to equip the Resuscitation Critical Response Room at Children's Hospital with exceptional diagnostic equipment and fourth to focus on Federation's Centennial.

She felt that without PRIDE IN MEMBERSHIP, Federation would never grow and prosper. Her personal approach of sharing with members the problems, the accomplishments and the joys of Federation resulted in a positive attitude change. Sisterhood was at an all time high with the Juniors and the EMD; attendance was up at the 99th Convention and even more members were expected for the 100th. Reporting took an upturn and club members felt comfortable giving input.

Mrs. Hunt often stated, "Wouldn't it be nice if ......?" and all through her Presidency this was said again and again. Always it was answered willingly by the membership.

Pride in Membership - "Wouldn't it be nice if....?" The yearly loss of members was held in check. State Membership Chairman, Carol Hancock, worked hard to increase the ranks. As this book went to press, there were 9 new Centennial Clubs formed and one Medallion Club (a club of 280 members) inquired about rejoining.

Pride in the Districts - her "Wouldn't it be nice if...?" was answered by Marie Drake and Rose Schmitt, both members of the Eighth District, who created district banners. It was a beautiful sight to see them used for the first time during the processional at the 99th Annual Convention. District Vice Presidents now had identifying banners to use at all District events, thanks to the gift of these two talented women.

Pride in being a member of the Board of Directors - Board meetings were always productive; educational videos were often shown. She felt meetings should have content, be meaningful. Historian Anita Rosen prepared and read a Historical Moment as part of the opening exercises, educating

296

the Board about their Federation roots. Mrs. Hunt began this when she assumed the responsibilities of the presidency for many months while her predecessor was recovering from serious surgery.

Her "Wouldn't it be nice if...?" was answered once again. The Board's sisterhood was documented first with bios on every member, which were put into book form and presented as a gift at the Holiday Party, by the Historian. Then it was with the creation of a beautiful Centennial Table Cloth, designed by Anita Rosen. Board members signed their names around the centered logo; and these were expertly embroidered by Rose Schmitt, who generously made this a gift to the President for Federation.

Another "Wouldn't it be nice if...?" A magnificent new Centennial Banner, which was proudly displayed at the 99th Annual Convention, was a gift to Federation.

"Wouldn't it nice if....?" was heard by Doris Psak and Dorothy Berrien, who contributed the funds for the gorgeous new NJSFWC Banner, which was donated by the Fourth District.

"Wouldn't it be nice if...?"Magnificent daffodils and tulips were planted in the front of Headquarters, a gift of friend M. Hope Diggs.

"Wouldn't it be nice if...?" The inside of the building was painted when Arts Performing Chairman, Dodie Waters, took her job literally, and personally painted many walls.

Pride in NJSFWC's past - Mrs. Hunt discussed with the Executive Committee the need to have the American Flag lowered to half staff at the death of a Past State President, Director of Junior Clubs or Evening Membership Department Chairman and they concurred. This is now tradition. She approached Marie Drake and Rose Schmitt with another "Wouldn't it be nice if...?"; a "grieving rose" was created, which would be hung on the front door on such bereavement occasions. Once again these caring women used their talent for Federation. The flag was lowered and the "grieving rose" placed on the door for the first time in May 1993 for Laura Teachman, EMD Chairman 1968-70.

Pride in GFWC - All General Federation of Women's Clubs information was shared with the Executive Committee and Board members. "Wouldn't it be nice if...?" Deen Meloro, Corresponding Secretary, volunteered to write a column for the "Almanac" containing GF news, etc. "Suzy Scoop" was well received. During her administration, NJSFWC's Departments were finally in sync with GFWC and the GF Outlines were used, with a supplement from the New Jersey State Chairmen.

When Sister Federations were devastated by 1992's "Hurricane Andrew" members were encouraged to send money to the Florida and Louisiana Federations. And, through the efforts of NJSFWC's Juniors, packages of items such as diapers were also delivered from the NJSFWC Board to the Juniors of Homestead, Florida. Their appreciation was so great that, not only did members receive personal thank you letters from the State Presidents, but at the 99th Convention, the Florida President sent a magnificent plaque thanking the women for their help.

The large number of states devastated by the massive 1993 floods necessitated asking the members to send their donations directly to the American Red Cross or Salvation Army. Members helped again.

President Hunt heard the needs of the membership, offering additional new and informative Seminars and Workshops on Finances and the Displaced Homemaker, both organized by the Home Life/Social Service Chairman, Dolores Farrelly; Club House Problem Solving, originated and implemented by Mary Ellen Brock, NJSFWC's Financial Secretary, and more. Mrs. Brock also compiled an informative Club House Directory for distribution to members, to help with rentals.

Realizing the average club leader was confused when it came to the proper protocol to be used at events, she requested that the Parliamentary Consultant to the Board review the protocol material Federation had distributed and simplify it. It was completely revised. Now that it is standardized, the information will be used by the Women's Clubs, Juniors and EMD, as "One Federation".

Mrs. Hunt had the privilege of being the President when Douglass College celebrated its 75th Anniversary. The Hunts attended a gorgeous Gala at the State Theater in New

Brunswick, kicking off the college's fund raising campaign. Later in the year she was honored at their exceptional 75th Anniversary Founders' Day Celebration, an extraordinary time of pomp and circumstance; followed by her own induction into the Associate Alumnae of Douglass College. As the founders of Douglass, she felt it was important for Federation to make a sizable donation to the campaign. "Wouldn't it be nice if...?" The request was added to the Continuing Funds Sheet and many clubs contributed. She then persuaded the Board of Directors to release additional funds and make a presentation at Founders' Day of $7,500, representing $100 for each year of the college's existence.

Federation became more involved with Women's Issues and Legislation. The 1993 State Fall Conference reflected this. She made it a point to attend all important events in New Jersey and thus Federation became better known. Federation was now included in surveys and often asked for assistance in promoting various bills, etc. Mrs. Hunt was invited for breakfast with Governor Florio and his wife at Drum-thwacket, where she had the chance to speak personally with him concerning funding for Children's Hospital. She was appointed as a Consultant to the first Women's Advisory Council, mandated by the New Jersey Legislature. Federation's Legislation Day was re-activated, under the direction of Mary Lou Phifer, NJSFWC's Legislation Chairman, giving the women the opportunity to meet with Legislators.

Marianne Kremer was appointed the Special State Project Chairman and entrusted with the responsibility of raising the phenomenal moneys necessary to equip the RCR Room at Children's Hospital. In the first year she raised over $ 59,000 with her many innovative sale items. She will certainly triple that sum by the end of this administration.

During Joan Hunt's term of office the Juniors' State Project was the Community Food Bank, with Kathy Rubin as Chairman. The EMD chose to join with the Women's Clubs and work with Children's Hospital by purchasing an exceptional pediatric ambulance; Bery Smithouser was the Chairman. All of these projects made a valuable contribution to the people of New Jersey.

State Fall Conference Chairman, M. Hope Diggs, organized two outstanding Conferences held at the Pines Manor, Edison, New Jersey. The first Conference was devoted to Child Abuse, with speakers on the subject and an original play dealing with it. Dr. Richard Rapkin discussed Children's Hospital. Mrs. Hunt was persuaded to tell little John's story, the story behind the Special State Project. When her grandson John was 11 months old, as the result of a freak accident, he was projected out of a second story window to the cement ground below. He was evacuated by helicopter to the Pediatric Trauma Center at Parkland Hospital in Dallas, Texas. Through the prayers of many and the superb care he received, today seven year old John is happy, healthy and an excellent student. She wanted the children of New Jersey to have the same opportunity for specialized care, and thus the project.

While researching this project, she became aware of Dr. Richard Flyer, a dedicated Pediatrician. He was desperately trying to get a bill through the Legislature, which in essence mandated that all hospitals must have pediatric trained personnel in Emergency Rooms. NJSFWC passed an Emergency Resolution concerning this bill and worked for its enactment with the Junior League; they succeeded and today

301

this bill is in the process of being implemented.

Convention Chairman, Ruth Rockhill, and Vice Chairman, Enid Bernabe, with their capable committee, produced a fantastic 99th Convention at the Renaissance Hotel, in East Brunswick, New Jersey.

Mrs. Hunt asked "Wouldn't it be nice if we had a special effects committee to handle all the decorations, etc.?" Mary Ellen Brock, NJSFWC Financial Secretary, volunteered to handle the decorations for the Tuesday evening banquet. Hundreds of empty tissue boxes were collected and turned into glamorous centerpieces with the aid of her club members, the North Jersey Woman's Club. The Clifton Woman's Club President, Barbara DiDonna, volunteered to handle the back drop. Marianne Kremer willingly did the gorgeous giant red poppies for Wednesday evening's decorations, assisted by Ninth District members. Anita Rosen and members of the Fifth District EMD came up with outstanding Unity Day centerpieces; again her "Wouldn't it be nice if ?", was answered.

Convention took off with the powerful motivational speaker "Mac" McDonald. At the Tuesday banquet, The National Colors were presented by Kinnelon Senior Troop 503. Ailene Kearns sang the Pledge of Allegiance to the Flag of the United States of America, (a first). Mary Higgins Clark, the famous mystery writer known as the "Queen of Suspense", and personal friend of Mrs. Hunt, was the keynote speaker who amazed all with her "no notes" delivery! UNICEF's representative was James Kiberd, a well known soap opera star in "All My Children"; he thrilled members by table hopping. President Hunt presented him with a check for $15,281.98, the balance of the moneys raised for UNICEF;

a check had already been sent in February in response to an SOS from UNICEF. Wednesday morning the dynamic and prominent attorney, Cecile C. Weich, spoke on "Women's Legal Rights" and that evening Karen Edson, a member of the Woman's Club of Dumont, performed a magnificent classical program "A Musical Tribute to Joan". Mrs. Edson then accompanied a gifted singer, Kristen Ann Olsavsky, a recent GCl Delegate.

Convention ended on a real high. Dr. Helen Vassallo's motivational speech, "Give Me Your Hand", received a standing ovation. Mrs. Hunt made the presentation of her President's Award, the "Board of Directors Volunteer of the Year Award", to Deen Meloro, NJSFWC Corresponding Secretary. Mrs. Meloro had been selected by secret ballot of Board members. She received a wrist watch inscribed with "Thank You for Volunteering". Alarms went off and all were asked to vacate the premises due to a fire. There was some hesitation to leave since everyone thought it had been arranged by Mrs. Hunt's Assistant, Marianne Kremer, as special effects, because the flickering ceiling alarms looked like stars. (Stars were Mrs. Hunt's personal logo). Fortunately, the fire was minor in nature and members were able to return to the building. The Unity Breakfast closed with everyone holding hands and singing "That's What Friends Are For"; tears of joy were shed.

The expression, "One Federation" (the Women's Clubs, Juniors, Juniorettes and EMDers), was used constantly by Mrs. Hunt; meaning, inclusive. She felt no segment should be left out; therefore, the second year of her administration the State Fall Conference was scheduled on a Saturday, allowing young mothers and working women to attend. Issues important to women were presented: Zulima Farber, the

Public Advocate, was the keynote speaker, and there was a speaker on the important subject of electing women candidates. Since October was Breast Awareness Month a physician from the Cancer Society was invited to speak. Feeling strongly about prevention, Mrs. Hunt has arranged for a Mobile Unit to be on site at Convention 1994 for women desiring a mammography. Yes, scheduling a Fall Conference on a Saturday was a challenge, hopefully the next administration will do even more.

The privilege of being State President during part of the 100th Anniversary, and having the Centennial Convention, was exciting. Plans had to be made for this special occasion. Joan formed a committee consisting of the three Vice Presidents, the Financial Secretary, the current Centennial Chairman, Doris Jones, and the incoming Centennial Chairman, Ruth Supp. Past State Presidents were contacted for their input and Elizabeth Alton, Past State President (1958-60) acted as an advisor.

A time capsule will be designed by "resident artist," Anita Rosen, to be dedicated by the next administration, on November 16, 1994, Federation's birthday. It will be on permanent display in the Library at Headquarters.

M. Hope Diggs chaired a Premier Event on January 6, 1994 at Federation Headquarters as a kick-off for the Centennial. Many important and influential guests were invited, including the Past State Presidents, members of the NJSFWC, Junior and EMD Boards and representatives from the Charter Clubs and the District Centennial Chairmen. June Warren, a gifted actress and member of the Woman's Club of Ridgewood, wrote an original vignette about "Jennie June" and Federation's beginnings. She thrilled the guests with her performance. At this time, Eileen Becker, Vice President of the Eleventh District, and Evelyn Barton, District Centennial Chairman, presented a Centennial Flag to honor the Federation. The flag will fly over Federation Headquarters, during the Centennial period.

"Wouldn't it be nice if...?" Mrs. Hunt, contacted Past State President Mary Bixby (1972-1974) to see if she could interest Helen Boehm, Chairman of the Boehm Porcelain Studios, to create a special porcelain to honor Federation and its Centennial. At the 1994 Convention Mrs. Boehm will present "The New Generation Eagle" — a treasured piece of art, valued at $975. Boehm porcelain is internationally respected and this will be a wonderful gift.

Betsy Davis Foster arranged for a visit to the Watch Tower in Federation Park on the Palisades for April 30, 1994, on the occasion of its 65th Anniversary. The Monument was built to honor Federation for all it had done to save the Palisades. Provisions were made to keep the area in its "wild" state so that future generations would realize its natural condition at the time of the Monument's presentation in 1929. Wearing the Centennial pin was the "fee" required to attend this Federation event. The women also visited Blackledge-Kearney House (Cornwallis' Headquarters) and Greenbrook Sanctuary, sites Federation supports. President Hunt presented a check from the Federation for the continued upkeep of these two areas.

Many Centennial items were sold to raise money for the celebration, i.e. a rose bush, called Perfect Moment; the demand was overwhelming. Mrs. Hunt's dream was realized, a garden of Perfect Moment roses was planted at Headquarters; members of the JWC of Greater Brunswick Area care for the garden.

There was no doubt that the same Convention Committee, headed by Ruth Rockhill, would develop an exciting Centennial Convention at the Brunswick Hilton, formerly the Renaissance. And the Special Effects Committee volunteered without a "Wouldn't it be ?" Following are the 1994 Convention plans:

CELEBRATE FEDERATION will begin Tuesday afternoon with a motivational seminar conducted by Jackie Pierce, the President of the Illinois Federation and personal friend of Mrs. Hunt. That evening at the banquet honoring Club Presidents, special guests will be invited such as Christine Todd Whitman, the Governor of New Jersey, along with Hillary Rodham Clinton, wife of the President of the United States. There will be a celebrity keynoter and celebrity representative from UNICEF. At each scheduled meeting, vignettes are planned depicting a period in Federation's history. There will be special mementos given out daily. Richard Rapkin, MD will be presented with a check to equip the Resuscitation Critical Response Room at Children's Hospital. A Reception honoring the Club Presidents will follow.

Convention on Wednesday is devoted to nostalgia, A GLORIOUS PAST. There will be a short Parliamentary Workshop prior to the Business Session, to prepare the women for voting on Bylaws. Following the Business Session, the Past State Presidents will be honored at a luncheon hosted by the State President. All day long there will be a festive atmosphere with contests, prizes, entertainment and celebration. An open house will be held at Federation Headquarters, with bus loads of women transported from the hotel to participate in the Rose Garden's dedication to the Past State Presidents. The mood will continue to be festive, hostesses will dress in period costumes and the Meta Thorne Waters Scholarship students will entertain with Chamber Music.

Karen Edson wrote a new Federation Song in Mrs. Hunt's honor. It will be sung by the State Chorus, for the first time Wednesday evening, under the capable organization of Choral Director, Ailene Kearns. Seated on the dais for the banquet will be the President and the Past State Presidents, with each sharing a special moment from their administration. Club members will be encouraged to dress in period costumes to add to the festivities. Before the announcement of the 50th recipient of the Cecilia Gaines Holland Award, Chairman Elaine Villani will read the treasured Cecilia Gaines Holland Speech describing the 1890's. The Charter Clubs will be honored and Happy Anniversary will be sung during the cutting of the cake. The program will be a professional Heritage Fashion Show, followed by a special Centennial Reception and the serving of the Anniversary Cake with fountains of sparkling beverages.

Federation will be privileged to have both the GFWC International President, Ann Holland, and the GFWC President Elect, Jeannine Faubion, attending the Centennial Convention.

The 100th Centennial Convention's closing event, the Unity Breakfast, should be beautiful to the eye - the room will be decorated with red and white roses, which mean Unity....One Federation. And it will end on a high note with the thrilling voices of Gospel Singers, directed by Karen

Edson, celebrating A BRILLIANT FUTURE with the Installation of Officers. Dorothy Lowe Greene will become the 44th NJSFWC President.

Mrs. Hunt's assistants, formerly referred to in other administrations as Aides, were M. Hope Diggs and Marianne Kremer. Joan stated time and time again it was only because of these two wonderful women that she was able to maintain the pace she did throughout her term of office.

GFWC President Elect, Jeannine Faubion, has asked Mrs. Hunt to serve on the 1994-1996 GFWC Board of Directors in a vital new General Federation role when she completes her NJSFWC presidency - one which will prove to be another challenge.

The publication schedule for this book made it impossible to include all of the extensive accomplishments of Joan M. Hunt and her outstanding associates who epitomized women who faced and met all challenges.

1992-1994 NJSFWC Executive Committee

STATE DIRECTORS JUNIOR MEMBERSHIP

*1923-25	Mary S. Daniels (Miss)
*1925-26	Mrs. G. Malcolm Shelmire
*1926-29	Florence L. Robinson (Mrs. Myron W.)
*1929-32	Emma R. Dunaway (Mrs. C. O.)
*1932-35	Louie C. Francisco (Mrs. Stephen J.)
*1935-38	Agnes Shirley Polhemus (Mrs. P. Garretson)
*1938-41	Rachel L. Mecray (Mrs. Jay E.)
*1941-44	Velma Moersdorf Garrett (Mrs. Thomas A.)
1944-47	Arlyne W. Reed (Mrs. Roy L.)
1947-50	Mildred E. Ansink (Miss)
1950-53	Geraldine Brown Sentell (Mrs. Douglas P.)
1953-56	Evelyn T. Borea (Miss)
1956-58	Dorothy L. Furness (Miss)
1958-60	Jean Hamilton (Miss)
*1960-62	Evelyn P. Colgan (Miss.)
1962-64	Barbara Farrell (Mrs. Robert M.)
1964-66	Dorothy A. Krivancik (Miss)
1966-68	Joan Buchanan (Miss)
1968-70	Jacqueline Wershing (Mrs. Glenn A.)
1970-72	Joan Quigley (Mrs. John J., Jr.)
1972-74	Jean Porte (Miss)
1974-76	Patricia Moore (Mrs. James M. P.)
1976-78	Dorothy Lowe Greene (Mrs. James B.)
1978-80	Margie Waer (Mrs. Robert E., Jr.)
1980-82	Barbara Spillane (Mrs. Thomas)
1982-84	Ann Quinn (Mrs. J. Anthony)
1984-3/86	Linda Rissel (Mrs. John M.)
3/86-5/86	Anne Redlus (Mrs. Howard)
1986-88	Roberta Dyrsten (Mrs. Gerald)
1988-90	Mary Lou Sullivan (Mrs. W. Timothy)
1990-92	Deen J. Meloro (Mrs. Daniel)
1992-94	Sandra L. Johnston (Mrs. Gary)

JUNIOR CLUBS — NJSFWC LIFELINE

The Junior Membership Department, like other departments within the Federation, evolved over time in response to the needs and changes within our society. Reviewing early history, the first group of "Juniors" existed in New Jersey in 1890 (although the Woman's Club of Redlands in California was awarded official status as the nation's first Junior Club). At that time, the Ladies of Clio Literary Society in Roselle Park, NJ felt the need to incorporate their daughters, as well as other younger women, into their semi-monthly programs. Thus a Junior Committee was founded.

The group achieved such recognition for their work within the community that they were approached to join as Federation members, and immediately began paying regular dues to NJSFWC. In 1896, these new members worked tirelessly to help petition the State Legislature to preserve the historic beauty of the Palisades. Four years later, as a result of these efforts, coupled with the success of the Clio experiment, other clubs began forming Junior Committees.

Over the next twenty-five years the work of the Juniors flourished. In 1923, NJSFWC President Etta Gould Lee appointed Mary S. Daniels, Second Vice President, as Chairman of a special committee to study and plan for the integration of the Juniors as an organized department within the Federation. At the Federation's State Fall Conference in October 1924, Miss Daniels announced the appointment of Mrs. G. Malcolm Shelmire as Junior Chairman. She was succeeded in January 1926 by Florence L. Robinson who was chosen to fill the unexpired term.

During her term, Mrs. Robinson put into place many of the elements that would later become part of the Junior tradition. Among these were the State Junior Pin and the Junior Past President's Pin. Also chosen were the Junior banner and the motto — "JOY in Service, PRIDE in Achievement". The first Junior Presidents' Councils were organized as was the establishment of an educational fund to provide scholarships enabling Juniors to continue their education. One of the first projects of the newly-organized Juniors was the donation of twelve Braille books for the blind.

By 1926 there were 61 Junior Clubs with 2500 members. Two years later, the country's first Junior State Convention was held at the New Jersey College for Women, now Douglass College. Mrs. Robinson presided over this historic meeting and welcomed 17 new clubs into the Federation. By unanimous vote, it was recommended to hold Annual Conferences and Conventions and to pay a five cent per capita tax to defray the expenses of those meetings. Also, the Junior Penny Art Fund was established for the purpose of helping students at the New Jersey College for Women to continue their education in the Arts. At the same Convention, it was agreed that the Junior Braille Fund would be a permanent account and it was renamed the Florence L. Robinson Braille Fund in honor of that Chairman of the Junior Committee.

The Juniors grew to a membership of 6800 during 1929 and under its new chairman, Emma R. Dunaway, the age limit was set at thirty. It would later be changed to 35 and eventually increased to age 40. Louie C. Francisco held the status of a non-voting member of the Federation Board of Directors. District Junior Past Presidents' Clubs were first formed in 1935, and by 1938 the Junior Committee became the Junior Membership Department with the Junior Chairman Rachel Mecray, an elected Trustee.

In 1935, under Chairman Agnes Polhemus, major Junior State Projects included raising over $10,000 to supply "talking books" and their accompanying machines. Two years later, $500 was earmarked for two travel scholarships. One was for a student from the New Jersey College for Women and the other went to a foreign student. The organization of Sub-Junior groups in 1948 allowed girls too young to join the Juniors the opportunity to engage in Federation activities.

The hardships and upheavals of World War II were addressed through the many projects engineered by the Juniors. Over 1000 "buddy bags" were made for the servicemen stationed on the Battleship USS New Jersey. The Juniors also helped to furnish company "day rooms" at various Army installations throughout the state. Fort Hancock at Sandy Hook was one of the bases to benefit from this program. Great effort went toward amassing $22,000 to purchase fifteen Army ambulances which were sent overseas for field service. Juniors provided entertainment and hospitality to military personnel and played an active role in

312

all branches of the American Red Cross. For their work, the Juniors received several citations from the War Department for meritorious service.

Velma M. Garrett

Arlyne W. Reed

In the months following the end of World War II, the Junior Membership Department embarked on a campaign to support refugee relief programs. Thirty-five needy families were adopted and 2500 pounds of food and clothing were sent to them. Three thousand packets of seeds were sent to war-ravaged countries as part of an international renewal program.

Junior State Projects included raising over $12,000 in 1945 to purchase, equip and operate a traveling van which toured the rural areas of New Jersey providing free eye examinations. Also, in the late 1940's, the Navajo Indians would benefit from nearly $10,000 contributed to improve their living conditions. In addition to the donations of clothing and infant layettes, the Juniors lobbied for pushing a $10 million appropriation bill through Congress to provide much needed relief for the Native American population.

Another activity which would continue for a few years was the "Stamps for the Wounded" program that began as a GFWC Junior project. In 1950, Junior Chairman Geraldine V.

Brown (who later became Mrs. Douglas Sentell) reported that over 100,000 stamps were collected. During her tenure, $18,378 was raised to purchase, equip and staff a traveling unit for education in early cancer detection. The Mobile Cancer Unit was a familiar sight throughout New Jersey.

Mildred E. Ansink   Geraldine Brown Sentell

In 1954, JMD Chairman, Evelyn T. Borea reported an even larger total of 442,537 stamps for the wounded. In that same year 101,507 hours of service were contributed by the Juniors to various charitable causes. Among these was the establishment of the Upper Extremity Amputee Fund, the first of its kind in the United States. During that initial year, over $30,000 was raised to provide training and prostheses for New Jersey residents who had lost portions of their hands and arms.

In 1956, the term of office for the Junior Membership Chairman was changed from three to two years. The practice of embarking on a major Junior State Project during each administration has continued.

During the 1950's and 1960's, Junior Clubs had entered in the Shell Oil Program. Some of these projects included third grade science fairs, a humane education program, a poison

314

awareness campaign, a thrift shop to benefit a local library and baby sitting management courses. In other programs, such as "Understanding Through Brotherhood", clubs participated in visits which observed various religions.

For American Education Week, schools were visited and hours were donated to improve educational opportunities for under-privileged children. Juniors volunteered as teachers and aides in Head Start programs. They also served on committees which provided recreational activities and study centers.

Clubs provided assistance in state mental hospitals, private schools, local education groups for the mentally-challenged and participated in patterning programs for brain-damaged children. Juniors worked as "Teaching Mums" at a school for retarded children. Other groups of children were sent to camp. Clubs also were involved in Project Fresh Air Fund in their communities. The Helping Hand Block Parent Programs were initiated through many Junior Clubs. One notable project was the establishment of a children's zoo.

Chairman Dorothy L. Furness, 1956 - 1958, chose "ABC" — A Better Community — as her theme and State Project. Juniors served on a number of beautification committees and an outgrowth of these was a garden for the visually-handicapped with Braille plaques that described the many flowers planted there. Clubs embarked on a successful letter writing campaign to get a bill passed in the State Assembly to establish a separate division for narcotic and drug abuse. Thousands of hours were donated to hospitals, including the making of tray favors and hand puppets for children. The Walter D. Matheny School benefited from the collection of more than $3000 worth of coupons.

In 1960 Junior Membership Chairman, Jean Hamilton, reported that the Trenton State Home for Girls received $34,545 to build and equip an athletic field. Two years later, in another State Project entitled "Four Plus One", Junior Membership Chairman, Evelyn P. Colgan, proposed that clubs should be offered the opportunity to provide service on five levels — international, national, statewide, district and community. One outgrowth of this was the donation of over $9,000 to the New Jersey Chapter of the American Cancer Society for the training of six cytotechnologists.

Evelyn T. Borea

Jean Hamilton

During these years other charities received Jersey Junior financial aid such as the medical ship SS Hope, CARE, the Salk Foundation, the Peace Corps and the Braille Fund. Other projects included money donated to the Cystic Fibrosis Foundation, mental health associations, the Midland School, Operation Healthy Babies, the restoration of Independence Hall and Radio Free Europe.

In addition, Juniors raised extensive funds and donated countless hours towards scholarships. In 1950, Junior Membership Chairman, Mildred E. Ansink, reported that $1650 was raised to provide a scholarship for a student from the

Philippines to attend the New Jersey College for Women. In 1954, Junior Membership Chairman, Evelyn T. Borea, announced the creation of the first Junior Drama Scholarship. Another $836 was earmarked for Home Economics Scholarship Funds. In that same year, two art scholarships were given to students attending the New Jersey College for Women and another $15,000 was allocated for two special Braille training scholarships. In 1962, Junior Membership Chairman, Evelyn P. Colgan, reported that over $415 was raised for the Meta Thorne Waters Music Scholarship and four years later, Junior Chairman, Dorothy A. Krivancik, stated that a total of over $12,000 was awarded to students seeking higher education.

Evelyn P. Colgan   Barbara Farrell

In 1964, Junior Membership Chairman, Barbara Farrell, reported that over $20,000 was raised for that year's state project — The Children's Aid and Adoption Society. This provided for the medical examinations and treatment of babies in the care of that society prior to their adoption or placement. Two years later, JMD Chairman, Dorothy A. Krivancik, stated that the Juniors earned $12,500 toward the NJSFWC Headquarters Building Fund, in addition to assisting four state hospitals. In 1968, the next Junior Membership Chairman, Joan Buchanan, reported nearly

$30,000 contributed for the establishment of programs for pre-school children and young adults who suffered from brain injuries.

Structurally, the New Jersey Juniors evolved into a Department of the NJSFWC. It holds a unique position in that the Junior Chairman, now called the Junior Director, serves a two-year term as a member of NJSFWC's Executive Committee. She also presides over a Junior Executive Board consisting of the Junior Officers, District Advisors, Department and Committee Chairmen. Subject to the approval of the Federation, the Juniors have their own projects and budget, as well as their own Convention.

 TEL-A-JUNIOR

Tel-A-Junior, the official Junior publication originated when Geraldine V. Brown was JMD Chairman in 1950 - 1953 (previously, the New Jersey Juniors were featured in the "New Jersey Club Woman" under the direction of a Junior Editor). It started with the masthead of the first issue which included a series of question marks announcing a contest to name the new publication. Holly Marie Parizot of Bloomfield submitted the winning one-word title "Telejunior". At the 1963 Junior Convention, it was voted to hyphenate the title and make it "Tel-A-Junior". During the first year of publication, there were 1092 subscribers. By 1968, there were 2676 readers from 111 clubs.

Another Junior publication, EUREKA, (first published under Evelyn T. Borea's term in 1954), has been printed

318

annually in booklet form containing the Department and Committee Outlines for the entire Junior Membership program. This booklet is distributed at the Junior State Fall Conferences as a reference tool for club presidents.

Highlights during these years included a number of citations from legislative officials and national organizations. In 1950, the Juniors received commendation for their work in contributing over $10,000 to establish Curative Workshops for the New Jersey Chapter of the National Society for Crippled Children and Adults. At the GFWC Convention in Washington, DC in 1962 the New Jersey delegation received two awards — one for outstanding work in the field of health and the other for their work in establishing a nursery school for the blind in Santiago, Chile. In 1964, the Jersey Juniors were cited by the General Federation for their work for the medical ship SS Hope, CARE and the Salk Foundation. They also placed first in the nation for outstanding achievement in the Public Affairs and the Fine Arts Departments. New Jersey was the only Junior group to endow a seat in the John F. Kennedy Cultural Center at Washington, DC. Of great significance in 1966 was Governor Richard Hughes' proclamation of Junior Women's Clubs Week during November 7-13. He urged all state residents "to pay tribute to the women who are performing such important services throughout the state and to join in those humanitarian efforts." Two years later, the Jersey Juniors received the Grand National Award given by the National Foundation March of Dimes for their work with Operation Healthy Babies. New Jersey State Chairman, Joan Buchanan, was honored as the Top Junior Director for 1966 - 1968 by GFWC. She later became GFWC Junior Director.

Dorothy A. Krivancik   Joan Buchanan

As the 1960's ended, a network of Committees and Departments was in place which allowed the Junior Membership Department to implement its programs and activities in a very effective manner. These included: American Home, Art, Braille, Civics, Club Yearbooks and Scrapbooks, Community Improvement, Drama, International Relations, Literature and Education, Membership and Parliamentary Procedure, Music, Program Assistance, Public Relations, Public Welfare, Sub-Juniors, Tel-A-Junior, State Projects and Youth Cooperation. The State Junior Board met nine times a year to plan programs for the membership. The overall direction of the programs was determined at the State Convention held in Atlantic City each May. Yearly goals were implemented at the State Fall Conferences held in Newark each September as well as at District Conferences and other sessions. The entire membership was encouraged to attend these meetings.

Junior involvement at all levels of society continued as JMD Chairman, Jacqueline Wershing, reported letters and articles being sent to American troops in Vietnam as well as to veterans in hospitals and to USO stations. The Junior Woman's Club of Woodbury was one of the ten national CIP finalists for their project "Robin's Nest", a home for girls. One hundred per cent of the Junior Clubs had subscribed to Tel-A-Junior. The JMD State Project, Ranch Hope for Boys, had received over $30,000 in donations which went toward food products, clothing, household items, medical and automobile supplies, books and garden equipment. This unique facility has continued to receive Federation support.

The Juniors were ready to meet the challenges of the 1970's with many new objectives. The leadership for this Department would assume a much more prominent role in directing the activities of the individual clubs at all levels. Beginning her term in May 1970, Junior Membership Chairman, Joan Quigley, reported a year later that, in reviewing projects and departments within the state membership, some programs would have to be eliminated and others would be revitalized. Two new Departments were created to promote more interest in national Junior goals and to focus attention on the problems of conservation, beautification, pollution, safety and overpopulation. Clubs would be judged on their accomplishments rather than on their participation.

Fall Conference also underwent some modifications. The Mid-Year Rally featured a Leadership Workshop conducted by professionals; and all District Conferences had Department Workshops. The Convention format was completely revised to allow more time for communication, education and recreation. Reporting and judging procedures were completely reorganized. Report questionnaires were standardized; judging criteria was not. As a result, all Junior clubs were able to report their goals and how these were accomplished.

According to information submitted to her, Joan Quigley reported that the composite for the "average" Junior was that she was 29 years old with two and one-half children. She belonged to a number of church and school-related organizations and was employed in a part-time position. She had been a member of her Junior Club for less than three years, and her favorite projects were those which benefited children and met the special needs of her own community. This "average" Junior had lived in her town for less than five years and considered her community attractive, suburban and political.

That same year, clubs sponsored programs to focus attention on the plight of American prisoners of war by petitioning local governments for resolutions. Day care centers were established and health clinics for migrant workers started. Also implemented were special classes for the mentally retarded and transportation services for the physically handicapped.

Jacqueline Wershing   Joan Quigley

Membership increased by 244 members with the addition of three new Sub-Junior clubs.

In 1972, Quigley reported that the Mobile Craft Bus, which has been purchased by the Juniors the previous year, had been in operation throughout New Jersey and was often staffed by Junior Clubwomen. Members who learned Braille had prepared many pages for the visually-impaired while other Juniors tape-recorded thousands of pages for use by the blind.

The Junior State Project, the Ruth Gottscho Kidney Foundation, had received overwhelming support through public relations efforts, the maintenance of the kidney transplant hotline, patient assistance and the collection of donor cards. More than a million Betty Crocker coupons were collected for dialysis machines. The total Junior financial contribution to this project was over $56,000.

The following year, Junior Membership Chairman, Jean Porte, stressed the themes of "involvement" and giving" to incorporate into her administration's projects. Membership was emphasized and there was another increase of members with five new clubs established. Two more Junior clubs would be ready to become federated by September 1974.

Clubs conducted 200 Arts and Crafts Workshops for the handicapped, the hospitalized, the retarded, the orphaned and the senior citizens in their communities. Four hundred Arts and Crafts Workshops were held specifically for teenagers and children. District Art and American Home Workshops were begun for the first time.

Juniors visited jails and sponsored projects to improve the corrections system. Voter registration drives and candidates' nights were held. Juniors participated in recycling efforts and conservation programs. They provided clinics for measles, dental care and audio screening. Clubs either started or continued work with Big Sister groups and Youth Good News campaigns.

In 1974, Chairman Porte stated that the Junior State Project, Spaulding for Children, had realized over $58,000. Group meetings were held for interested parents and nearly 400 referrals were made. Several children were in the process of being placed in permanent homes with four Juniors participating in the adoption process.

Clubs supported the Justice for Juveniles Bill #2141 and many hours were spent working in detention centers and children's shelters. Juniors also worked with the Education Committee of the Friends of Channel 13 in order to conduct a state-wide survey to determine the future use of educational TV in schools.

Two other important projects were the complete refurbishing of a veterans' rest home and the furnishing of an apartment to be used as a transitional residence for patients from mental institutions. A goal of providing for a fifteen bed hospital unit in Southeast Asia for the Dooley Foundation was realized.

In 1975, JMD Chairman, Patricia A. Moore, had as her administration's theme: JOY of giving; PRIDE in accomplishment; SERVICE to others; and ACHIEVEMENTS far beyond expectations. To this end, thousands of volunteer hours were spent in youth-related activities, drug and alcohol treatment centers and in assisting senior citizens. Consumer awareness and better home management were promoted through food co-ops, swap shops and comparison shopping guides.

324

In the area of crime prevention and law observance, some of the projects covered by the Public Affairs Department throughout the state included Operation Identification, Neighborhood Watch, juvenile justice and vandalism. Attention was drawn to the problems of child molestation and rape.

For the following year, Chairman Moore also served as a Trustee for the NJSFWC and as a member of the GFWC Board of Directors. There were 132 Junior clubs and 32 Sub-Junior clubs. Art objects, books and prints were donated to institutions and libraries. Work continued in the area of the prevention of vision disorders and aid for the blind.

The Institute of Medical Research was chosen as the Junior State Project. Over $56,000 was raised and hundreds of hours were spent in the service of one-to-one care at home and volunteer work at hospitals. Equipment was donated to cancer units and there was increased public awareness as to the need for early cancer detection and cancer research.

Dorothy Lowe Greene, Southern Vice Chairman, became JMD Chairman in September 1976 when Delores Thierfelder (who had been elected in May) found it necessary to resign for personal reasons.

Mrs. Greene emphasized the qualities behind the concepts of "concerned" and "committed". Over 7000 children viewed "Here's Looking at You", which was an original Junior puppet show on eye safety. Juniors worked to revamp parks and highways. Clubs advertised energy conservation and environmental awareness with over 1000 pieces of literature distributed to the public.

Jean Porte   Dorothy Lowe Greene

Drug and alcohol rehabilitation centers were given clothing and monetary support. Service hours and programs were donated to these facilities. UNICEF received over $11,000 through various projects. Financial support was given to other international organizations and hundreds of foreign students and visitors were welcomed by Juniors.

Twenty-two copies of "The Songs America Loves Best" were sold for the Affiliated Artists National Trust. Lending libraries, story hours and book drives were implemented to help communities and to provide services for the handicapped. Other programs that received Junior support included Neighborhood Watch, Women Against Rape (WAR) and Operation Identifax. Several hundred Juniors volunteered their time at Swine Flu clinics.

Several clubs had "Junior Week" proclaimed in their communities and the bumper sticker campaign entitled "Creating Junior Awareness" was a huge success. For the first time, a separate Sub-Junior Drama Tournament was held with the participation of six clubs.

In 1977- 1978 Chairman Greene reported that 2400 children throughout the state witnessed performances of "Let's Be

326

Friends", a preventive drug abuse puppet show. Many projects were instituted such as Child Shield and Neighborhood Watch. Juniors were appointed to Community Crime Watch Boards and lobbied state officials to establish a Uniform Crime Prevention Code and a Crime Prevention Resource Center.

Participation in the GFWC CARE Junior Project — Guatemala Highlands — was successful. The Junior State Project, the National Burn Victim Foundation, benefited from 15,000 volunteer hours and thousands of dollars. Over one-quarter of a million dollars was raised for all of the projects that year.

With the theme "Harmony Through Understanding", incoming JMD Chairman, Margie R. Waer, in 1978 began her administration with a look to the coming decade and a call to have the Juniors meet the needs of members by understanding new priorities and adjusting programs accordingly. In celebrating the International Year of the Child, special emphasis was placed on the support of the 1980 Olympic Games and 23,000 cancelled stamps were sent to "Stamps for Children". Also, $38,000 was raised for scholarships.

Ninety percent of the clubs worked in shelters and with officials to aid in assisting battered wives and abused children. Club members spent hundreds of hours working in nursing homes, conducting blood drives, working at Health Fairs and dental clinics as well as centers for the handicapped and the retarded. Facilities for veterans also received Junior support.

In 1980, Mrs. Waer reported that many Juniors had helped

with pre-school vision screening, and many dormant eye problems were diagnosed and treated as a result. In the Drama Department, more emphasis was placed on actual service work in schools, hospitals and senior citizen centers.

Some clubs entered the GFWC Home Energy Check Contest and distributed over 12,000 check lists to the public. Juniors also raised over $11,000 for UNICEF and had sent more than 25,000 stamps to CROP and other international organizations. Foster children were sponsored with contributions of over $15,000. Clubs actively participated in sending Christmas mail to the American hostages imprisoned in Iran.

By the end of 1980, over 150 Juniors held dual memberships in their Junior and General Clubs. This was a program in its second year. It was judged to be a success by a committee appointed by the NJSFWC President.

Of great importance was the over $54,000 which had been raised for the Junior State Project, the New Jersey Hemophilia Association.

In assuming the position of Junior Membership Chairman upon the resignation of JoAnn Rivard, Barbara Spillane reported, in 1981, of the club members' involvement in the community and with international organizations. American Energy Week was proclaimed by 55 clubs. Juniors continued to support recycling programs, the restoration of old buildings, the maintenance of mini-parks as well as beautification and conservation programs.

UNICEF and CARE received donations of nearly $3,000. Some clubs hosted foreign exchange students. Juniors

328

supported and publicized crime reduction projects such as "Mr. McGruff". The hostages in Iran were remembered with yellow ribbon ceremonies by nearly all of the clubs.

The revitalization of Sub-Junior clubs was encouraged. A mini Sub-Junior Conference was held in the fall and a Federation briefing at Headquarters took place in the spring. There was a decrease in the number of <u>Tel-A-Junior</u> issues from five to four a year.

Margie Waer   Barbara Spillane

In 1982, Chairman Spillane reported that the state project, National Sudden Infant Death Syndrome (SIDS) — New Jersey Chapter, received overwhelming support. The Junior slogan, "Stick Your Neck Out for SIDS" was most effective. Clubs promoted interest in SIDS through stay-at-home teas and by having the week of April 11 - 17 declared Junior SIDS Awareness Week.

In their efforts to raise money for SIDS, the Juniors held their first state-wide fund raiser, an exhibition basketball game between the New York Giants and Philadelphia Eagles football teams. This event, together with other fund-raising projects, helped the Juniors to collect more than $100,000 for SIDS. New Jersey would also benefit from two open evaluation centers to help children with SIDS. Linda Rissel chaired this project.

Ann Quinn, the next Junior Membership Chairman whose title was officially changed to Junior Director to conform with GFWC, reported in 1983 on the thousands of hours that were donated to the Visual and Creative Arts Department in support of the GFWC logo "You've Gotta Have Art!" Clubs proclaimed Youth Art Week throughout the state and conducted art contests and festivals. Art programs were developed and art auctions, house tours and fashion shows held.

In the area of education, Juniors made an impact in their communities by serving on local School Boards, volunteering at libraries, participating in the Seedlings Reading Program, conducting contests and supporting Reading Is Fundamental (R.I.F.) programs. Members also helped with kindergarten pre-screening and Head Start projects.

Other projects promoted were mandatory car seat restraints for children and Ident-A-Kid, which involved the finger printing of children. A full 100 percent of the Junior Clubs were enrolled in Partners for Progress through the Community Improvement Program (CIP).

Ann Quinn

Ann Redlus

Director Quinn acknowledged that the greatest challenge for her administration was in the area of membership. She recounted that there had been a 50 percent loss of members over the previous nine years, with an accelerating decline in the last three years. Mrs. Quinn stressed the importance of periodically evaluating the Junior Program to make it more adaptable to current situations. Some changes were implemented which provided for a simpler and more realistic method of report writing. Formation of new Sub-Junior Clubs was encouraged by lowering the entry level age to twelve.

For the following year, Quinn continued to emphasize the need to enroll more new members by reporting on some of the programs implemented. "Project +1" encouraged clubs to attain a net increase of at least one member through traditional "teas" and by word of mouth. New membership pamphlets, highlighting the appeal and achievements of Juniors, were introduced to coincide with a state-wide campaign. A proclamation was issued by Governor Thomas Kean which declared that November was to be "GFWC Junior Clubwoman Recognition Month".

Clubs were encouraged to set realistic goals to avoid "burnout". Tel-A-Junior had acquired a new format which led to increased subscriptions. Problems of small clubs were addressed through visits from the "Membership Team" and the introduction of a handbook for their use.

Five new Sub-Junior clubs were started and one club was reinstated. Juniors and Sub-Juniors raised over $60,000 for their state project, the American Liver Foundation. A TV Documentary entitled: "Liver Disease — The Silent Killer" was produced and later broadcast to one million viewers over the New Jersey Cable Network Station. Mary Lou Sullivan, an active members of the Jersey Juniors, was designated as that year's "GFWC Outstanding Junior of the Year".

In 1986 Junior Director Linda Rissel, who was later asked to resign, reported on the Juniors' concerns over environmental issues, particularly toxic waste. There was a "Sacks Appeal" campaign in which club members used brown paper bags to clean up areas. The General Federation would make use of the project for the following year.

The Junior mascot, Poppi the Panda, generated financial support and interest for the plight of the Panda Bear. In the International Affairs Department, Juniors sponsored a half-time show of the Sydney Conservatorium Symphony in conjunction with Somerset County College to benefit CROP, CARE and UNICEF.

Ann Redlus, who replaced Rissel, reported in 1986 on the strengthening of communications between the State Department Chairmen and the Club Department Chairmen. District Advisors would play a key role in doing this.

Learning disabilities and literacy were spotlighted throughout the year. In addition, cuddly bears were collected and distributed to hospitalized children. The Radio Information Center for the Blind in South Jersey was completed through years of donations to the Florence L. Robinson Braille Fund.

Juniors throughout the state supported the Missing Children's Day Balloon Launch and $11,000 was raised for the Foundation to Protect and Find New Jersey's Children. Two new Sub-Junior clubs became federated.

In 1987, Junior Director Roberta Dyrsten reported that the 92 Junior Clubs and 16 Sub-Junior Clubs had raised over $400,000 for various projects throughout the year. Juniors supported such GFWC programs as Make-A-Wish Foundation, Support Dogs for the Handicapped and Family Financial Planning Seminars.

Roberta Dyrsten

In 1988 Mrs. Dyrsten reported on the emphasis of creative arts. Clubs throughout the state held creative writing, scrapbook and poster contests as well as craft classes. Youth Art Month was proclaimed and art festivals were held over the year in response to the theme, "Be A Part of Art!"

A special focus of the Health Department was "Prevention Programs for Youth", whereby problems such as teen suicide, drugs and smoking were highlighted. The prevention of child abuse and child abduction received special attention. Juniors distributed thousands of promotional items for S.O.B.E.R. and either supported or founded SADD or MADD chapters. Linda Caputo chaired the Junior State Project, Tourettes Syndrome Association, which successfully raised money and public awareness. Roberta Dyrsten was elected GFWC Junior Director for 1992 - 1994.

With the approach of another new decade and new

challenges, Junior Director, Mary Lou Sullivan, reported in 1989 of growing concern over declining membership. The Membership Development Campaign Committee was formed to address some of these problems. Charter ceremonies were conducted for two new clubs, the Greater Linwood Juniors and the Little Falls Juniorettes. (It should be noted that the term Sub-Juniors had been dropped in favor of "Juniorettes".)

Mary Lou Sullivan   Deen J. Meloro

For the following year, funds and public awareness were generated for the Junior State Project, the Lupus Foundation. Of particular importance was an Amendment of NJSFWC By-Laws which made the Director of Junior Clubs an Officer of the Federation and a member of the Executive Committee. Of great consequence were the establishment of a Membership Committee to address solutions to declining membership and the initiation of Leadership Institutes. More changes included the reactivation of the Top Five Awards (for the most active clubs), the combination of the Little Theater Tournament and Music Festivals and the procurement of corporate sponsorship for the statewide Spelling Bee. Mary Lou Sullivan would continue representing her state at the national level by assuming positions as the GFWC Junior Membership Chairman from 1990 to 1992 and then as GFWC Membership Chairman, 1992 to 1994.

When Deen J. Meloro was Director of Junior Clubs (1990 - 1992) the Juniors donated $1.4 million to worthy causes. This included over $20,000 to NJSFWC's Special State Project, Children's Hospital AIDS Program (CHAP). The Juniors own Special State Project was Lyme Disease with the $56,000 raised creating a videotape and booklet distributed to schools throughout the state. These taught children self-protection against the "tick" causing Lyme disease.

In 1992 the Juniors fourth Spelling Bee involved 47 clubs and over 9,000 children. Juniors participated in the Care Box for the Homeless, implemented spring clean-up programs in their towns and continued to collect funds for UNICEF. The Rutherford Juniors received the Woodrow Wilson Good Government Award and the Juniors of Hasbrouck Heights received the Governor's Highway Safety Award.

During Mrs. Meloro's tenure the Flemington Area Juniors and the Vineland and North Huntington Juniorettes were chartered to add three new clubs to the Federation. A questionnaire format revamped report writing which resulted in a ten percent increase in clubs reporting. A President's Handbook was prepared for all clubs, and a videotape on membership was created for distribution to the districts. New Jersey Juniors were recognized by GFWC for their outstanding work in education, conservation, international affairs and leadership.

Deen Meloro went on to serve as NJSFWC's Corresponding Secretary (1992-1994) and as GFWC's Junior Conservation Chairman.

1992 - 1994 found Sandra L. Johnston serving as Junior Director. When "Hurricane Andrew" hit Florida and

Louisiana in August, 1992 the link among clubwomen became stronger as the Juniors initiated truckloads of help sent by all NJSFWC members to the victims there. The clubs in the stricken areas serving as coordinators. The Juniors of New Jersey held three Mid-Year Rallies and hosted a counterpart luncheon meeting with the Junior Executive Board entertaining the NJSFWC Board of Directors.

Sandra L. Johnston

Juniors continued their varied projects in 1992 - 1993 and selected the Community Food Bank as their 1993 - 1994 State Project.

The past and present Junior Directors and Assistant Directors have long recognized the challenges that are still facing the overall Junior membership. These problems have their roots in the overwhelming demands and tasks that have been placed on women in order to meet the growing financial and emotional needs of their families in these uncertain times. Yet, in the face of increasing odds and declining members, the Junior Women's Clubs expect to continue their aims and objectives that were put forth in their Collect: "To live each day trying to accomplish something, not merely to exist". Certainly their glorious past points to a brilliant and hopeful future!

336

STATE CHAIRMEN

EVENING MEMBERSHIP DEPARTMENT

* 1938-41	Marie Catlin (Mrs. Arthur A.)
* 1941-42	Mary S. Curtis (Mrs. Clifford B.)
* 1942-44	Renette H. Casebolt (Mrs. George H.)
* 1944-45	Ethel Lawrence (Mrs. Howard C.)
* 1945-48	Caroline C. Almond (Mrs. George B., Jr.)
1948-51	Ann Emrick (Mrs. Harold E.)
* 1951-54	Gladys M. Blauvelt (Mrs. Clarence L.)
1954-56	Madeline Pallo Garfin
1956-58	Anita Nussbaum (Mrs. William L.)
1958-60	Seraphine Mayer (Miss)
1960-62	Emily Brundage Haddad (Mrs. Theodore R.)
1962-64	Annabelle McCormick (Mrs. Thomas)
1964-66	Jan Denniston (Mrs. A. Lynn)
1966-68	Marie Wyatt (Mrs. Richard H.)
* 1968-70	Laura Teachman (Mrs. Russell R.)
1970-72	Margaret Kipple (Mrs. Arthur E.)
1972-74	Jeanne C. Decker (Mrs. Thomas E.)
1974-76	Ethel Richards (Mrs. Stanley H.)
1976-78	Helen J. Sparacio (Mrs. Carl)
1978-80	Dolores Plasket (Mrs. George K. Jr.)
1980-82	Carol White (Mrs. Allan W.)
1982-84	Joyce Farnham (Mrs. Walter A.)
* 1984-86	Joan Handschuh (Mrs. Robert)
1986-88	Shirley A. Kiefer (Mrs. Walter F.)
1988-90	Sharon L. Cartwright (Mrs. Donald)
1990-92	Mary Lou Phifer (Mrs. William A.)
1992-94	Phyllis W. Schneck (Mrs. Ernest J.)

EVENING MEMBERSHIP DEPARTMENT— THE VITAL LINK

The year was 1928. Most of the clubs in NJSFWC, except for Junior clubs, held daytime meetings. There were women who were employed and/or cared for children or others at home who, if they were above the age limit for Junior Membership, could not participate. Mrs. William P. Campbell, a former President of the Long Branch Woman's Club, saw a need for this segment of the population to become involved in the activities and pursuits of club work. Fourteen women met in the basement of the Long Branch Public Library to form an evening group. In 1933 the Little Falls Woman's Club followed by organizing the Business and Professional Department of their club. The first meeting of the "B's and P's" took place on October 5, 1933. By 1936 the Haddon Fortnightly, still one of the largest clubs in the Federation, took action to form an Evening Section. These three organizations are still active in 1994.

By 1936 the Federation realized that "Evening Sections"

represented a growing trend which could enrich membership in NJSFWC. State President Mattie Driscoll appointed Mrs. Robert G. Bellah and a committee of six members to investigate the need for forming more Evening Departments. At the 1937 Convention the committee reported that there was a vast need and desirability of offering the benefits of club membership to mature women who were unable to attend daytime meetings. By Federation action in 1938 the Evening Membership Committee was created with Marie Catlin to serve for three years as its first Chairman . During her term of office the framework of this very important Department was developed. All clubs were asked to study their individual community needs in this field and, if desirable, to form an Evening Membership Department (EMD). The Evening Membership Committee introduced the idea to clubs, suggested changes in their Bylaws and/or Standing Rules as needed, aided in the installation new officers and outlined activities, dues and program procedures.

Marie Catlin

The first EMD Supper Conference was held in 1939 with 54 women, representing 14 groups, attending. The idea "took off" and by the Second Annual Conference in 1940 there had been a fifty percent increase in membership. Individual EMD's introduced club yearbooks and formed American Home, Arts, Civics, Literature, Drama and Public Welfare

Committees with members actively participating. The Evening Membership Department idea was unique to New Jersey — the only State Federation who seemed to have thought of it — and it was soon brought to national attention through an article in the General Federation Club Woman Magazine.

By 1941 EMD's had increased to a total of 30 with notable projects such as Exchange Scholarships and a wide variety of Civic and Public Welfare Projects. By the time Mary S. Curtis became State EMD Chairman in 1941, the Fourth Annual Conference reported a total of 36 Departments with over 1,000 members! EMD-ers (often referred to as EMD-doers) raised funds with rummage sales and card parties, worked with the American Red Cross, War Relief, Institutions for the Blind, the Vineland State School and the TB Association. They served as hospital volunteers along with establishing scholarships and sending fourteen scrapbooks about the American Way of Life to South America as part of the "Good Neighbor" policy.

When Renette H. Casebolt became Chairman in 1942, World War II had come along. The Departments furnished a day room at Fort Dix along with many such local rooms in their communities to provide a "home place" for military personnel. Members became air-spotters, ambulance drivers, air raid wardens and went to work in shipyards and defense plants.

By this time, the Evening Departments were able to assume many financial responsibilities previously taken care of by their respective Women's Clubs. Some of the groups had their own officers and their own funds, paid their own NJSFWC dues and contributed to the clubs to which they belonged. In addition to their own projects, they substantially supported Federation projects and funds. In 1945 a revision in the NJSFWC Bylaws officially changed the designation from Evening Membership Committee to Evening Membership Department. Ethel Lawrence was the first State Chairman appointed for 1944-45 under the new designation. Her year proved the unspoken motto, "To be not for ourselves, but for others". Members continued their war work and volunteer services, sent Buddy Bags to the Battleship New Jersey and supplied food and cigarettes to army camps. Department scrapbooks, flower shows and more rummage sales were added to the list of activities. EMD's contributed to the College Committee Fund at the New Jersey College for Women (now Douglass College).

Caroline C. Almond

Due to the war, the Annual Convention of 1945 was held by mail. This was the first year that an EMD State Chairman was to be elected by the members and Caroline C. Almond, who served from 1945 to 1948, made it despite the vagaries of the U. S. Post Office. Mrs. Almond saw the addition of 20 new EMD's bringing the total to 62. Former Juniors formed many of the new Departments. Although members of Evening Departments were technically members of their respective Women's Clubs and full members of the Federation, they also had quite independent interests.

The majority of Evening Departments contributed to two projects: (1) looking toward equal economic and educational opportunities for all citizens and, in furthering a program for national peace, sponsoring a fellowship fund to send a black, Jewish, or foreign-born woman to a professional school. This resulted in two scholarships being awarded. (2) to continue a fund for an EMD room at New Jersey College for Women (Douglass College) and to cover any necessary replenishment of furnishings for the room. This marked the beginning of "official" State Projects for EMD — something which has been continued to the current time.

In October, 1946 the custom of holding two Round Table Programs began. EMD Chairmen from the southern part of New Jersey met at the Molly Pitcher Hotel in Red Bank and the northern Chairmen met at Bamberger's in Newark. During this time a family of orphans in Holland was adopted, food and clothing supplied to stricken families, surgical instruments were given to a hospital and $900 for the EMD State Project went to a student at Columbia University who was granted a degree in Nursing Education. In 1947 a Montclair resident who had graduated from Upsala College became the second recipient of the Fellowship. Over $1,000 enabled her to attend the University of Pittsburgh for an M.A. Degree in Economics which prepared her for work in the field of Industrial Relations. Evening Departments contributed $1,943.33 for a fireplace in the main lounge of the Student Center Building at the New Jersey College for Women.

Ann Emrich, EMD Chairman 1948 - 1951, formed a Project Committee. The committee developed ideas for EMD State Projects and presented them to the membership for consideration and selection. Following World War II, the first project selected was to raise money for the Philippine Women's

Clubs to enable them to distribute medical and nutritional needs to thousands of destitute children. This resulted in $1,580 being sent to the Philippines. The Vineland Training School (now the Vineland Developmental Center) received more than $8,000 from EMD members as the total of 72 Departments grew in service and prestige throughout their communities. EMD was making a place for itself in the Federation!

Mrs. Emrich initiated the Community Welfare Project which has continued to become an annual competitive feature in EMD endeavors. Awards are presented annually, in membership classifications, for outstanding community welfare activities.

Separate conferences for EMD Chairmen were continued and held in New York and Trenton, with a state-wide one day meeting in New York City. With Gladys M. Blauvelt at the helm from 1951 to 1954 membership was reported at over 4,000 in 77 Departments. Round table sessions were expanded to include International Relations and Public Welfare; during the EMD Convention session. Department Chairmen were instructed in parliamentary procedure. A safety program through the bicycle Scotchlite Campaign was instituted, a Student Nurses' Loan Fund and Nursing Scholarship established, books transcribed into Braille, cancer dressings and many national service campaign functions continued to receive the unselfish efforts of members. Mrs. Blauvelt served on the committee of the "New Jersey Club Woman" magazine and Department members added to the success of Club Woman Day at Hahne & Company in Newark by presenting an original skit written, directed and performed by EMD-ers. Kessler Institute was the State Project for 1954 with an anticipated goal of $7500. Since

$12,212.88 was contributed to the Institute, the Evening Departments had again under-estimated their capabilities. Departments realized the value of good citizenship and began sponsoring delegates to GCI.

Madeline Pallo Garfin   Anita Nussbaum

The terms for Trustees for NJSFWC had been changed to two years, and Madeline Pallo Garfin served the 78 Departments with their total of 5,811 members in 1954 - 56. Attendance records at state events were broken, and the growth in membership found the State Chairman understanding a need for District Chairmen to hold evening conferences and disseminate Federation information at the District level. Active participation continued in all projects and departmental activities within the individual EMD groups. Choral groups were formed and children's symphony concerts sponsored; drama enthusiasm increased with EMD participation and the winning of District Drama Festivals. Scholarships were awarded, press book awards were received and literary contests were won by members. Over 30,000 hours of volunteer service were contributed in 1956 to local charities as well as to state and national campaigns. The Totowa Nursery Project (equipping a laboratory at the Alfred Muse Nursery) overflowed the anticipated $10,000 and a check for $25,368.21 was presented.

Anita Nussbaum, who served as State EMD Chairman 1956 - 1958, stressed association and reciprocity which honed the harmony among Junior, Daytime and General membership groups to a fine degree. EMD's contributed well over $4,000 toward upkeep and renovations of the club houses owned by their General Clubs. The unifying tie to the "New Jersey Club Woman" magazine was notable with 715 subscribers. An "EMD first", instituted by Mrs. Nussbaum, was the Federation Study Group Workshop at Convention. Contributions of $1,000 were made to youth-oriented activities such as a Youth Council and a Children's Room at a local library. Mentally and physically-challenged children benefited from an excess of $3500 in contributions. Hospitals received over $2500, and educational scholarships (other than those of the Federation) received more than $1500. The EMD State Project was New Jersey Boys Town with EMD's raising $30,825.96 for this facility.

By 1958, when Seraphine Mayer took office as State Chairman, the Executive Committee had grown to 20 members and EMD celebrated its 20th birthday. Membership received special recognition at this time and progression was practiced as 142 members of EMD moved on to their Women's Clubs and 46 Juniors became EMD-ers. This furthered the ideals of unity among the segments of NJSFWC.

Seraphine Mayer   Emily Brundage Haddad

One Department raised $2500 in a drive for a local leukemia victim during 1959 - 1960; libraries were refurbished by another group and one Department aided in the purchase of equipment for the infirmary of the State Colony for Retarded Boys at New Lisbon. Special shoes and braces were contributed to Cerebral Palsy victims by another EMD. Efforts continued for national fund drives, scouting, hospitals, nursing homes, shut-ins and under-privileged children. Mental and dental care were sponsored in communities where there was an EMD. The EMD State Project was the Vineland State School for Girls which received $25,263.75. Fifty-one of these mentally retarded girls were "adopted" by Departments for year-round remembrances.

In 1960 - 1962 State EMD Chairman Emily Brundage Haddad guided a continually growing membership. The Departments continued to add new projects, but maintained their interest in previous activities. They gave untold hours of service to their communities and donated countless numbers of items to many institutions in New Jersey. It would seem that anyone in a New Jersey institution must have received at least one article made by the many hands of the EMD-ers. The State Project — Babies' Hospital in Newark — received $29,559.16 for education and research. State Projects were astonishing in that the monies raised were all accumulated within one year.

Annabelle McCormick chose a theme for her Chairmanship in 1962 - 1964 — "It is more blessed to give than to receive". During her term $26,683.38 went to communities' needs, but money was not the only goal. Members collected 854 pairs of eye glasses for the needy, made over 35,000 cancer dressings and leper bandages, collected 535 pounds of used nylon stockings, made 5,565 tray favors for hospitals and provided 17,610 hours of volunteer community service. They distributed holiday baskets and 1021 toys to less fortunate children. Golden Age Clubs were supported and one Department purchased an organ for a blind girl who had the ability to become a concert organist but had no access to an organ. A Braille typewriter was given to a girl and she was trained to use it. In 1962 - 1963 total monetary contributions amounted to a monumental figure of $51,629.57. Cooperating with the rest of the Federation EMD members helped to send a high school choir on a five-week tour of Europe in 1964 as part of the Tercentenary Year celebrated by New Jersey. A check for $28,000 was presented to the South Jersey Medical Research Foundation from the EMD State Project. It was used to purchase an electron microscope to further the work of the staff who were discovering more about the facts of cancer control.

Annabelle McCormick   Jan Denniston

In 1964 - 1966, when Jan Denniston was the EMD Chairman, the Headquarters of NJSFWC had become a reality. Mrs. Denniston, along with the Junior Membership Chairman, had the honor of laying the corner stone for the Headquarters. EMD had contributed $10,753.41 towards the Headquarters and 24 departments participated 100 percent in the "Stamp of Approval Plan" for the building fund. This

347

was the year of a dual project. Along with the Headquarters Project the Multiple Sclerosis Organizations' Nursing Home in Chester received $12,753.41 to purchase a combination Hubbard and Wading tank.

When Marie Latcham Wyatt became Chairman in 1966, it was a community project year when members continued with work they had started many years before. One Department recruited 550 new blood donors while another made it possible for every resident in the city to be eligible to receive blood if necessary. Cerebral Palsy Swim Programs were activated and hours were spend by members patterning brain-damaged children. Thousands of cakes and cookies were made and distributed to institutions, 15 needy families were supplied with bread, rolls and cake each week for eight months and eight families were provided with completely cooked dinners. Old projects were continued and many new ones were inaugurated. Community welfare contributions in 1967 amounted to $38,507.81. The theme was "The world is round so that friendship may circle it" which truly exemplified the world of the EMD. The Ruth Carole Gottscho Kidney Foundation was the 1968 State Project which received $33,014.13 to aid in the battle of kidney disease and uremia. An additional $35,653.75 was raised for local community welfare.

Laura Teachman   Margaret Kipple

Laura Teachman was elected EMD State Chairman at the 1968 Convention by the vote of the entire delegate body. A Bylaw change adopted that year permitted future State Chairmen to be nominated only by EMD members.

Community welfare and EMD State Projects continued to earn awards for EMD as they furthered the work of women's clubs and the Federation. By this time, the success of EMD had become widely known in the General Federation of Women's Clubs — leading the way for other State Federations to now include Evening Membership Departments.

Margaret Kipple was the first State EMD Chairman to be nominated solely by Evening Membership. The State Project during her term of office (1970 - 1972) was Camp Merry Heart, which at that time was the only camp for handicapped children in New Jersey.

Ethel Richards

1972 - 1974, during the term of Jeanne C. Decker, it was noted that membership had declined by 33 members. The Walter Matheny School was the EMD State Project. This was a school for severely handicapped children with average or above average intelligence. The $36,271.35 which was raised was used to construct and equip secondary school facilities.

The next Chairman for 1974 - 1976 was Ethel Richards, a former Junior District Advisor and later President of Somerville Civic League, who saw new issues being addressed by EMD. These included barrier-free buildings for the handicapped, disturbed children from problem homes and drug abuse among children. The Institute for Medical Research in Camden was adopted as the State Project.

Helen Sparacio   Delores Plasket

There was a surge of enthusiasm during the term of Helen Sparacio, who served in 1976-1978 as the first EMD State Chairman to be a member of the NJSFWC Executive Committee. Funds were raised for the Betty Bachrach Rehabilitation Hospital which was the EMD State Project.

"Look forward to the future for challenging goals. After these are achieved, you may then look back to the past with satisfaction" was the theme of Dolores Plasket, EMD State Chairman in 1978-1980. Several EMD members were appointed by various NJSFWC Department Chairmen to serve as committee members. The Burn Center at St. Barnabas Hospital proved to be a most popular State Project.

Carol White, EMD Chairman in 1980 - 1982, spoke of the modern woman facing a changing and complex society and the important role which Federation played in her life. She

350

stressed the value of the service given to those in need. The Hematology Department at St. Michael's Hospital in Newark was the EMD State Project.

Carol White

Joyce Farnham

During the administration of Joyce Farnham (1982 - 1984) EMD members continued to spread their wealth of caring and sharing. Members chose as their State Project, the Children's Specialized Hospital in Mountainside.

"EMD has made Valerie the apple of our eye" is a quote from the annual report of Joan Handschuh in 1984 - 1986. The Valerie Fund for Children with cancer and blood disorders turned out to be an extremely well-received State Project. Joan combined her term of office with the care of her husband and two young sons.

Joan Handschuh

Shirley Kiefer

351

Shirley Kiefer served as State Chairman from 1986 to 1988. The State Project during her term was The Childrens' Seashore House, one of the oldest children's hospitals in the state, located on the ocean front in Atlantic City. It was founded to give children from cities who were chronically ill the advantages of the fresh sea air. Eventually, it became a year-round facility connected with Children's Hospital in Philadelphia.

Sharon Cartwright   Mary Lou Phifer

Increase in membership was the goal of State Chairman Sharon Cartwright during 1988 - 1990. Although the gain in membership was not significant, there was no loss. The Pediatric Department of The Eye Institute of New Jersey was the State Project, a most important one because of the lack of such facilities for children.

When Mary Lou Phifer became State Chairman from 1990 to 1992 many new problems were addressed by members. These included the rape crisis, AIDS, temporary help for those unemployed due to the recession and fatalities caused by drunk driving. The Deborah Heart and Lung Center was an outstanding EMD State Project.

Declining membership and loss of Departments faced Phyllis Schneck at the beginning of her term in 1992. The problem was faced head on and Departments were challenged to retain and gain members. Clubs were urged to start EMD's. The State Project was an Emergency Pediatric Ambulance for the United Hospitals' Medical Center.

EMD received national acclaim when an award-winning photo taken by Mrs. Schneck appeared on the cover of the General Federation Club Woman Magazine in 1992.

The hope of the Evening Membership Department of the NJSFWC is that the decline of membership and the country-wide slump in volunteerism is temporary. The need does not decline, nor is it temporary. There is so much to be done now-as always!

Phyllis Schneck

STATE ORGANIZATIONS

During the first decade of the annals of the Federation it became apparent that there were other organizations of women in New Jersey who were interested in being affiliated with NJSFWC. Arrangements were made to provide a special category of membership for such groups. They became known as State Organizations, and were given the opportunity of affiliation by paying a flat rate of dues. The current NJSFWC Bylaws provide for such State Organizations which are "composed by one or more chapters or branches unrelated to the New Jersey State Federation of Women's Clubs whose objects are and remain in harmony with those of the Federation, each of which shall have qualified for membership in accordance with the Bylaws of the Federation." These organizations are entitled to one voting delegate at Federation Conventions and their representatives often march in the processional at the opening banquet honoring club presidents.

Those currently affiliated include the New Jersey Woman's Press Club (organized and federated in 1904); the Ex Club of NJSFWC (organized and federated in 1915); The Daughters of the British Empire in New Jersey, Inc. (organized in 1909 and federated in 1920); the Associate Alumnae of Douglass College (organized in 1922 and federated in 1927); The Junior Ex Club (organized in 1947 and federated in 1948); the EMD Ex Club (organized and federated in 1958); the PM Club (organized in 1954 and federated in 1959); and the Ukrainian National Women's League of America, Inc. (organized in 1960 and federated in 1971).

There have been many others which, for various reasons, are no longer affiliated with NJSFWC. Some of these include the Auxiliary of the Society of New Jersey Chiropractors, Inc.; the Kalomathia Club of Hightstown; the New Jersey League for Nursing; the New Jersey State Nurses' Association; the Nitis Club; and the AM Club (now the Phoenix Club). Undoubtedly there have been others; however, the "archives" do not provide information.

Although it is not a State Organization, NJSFWC has always maintained a cooperative link with the New Jersey State Federation of Colored Women's Clubs (NJSFCWC) and their State President is customarily a guest at the opening banquet of NJSFWC Conventions.

State Organizations such as the Ex Club of NJSFWC, the Junior Ex Club, the EMD Ex Club and the PM Club were formed of federated clubwomen in New Jersey who had served at various state levels and wanted to maintain close relationships formed during their various periods of service. These groups often meet twice a year to renew friendships and "socialize". However, they continue to financially support the Federation projects and to contribute additional time and energy to the work of NJSFWC. Mrs. Lemuel Skidmore of Summit expressed it beautifully when she said that such organizations are "an escape valve from extinction".

Similar Federated clubs with the same type of purpose are formed within their respective Districts. Their membership is composed of former Presidents of Women's Clubs, Junior Clubs or Chairmen of Evening Membership Departments. They are either known as "Past Presidents or Ex Presidents Clubs" or, like The Contemporary Club of First District, they are former Junior Presidents and/or former Junior Board members. Their love of Federation and its work keeps them actively involved.

NJSFWC Ex Club

IN TIMES OF PEACE AND WAR

NJSFWC is truly composed of "Women for All Seasons". Sprinkled through the Federation's eventful first century were years of peaceful living interspersed with major world conflicts. The active New Jersey clubwomen coped with all of them and successfully survived.

Shortly after the formation of NJSFWC came the Spanish-American War in 1898. We can be sure that the women helped the USA individually or collectively; however, the archives do not record any particular activities related to this conflict. On October 27, 1905 the Federation sent a letter to President Theodore Roosevelt commending the Peace Conference which resulted in a Treaty ending the Russo-Japanese War. In 1905 the New Jersey Peace Society was formed as an auxiliary to Federation work, and the clubwomen supported a program advocating the education of youth towards peace not war.

In the years preceding World War I many Resolutions were adopted by the Federation to support world peace and in

1914 clubwomen promoted interest in the Industrial Peace Movement, favored the proposed Court of Nations as well as an International Congress and an International Police Force. By 1915 the clubs expressed sympathy with the purposes of the National Women's Peace Party to end the hostility which had already begun in Europe. As the sounds of guns across the sea grew louder, the Federation urged Congress to provide swift and efficient military training for defense purposes and/or in the event of war.

When the United States entered World War I in 1917 New Jersey clubwomen not only sent the men in their lives into battle but became "mobilized" themselves. They supported three Liberty Loan Drives, the sale of Thrift Stamps and engaged actively in Red Cross and war relief work with many clubs turning their clubhouses over to the Red Cross for its use during the war. The Federation was honored by being the first state asked for assistance by the Department of Justice in Washington, D.C. to serve as a Bureau of Information and Patriotic Service. The Espionage Committee was formed to be the "eyes and ears" of the government by reporting suspicious actions, seditious remarks, interference with government meetings and the circulation of false reports concerning war organizations. There is every indication that reports sent through this committee were of material assistance to the government.

In October 1917 it was decided that the Federation would equip and maintain a Soldiers' Club at Camp Dix. The appointed committee inspected the Newbold Homestead on November 10 and signed a lease for rental on November 14. They moved in and began transforming the empty, dusty house into a building with a home-like atmosphere. The 200 clubs in NJSFWC at that time provided   money and furnishings. Doors to "The Haversack" were opened with appropriate ceremonies on December 12, 1917 — the clubwomen of New Jersey were experts at taking prompt and decisive action! Visited by half a million soldiers, "The Haversack" was operated for 21 months and was known all over the world as the only soldiers' club of its kind. And this was 25 years before the USO was even thought of! The volunteer hostesses worked sixteen hours a day to provide home cooking and family-type environment for their visitors. There was a canteen, living room, library, music room, card room and writing room — even pets were provided to make the men feel more at home. In 1918, the 26th Army Engineers enlarged the building to include a 48 x 64 foot "lounge", paid for by the hostesses who had raised $3600 for the purpose. Clubs paid for rent, lights, heat, water, insurance and stationery. Although food was sold in accordance with Government regulations rather than given free of charge, no profit was made on this venture.

When the War ended, "The Haversack" was closed on July 14, 1919 and the "lounge" was sold for $4300. This money was used to set up "The Haversack Scholarship" at Stevens Institute of Technology in Hoboken as a tribute to the 26th Army Engineers. The scholarship was used to benefit veterans or their descendents. The furniture, library books and musical instruments were sent to the State Home for Girls in Trenton to furnish club rooms. The Federation received a Citation from the War Department for their work at "The Haversack". Blanche Durgin, the Chairman, and State President Agnes A. Schermerhorn received much-admired War Service pins.

Despite concentrating on assistance to military personnel, the Federation continued to think of other people during

World War I. In 1917 a Resolution opposed legislation which would cause health problems for industrial workers in war plants through creating safety hazards, long hours etc. Petitions were signed to urge the prohibition of alcohol in New Jersey as a war measure to conserve grain. The slogan was "Make Bread not Liquor". The clubwomen asked Governor Edge to rid military encampments of "demoralizing camp followers" to protect soldiers from moral and physical contamination. On May 18, 1918 NJSFWC urged equal military rank for nurses serving in the armed forces and expressed concern that women in war industries were exposed to unhealthy conditions which could endanger future childbearing. Clubwomen urged that men be employed first, because industry was hiring women as "cheaper labor".

Obviously, feelings ran high during World War I and the Federation joined others in opposing the singing of German songs and teaching of the German language in schools as well as the sale of articles made in Germany. Clubwomen asked that the government consider having aliens who were accused of disloyal acts and utterances kiss the United States flag as part of their punishment. Patriotic fervor was evidenced when, in 1914, the Federation endorsed the "Star Spangled Banner" as the National Anthem, and in 1918, adopted a Resolution that men should raise their hats and women stand at attention when the Flag passes by and when the National Anthem is played. It was even suggested that women be given the vote as a war measure — the first evidence that the Federation favored Women's Suffrage.

By 1920 everyone felt that "the world had been made safe for democracy" and promotions for peace became paramount. The Federation adopted a Resolution favoring the reduction of armaments, espoused the cause of "no more war", established an "Education for Peace" Committee and distributed great quantities of literature to arouse public sentiment for peace. In 1925 NJSFWC supported the World Court and in 1932 the World Disarmament Conference.

Clubwomen conducted studies seeking an intellectual understanding of the true causes of war and to find out what could be done to eliminate such causes. The study was entitled "Preparing the New Generation to Make War Obsolete". The Committee joined with nine women's organizations at a Washington DC Conference on "Cause and Cure of War" in 1925. A similar conference was held on January 21, 1926 with 100 New Jersey clubwomen attending. The Federation was represented at the Fourth International Congress of the Women's International League for Peace and Freedom. The Kellogg Briand Pact denouncing war was signed in August, 1928 by fifteen nations and was promptly endorsed by NJSFWC. The Roerich Peace Pact was also endorsed by the Federation in 1929 and the hope for the World Court was still a topic for discussion in 1930. The Federation expressed great disappointment as the United States Senate continued to reject participation in the World Court. A New Jersey clubwoman attended meetings in Geneva, Switzerland of the Women's Committee on Disarmament in September and October, 1933 where she represented the Federation as an observer. New Jersey clubs supported cooperation with the League of Nations following World War I, despite the failure of adherents in this country to gain participation by the United States.

Although the next two decades were relatively "peaceful", the clouds of war began to gather over Europe as the 1940's approached. In 1939 the Federation went on record to prevent the growth of prejudice, intolerance, injustice, and religious discrimination in the United States. In May 1941 the clubwomen felt that anti-American influences were thought to be instigating strikes in defense plants. A Resolution was adopted asking that the government take action to ensure the cessation of such strikes. By May 1941, when Europe was again torn by strife, the Federation endorsed federal legislation to feed the starving children in the war-torn and occupied countries.

In spite of attempts to stay out of the conflict, which later became known as World War II, it was evident that the United States might become involved. Fort Dix was reactivated and the Federation became affiliated with the Fort Dix Community Service, a group of well known organizations. They began the renovation and remodeling of space in a rented building for a study or library. An Emergency Committee on National Defense (which later became the War Service Committee) was formed. Another committee established was that of the New Jersey Service Units, which later became the Committee on Recreational Work with the Armed Forces. The State President represented the Federation on the State Salvage Committee, Committee for Women's Participation under the Office of Civilian Defense and the state's War Service Committee. Two clubwomen were sent to Amherst College for training in Civilian Defense. The Federation had long been officially representated on the New Jersey Council of National Defense.

Classes were sponsored in consumer and market problems and food preservation such as canning, freezing, storage and dehydration. In cooperation with Public Service Electric and Gas Company and the County Extension Services canning centers were set up with instructions in methods and equipment. Victory Gardens were stressed with a goal of

250,000 gardens which was surpassed by sixty percent! Contributions were made to British War Relief for the purchase of seeds. All phases of Red Cross work were supported and club houses were again readied for possible emergency use.

The shock of the Japanese attack on Pearl Harbor — December 7, 1941 — was, as President Franklin D. Roosevelt said, "A date which will live in infamy". NJSFWC quickly geared itself to provide wartime services.

The sale of War Bonds and Stamps was aided by all clubs with spectacular amounts being sold as a result of club-sponsored activities. One club presented an original play eleven times and sold over $570,000 worth of Bonds and Stamps. In 1944 clubs were responsible for Bond sales of $3,729,907.47 in a six-week period, designated to supply six ambulance planes. In 1945 the $1,000,000 goal for the sale of Stamps and Bonds was exceeded by thousands of dollars which purchased eleven Hellcat Fighter Planes for the "Air Armada for Our Navy". Junior clubs raised funds to send fifteen Army field ambulances overseas and supplied 1,000 "buddy bags" for the Battleship New Jersey. Bedside radios were installed and kept in repair at Thomas England General Hospital operating in Chalfonte-Haddon Hall, Atlantic City. Bedside bags numbering 2300 were supplied to Tilton General Hospital at Fort Dix. Clubs collected furniture, radios, pianos and recreational equipment for Army posts throughout New Jersey and supplied washing machines and fur coats to Merchant Seaman while sending record players and musical instruments to Navy personnel.

The Federation furnished and equipped 130 "Company Day Rooms" at Fort Dix which was a major embarkation point throughout the conflict. This project was completed in six months and, at a meeting of morale officers from 145 camps in the United States, it was disclosed that only at Fort Dix had a fully-organized effort been made to furnish enough facilities of this nature to meet the needs! A Non-commissioned Officers' Club complete with kitchen and recreational equipment was furnished at Fort Dix as were Day Rooms for the WAC at this installation. Clubs compiled 6,000 USO scrapbooks and 16,000 holiday gifts went to service hospitals with the nurses at Tilton General Hospital also being remembered at this time.

At the close of World War II the Federation received many citations for "Meritorious Service", and State President Marion S. Spain was the only woman in New Jersey to receive a special USO citation for work in this field. The Federation and individual members were cited by the Second Service

Command for wartime activities and by the Office of Civilian Defense.

America entered into an era of "incidents, episodes, scrimmages, and conflicts" which marked our foreign policy in fulfilling commitments in far-flung corners of the world. The Federation urged that surplus grain stocks be released in 1946 to feed the starving post-war population of Europe and, in 1951, opposed measures used to create artificial scarcities in farm products. In 1947 NJSFWC fully supported the participation of the United States in the United Nations which (this time around) came about. It also urged that the country's armed forces be adequately maintained to keep the peace although, at that time, they had little idea how much "peace-keeping" would be required.

The Haddon Heights Juniors present a field ambulance to the Army.

FEDERATION SERVICE FLAG

Club women, both Junior and Senior who have
entered their country's service, or war industries.

WAACS

MISS EDNA EMES
Hackensack Junior Woman's Club

MISS BETTY HARVEY
Rutherford Junior Woman's Club

MISS JOAN BENNETT
Bogota Junior Women's Club

MRS. RUBY T. VLIET
Hackettstown Woman's Club

MRS. FRANCIS J. CAMPAGNA
Wanaque Woman's Club

WAVES

MISS DOROTHY O. MULVEY
Junior Woman's Club of Wenonah

MISS PEGGY HUESMANN
Rutherford Junior Woman's Club

ELSIE YORK
Woman's Club of Connecticut Farms

ELEANOR STREAT
Boonton Junior Woman's Club

MARY WOODWORTH
Hackensack Junior Woman's Club

War Department

MRS. NATHANIEL MERRILL
Woman's Club of Caldwell

War Industries

MRS. R. W. SCHOOLEY
Woman's Club of Caldwell

MRS. H. HALPRIN
Woman's Club of Caldwell

MRS. H. EASTON
Woman's Club of Caldwell

MRS. CHAS. CAPTAIN
Woman's Club of Caldwell

ELIZABETH W. GORDON
Woman's Club of Elizabeth

MRS. E. B. RAE
Woman's Club of Caldwell

MRS. W. J. RAE
Woman's Club of Caldwell

MRS. J. D. ROBERSON
Woman's Club of Caldwell

MRS. CHARLES CARR
Woman's Club of Caldwell

MRS. LEE BASTEDO
Woman's Club of Caldwell

MRS. FRANK RUGG
Woman's Club of Caldwell

MRS. GLENN ARMSTRONG
Woman's Club of Caldwell

MRS. WILLIAM PASCAL
Woman's Club of Caldwell

(Clubs having names to add to this list, please send them to the editor.)

The Korean Conflict in the early 1950's generated more wartime projects by clubs who were well-trained in this aspect of their work. The undeclared war in Vietnam found the clubwomen sending tons of reading material, holiday gifts, cards and other comfort items to those fighting in the jungles.

In 1965 hundreds of pounds of cookies were sent as part of President Lyndon Johnson's "Project Christmas Star". "Operation Candy Cookie" had begun in 1961 with boxes of home-baked cookies being sent to service personnel stationed in Greenland and Iceland during the Christmas Holidays. This became a popular annual project conducted by the American Home Department. By 1968 there were 4,080 boxes sent. The Federation received special Citations for this project from the Air Defense Command each year. When the need for cookies by military personnel diminished in later years, the clubwomen continued this project by distributing cookies on different holidays to local hospitals and nursing homes.

Between major wars the emphasis was on civil defense and disaster control with the Federation maintaining a steady effort of preparedness. In 1955 - 1956 clubwomen and their families served in the Ground Observer Corps and many received "silver wings". As the United States moved into the "Cold War" days of trying to keep Communism at bay, there were new flurries of anxiety inspired by the advent of the Hydrogen Bomb. Evacuation plans for strategic areas were studied and survival information was distributed via 325,000 pamphlets on "Home Protection Exercises". Sale of United States Savings Bonds and Stamps was supported and the "Bond a Month" programs stressed. Protection of civilians in the event of nuclear attack was paramount and the construction of "Fall-Out Shelters" urged. The Federation took on the project of building shelters in each District as display models with the eleventh shelter being opened on Steel Pier, Atlantic City on May 9, 1960 by the National Director of Civil Defense. Awards for this project were presented to the Federation for leadership in bringing to the attention of the public the need for shelters in homes.

The fears generated by the Atomic Age which had successfully finished World War II were responsible for many club activities. Keeping a watchful eye on the development of communist countries in Europe created much concern for several generations of clubwomen. It is interesting to note that in 1929 the GFWC President was quoted as warning of the dangers of Communism when she said, "Watch schools, churches and young people — even the very young children!" The clubwomen of NJSFWC are sincerely grateful that the Berlin Wall came tumbling down and that the USSR (Russia) is working diligently at becoming more of a democratic nation.

When "Operation Desert Storm" occurred in 1991, the Federation made hasty plans to provide its usual support and services. Fortunately, this conflict was short-lived and the plans were not implemented. Many women who are members of federated clubs did serve in the Persian Gulf War, and were remembered by the Federation "sisterhood". In 1993 clubs supported the rescue mission to help Somalia and continue to stand ready to give necessary aid wherever required.

ENDEAVORS IN EDUCATION

Because the earliest clubwomen were striving to enhance their own education, helping others to expand the learning process has always been an aspect of NJSFWC. Improving the educational system in New Jersey took the form of urging the establishment of Kindergartens in public Schools in 1896 when Federation formed a Kindergarten and Education Committee. By 1898 this became the Education Department, and more than half of the communities where clubs had been organized had Kindergartens available.   A Bill was introduced in the State Legislature in 1898 to establish Kindergartens in Public Schools, if requested by parents. This was a slow process. In 1934 the Federation was still working toward this goal.   Today, Kindergarten is an accepted program in the Public Schools as the beginning of young children's formal education. Many clubs volunteer time for private nursery schools and day care centers for young children in their own communities. These help to prepare very young children for that all-important "first day of school".

In 1900 the Federation began a movement to include Domestic Science classes in schools, and by 1909 seven cities in New Jersey had this type of program. The next effort was to include Civics in the school curricula, and many clubs claim to be responsible for having Art and Music taught in their local schools. A school lunch program was endorsed in 1906. In 1930 the clubwomen were urging that schools include the services of psychologists to assist in resolving emotional difficulties and learning disabilities. All of these important additions to education are now a part of the school system; however, they may not have become realities without the work of clubwomen.

As early as 1899 NJSFWC adopted a Resolution to support a Teachers Mutual Aid Association to start retirement funds which would provide assistance and comfort when dedicated teachers finished their careers. By 1902 clubs were urged to become better acquainted with the teachers in their schools and to become interested in the Teachers' Retirement Fund which had been established. By 1906 the Federation was urging higher salaries for teachers. In 1930 New Jersey was reported as the third highest state in the nation in regard to teachers' salaries. In 1915 the clubwomen urged free summer school classes for teachers, and they became active in movements to secure the right type of women to enter the teaching field. In 1923 the Federation recommended that training in the Normal Schools (where most teachers were being educated) be increased from two to three years. They sponsored the "Visiting Teacher" movement in 1924 -1925 and in 1959 - 1960 the Federation urged the support of a Bill to increase faculty salaries at the State Universities. In the 1940's many women were returning to the teaching profession as their children grew older and a large percentage of these teachers were clubwomen. Current Federation membership still includes a high volume of teachers and former teachers who continue the struggle for improvement in education.

The women of the Federation, as early as 1904, were interested in improving appearances in schools with the thought that better surroundings would stimulate learning. A survey conducted in 1911 revealed that 908 of the 2,133 schools surveyed were of the "one-room" type. In 1913 the schools were urged to use their facilities for recreational purposes and the various school boards were asked to appropriate $300 each year to use their auditorium for dances.

The clubs of NJSFWC became interested in school budgets by 1911 and passed a Resolution to amend laws which would allow women to serve as members of boards of education. Governor Woodrow Wilson approved of this and suggested that the request be sent to the proper state commission. This was a long-term effort — especially since women did not have the right to vote — but it was finally accomplished. Today, local school boards include women and many of them are members of NJSFWC.

All legislation affecting education has received attention from the Federation since 1906 when members began working for compulsory school laws. School was not mandatory in New Jersey until 1920, and by 1932 it was realized that some of the burden of taxation should be shifted from local to state taxes. The Federation endorsed a Bill for this purpose but, when the idea of Federal Aid for schools was voiced in 1938, the Federation was opposed on the grounds that such Federal money would result in too much Federal control of the school system. State Aid for Education was endorsed by support of several Bond Issues during the latter half of the Federation's first century.

Many special forms of education have been the concern of clubs since 1906 when they urged public instruction for blind, deaf, and mentally defective children. In 1925 the Federation cooperated with the Children's Aid Society in urging instruction for bed-ridden children. During the 1929 - 1932 period protests were registered over the loss of schooling for the children of migrant workers in New Jersey's farm areas. Vocational training was supported since 1933 when the "Depression Years" made it evident that unskilled workers were the first to join the ranks of the unemployed. School savings systems were introduced in 1924 with many clubs volunteering time to educate youth in the handling of money. The Federation also endorsed safety education and driver training when it appeared in the public school system.

Adult education has interested NJSFWC since 1915 when assistance was provided in a national campaign against illiteracy. At that time, a census had shown that five million adults in the U.S.A. could not read or write. Many of these people were newly-arrived immigrants, so it was resolved to establish evening classes to teach such prospective citizens English and other necessary subjects. Since 1963 clubwomen have been concerned over the increasing number of "high school drop-outs" and many clubs have since sponsored youth employment services in their communities. Evening classes and extension courses began to appear in community high schools and colleges by the end of the 1940's. Clubwomen encouraged others to attend such classes and became part-time students themselves. With more women returning to the work force since World War II such educational opportunities have become more available. Financial support was provided for the first time in 1977 - 1978 for qualified mature women at Douglass College so that they could attend classes on a part-time basis.

Several millions of dollars have been provided by clubs, and through NJSFWC, in the form of scholarships during its first century of achievement. The Margaret Yardley Fellowship Fund for women pursuing graduate study, the Louie C. Francisco International Exchange Scholarship Fund, the Continuing Education Scholarship, the Girls' Career Institute Scholarship, and the Federation Scholarship Fund are joined by many other scholarships presented under various Departments and Committees. A large number of students benefit annually from the moneys raised by federated clubs throughout New Jersey. Individual clubs present scholarships and other awards to graduating high school students in their communities.

Although "money" is essential for furthering educational endeavors, clubwomen in New Jersey go beyond that. They support their local schools vigorously through participation in the parent-teacher associations or home and school associations, by serving as consultants on local committees set up within the school system and by "getting out the vote" to elect qualified members of school boards. They attend meetings of their local Boards of Education and report to their members on current concerns. The Federation has supported the "Head Start" programs since 1965 with clubs contributing facilities, equipment and volunteer services.

The work of New Jersey clubwomen in founding and supporting local libraries is described elsewhere in this book as part of the educational process (see Literature, Libraries and Literacy).

The Federation is interested in education of children and young adults throughout the world. It has held programs in connection with the American Friends Service Committee and the American Field Service for Foreign Exchange Students since the 1950's. It has had a close connection with the Save the Children Federation and sponsored schools in poverty areas throughout the United States and foreign countries. Clubwomen have long been involved with the Vineland Research Fund, and an early project was that of sending a social worker into the New Jersey area known as the "Pines" in 1915. Elva Hughes, the Social Worker, was so successful in her efforts at teaching mothers at home and helping teachers in the little one-room school houses to abolish illiteracy that the State Board of Education endorsed this project and made it part of their program in 1919.

The establishment of what is now Douglass College was a crowning achievement for the clubwomen of New Jersey which has continued for the past 76 years. On the Federation's Seventy-Fifth Anniversary in 1969 Douglass College acknowledged the service given to education by presenting the Federation with an engraved silver tray which is proudly exhibited at the NJSFWC Headquarters.

College Day and Girls' Career Institute, sponsored annually by the Federation at Douglass College, are additional activities in the field of education. The "learning experience" is an integral part of NJSFWC and work in "Education" continues to grow and expand.

DOUGLASS COLLEGE: A TRIBUTE TO NJSFWC — THE FOUNDING MOTHERS

(by Louise Duus, Associate Dean of Douglass College)

The New Jersey State Federation of Women's Clubs is the only State Federation that can count among its achievements the creation of a women's college. Without the efforts of the NJSFWC, Douglass College, the women's college of Rutgers University, originally called the New Jersey College for Women (NJC), would probably not exist. It is a source of great pride to the college that for 76 years, though there have been massive changes in the structure of Rutgers University, we still enjoy a warm relationship with our Founding Mothers.

What began in 1911 as a campaign to get women admitted to Rutgers College, then an all male school, came to fruition on September 18, 1918, when the New Jersey College for Women opened its doors to 54 adventurous young women. At a District Federation meeting in 1911 Mrs. John V. Cowling, NJSFWC Chairman of Education, advocated the speedy admission of women to Rutgers College on the grounds that, as a state college, Rutgers received large sums of public money that ought to be used to educate all the youth of the state regardless of gender. Almost immediately the goal shifted to the creation of a college for women. For eight years, the women of the Federation, under the leadership of Mabel Smith Douglass, President of the College Club of Jersey City and the first Dean of NJC, planned, agitated, lobbied as high as the White House and raised money through a remarkable one dollar subscription plan. So vigorous was the campaign that one of the Rutgers trustees who attended the meeting in April of 1918, at which the establishment of the coordinate women's college was approved, argued with some force that "It is better to have 20,000 women with us and not against us!" What the women of the Federation had helped create was not a teacher's college or a vocational school but, in the words of Dean Douglass, "A true college for women," offering a traditional liberal arts education.

Mabel Douglass

The first year in the life of NJC was difficult, including as it did a flu epidemic, a broken furnace in mid-winter in the building that housed the college, and uncertainties about future finances. But that hard, cold winter strengthened all those who survived it. The Federation continued to provide both financial and moral support during the first decades of

376

the college's life. Federation Hall, the first Science Building, opened in 1922 and housed zoology and botany laboratories. (Today it houses the Educational Opportunities Program and Psychological Services) A more ambitious project, the Music Building, was dedicated in 1928. The dedication program listed 103 clubs that had raised $100,000 toward the construction of the building, which remains today the home of the Rutgers University Music Department. The first gift of books to the college, which formed the core of the library collection, was yet another Federation contribution to the college in its early years. In later years, the Federation contributed funds toward the building of both the Mabel Smith Douglass Library and the College Center.

Moral support was every bit as important as financial support. In January 1919, when Dean Douglass went to Trenton to appeal to the Legislature for $50,000 for the maintenance of the college for a second year, she took with her representatives of the Federation as well as other women's organizations in New Jersey and women members of boards of education. In 1928, when the Rutgers University Board of Regents mapped out a long range plan for the university in which the place of the women's college seemed somewhat ambiguous, the Federation stood firmly behind Dean Douglass in her efforts to maintain the integrity of NJC as an independent affiliated unit with its own faculty, administration, and budget. The Federation urged that, whatever resulted from the ultimate reorganization of the State University of New Jersey, instead of being merged into a co-educational institution, NJC maintain its identity as a college for women. And it did!

In the 65 years since that reaffirmation of the independent status of the women's college, the administrative structure of

Rutgers University has undergone a number of reorganizations, each of which has had an impact on the women's college. At each point of change, the Federation has stood firmly behind its creation. In 1954, for example, a group of efficiency experts made a set of recommendations that led the Trustees once more to review the entire position of the college within the university. Representatives of the Federation were invited to the November meeting at which the fate of the college was to be reviewed. L. Ethel Heine argued forcefully that it was time for the Trustees to get beyond their Victorian ideas that women were dependent on the men in their families and discuss the issues frankly and openly on the assumption that all participants were equal. Once more the women won the day!

The ties that link Douglass College, as NJC was renamed in 1956, and the New Jersey Federation of Women's Clubs are not as tight as they once were, but they remain strong. Every spring, the Associate Alumnae of Douglass College presents Founders Day in remembrance of that April day in 1918 when the Trustees passed a resolution to establish a College for Women. Distinguished college alumnae are inducted into the Douglass Society on that day. Since 1932, the college and NJSFWC have jointly sponsored a fall College Day to which high school students are invited to learn about the college. The original teas and musicales have given way to tours and workshops, but this remains a major recruitment event for Douglass College. The Girls' Career Institute, sponsored by the Federation, is held on the Douglass campus and provides yet another way of introducing high school girls to the benefits of attending a women's college. Since 1981, the college and the Federation have co-sponsored the New Jersey Women of Achievement Awards, conferred on women who are residents of New Jersey in recognition of their outstanding contributions in a variety of fields. The generous scholarships offered annually by the Federation represent yet another way in which our Founding Mothers continue to offer recognition to the academic achievement of Douglass students.

Douglass is now a mature college, with 3300 students who enjoy all the advantages offered by the distinguished university of which the college is a part. In addition, Douglass students benefit from such flourishing college-based programs as the Douglass Project for Rutgers Women in Math, Science and Engineering; the Douglass Scholars Program; and the new Certificate Program in International Studies. Leadership programs abound, ranging from the Emerging Leaders program for first-year students to the Public Leadership Education Network which offers internships in Trenton, seminars in Washington, DC and a new international seminar associated with the European Parliament in Strasbourg. The New Jersey State Federation of Women's Clubs can rightly take enormous pride in that long ago vision that the women of New Jersey ought to have a college of their own. A vision made concrete in the creation of a college that has grown to become the largest women's college in the United States and a leader in educating young women to meet the challenges of a new century.

* *

We are indebted to Dean Duus for writing the above tribute to NJSFWC.

****

MORE DOUGLASS DATA

New Jersey clubwomen were discussing ways to make education at the college level available to young women as early as 1903. Catherine C. Warren, NJSFWC President 1911-1913, appointed the first committee to work on founding a college for women. It was immediately evident that financing such a college was an enormous undertaking. At the 1915 Annual Convention a Resolution was adopted to attempt the founding of New Jersey College for Women. A slogan — WANTED A STATE COLLEGE FOR WOMEN — was adopted to arouse public interest. The needed funds were raised over the next three years, and the College became a reality in 1918.

The Federation's interest did not stop there. The clubwomen continued to support their "baby" by gathering $25,000 to build a Science Hall which was dedicated on June 8, 1922. The inscription says, "This Hall of Science is Presented by the New Jersey State Federation of Women's Clubs in Commemoration of the Vision Which Led to the Founding of the New Jersey College for Women. May the Spirit of this Place Inspire High Endeavor and Great Achievement." The first commencement held in 1922 saw five of the graduates elected to Phi Beta Kappa and a large percentage of the class planning to become teachers. A painting of Margaret Yardley, the Federation's first President, was hung in Federation Hall as a gift of the clubwomen to the students.

Student Center

Music Building

The Federation's next gift was the Music Studio, dedicated on October 3, 1928 when the College celebrated its 10th anniversary. The clubwomen had raised $100,000 for this purpose. By 1947 the Federation held discussions about building a Student Center at the college, and this was completed during the 1953-1956 administration with the clubs having contributed $28,908.52 toward it. The Evening Membership Department supplied $1,943.33 for a fireplace. In 1959-1960 the Education Department of the Federation had as its project furnishings for a Library Study Center and $6,573.19 had been raised by 1961. In 1962-1963 this became a one-year Federation project with $11,377.91 making it a reality by May, 1962.

In 1945 the College Committee had raised funds to furnish three rooms at the college for the use of foreign students. Others were supplied with accessories to make them more comfortable in succeeding years until the contributions by the clubs kept up to 12 such rooms available. In 1965 it became part of this project to give $100 each year to the Assistant Dean for her use as an emergency aid fund benefiting foreign students. A number of scholarships are given to Douglass College students each year from contributions made by clubs. NJSFWC gave a $500 gift to the college on its 50th anniversary.

On April 14, 1993 The Founders Day Convocation was devoted to the commemoration of Douglass College's 75th Anniversary. NJSFWC's State President, Joan M. Hunt, played a major role in this very special event. From the Processional (with dignitaries in full academic regalia) to impressive organ music, through the various addresses by honored guests, to the luncheon in the new Trayes Hall, President Hunt was justifiably proud to hear many complimentary references to the Federation for their part in the founding of the college. She presented a $7,500 check from NJSFWC — $100 for each year of Douglass' existence — as the Federation's gift to the 75th Campaign Fund. Following this, a beautiful tribute to NJSFWC was read and Mrs. Hunt received a card making her an Associate Alumnae of Douglass College, along with a handsome Douglass College pin. It was a "Day to Remember" and a special Convocation such as this one will not be held again until the 100th Anniversary of the College!

When Joan M. Hunt represented the Federation by lighting one of the candles on the Douglass College 75th Anniversary cake, she was very much aware that New Jersey clubwomen continue to take a very special interest in "their" college — a unique creation by women for women!

Joan M. Hunt presenting NJSFWC's 75th Anniversary gift to Douglass College.

MARGARET TUFTS SWAN YARDLEY FELLOWSHIP FUND

In 1929 NJSFWC established a fund to enable a selected woman to do graduate study in her chosen field at the education facility of her own choice. In memory of the Federation's first President (1894-1896) the fund was immediately named the "Margaret Tufts Swan Yardley Fellowship Fund" — usually referred to as the Margaret Yardley Fellowship.

The first contribution to the fund, in the amount of $5,000, was given by Mrs. Yardley's son, Farnham Yardley, in his mother's memory. By April 30, 1930 additional contributions had brought the Fund to $15,580. The first award of $500 was presented to Dr. Lillian Milgrim who went abroad for an intensive study of children's diseases.

Contributions made to this Fund are invested and only the interest is used to provide Fellowships to qualified recipients. Always well supported by club and individual contributions, the "capital" in the Margaret Yardley Fellowship Fund is currently over $100,000. The interest on the investments has made it possible to award larger amounts to recipients and to give Fellowship Funds to more applicants each year. In recent years, it has been possible to award at least 6 Fellowships of $1,000 each for a wide variety of study fields. Applications are submitted to the Margaret Yardley Fellowship Fund Chairman from all over the world, and the Committee selects those most qualified. On some occasions, when warranted, the Fellowship has been provided to the same student for consecutive years.

Selections are made on qualifications which include "High Standards of Character, Ability, Scholarship, Purpose and Potential Service as well as Financial Need".

The following women have been recipients of this award:

1930-31	Dr. Lillian Milgrim - Medicine
1931-32	Ruth W. Hughey - Literature
1932-33	Catherine K. Bauer - Housing
1933-34	Elizabeth Hoon - History
1934-35	Dr. Ruth Gruber - Sociology
1935-36	Lucy Ogden Norton - Collegiate Personnel
1936-37	Ruth M. Leverton - Science
1937-38	Margaret L. Hayes - Education
1938-39	Margaret LaFoy - International Relations & Organization
1939-40	Rachel B. Green - Child Welfare
1940-41	Claire E. Burton - School Health Education
1941-42	Claire E. Burton Reinhardt - School Health Education
1943-44	Claire Marcelotte Leake - Science
1944-45	Susan Isaacs - Romance Languages

1945-46	Jessie E. Parkinson - Pediatrics
1946-47	Pauline Tompkins - Soviet-American Relations
1947- 49	Doris T. Jones Ralston - Microbiology
1952-53	Lorene Rowan Warner - Psychiatrics
1953-54	Marijane Eastman - International Law
1955-58	Hannah Hall Todd - Medicine
1958-61	Vivian Chen - Medicine
1961-62	Louida Dayton Dare - Ed. Psychology
1962-65	Shirley Anne McMahon - Medicine
1965-66	Barbara Jones - Education
1966- 68	Barbara Damron - Creative Drama
1968-69	Jane Ann Underhill - Literature
	Karen Karwan - French Literature
1969-70	Margaret Bitters - Ed. Psychology
1970-71	Arlene Kirby - Human Behavior
	Penny Williams Cipolone - Classical Languages
1971-72	Jeannette Finan - Speech Pathology
	Georgette Liaskos - Law
	Elaine Razano - English
1972-73	Susan Lee Lennox - Law
1972- 74	Carol Ann Poh - Museum Curator
1973-74	Sharlene Linda Cygan - Business Education
1973- 75	Peggy Eugenia Starkey - Theology
1974- 76	Darcyjeanne Hansen - Pediatrics
1975-76	Margaret-Ann F. Mullins - Law
1975-76	Linda Sue Gassey - Political Science
1976-77	Denise Baxter - Finance
	Linda Gehron - Education
1977-78	Natacha Villamia Lowe - Pre-Med
	Florence D. Nolan - International Law
	Dolores Lusa - Law

1978-79	Lillian S. Cohen - Social Work
	Antoinette Costa - Medicine and Dentistry
	Wendy K. Westrom - Endocrinology
1979-80	Ann Marie Fegorello - Biology
	Darcelle F. Crooke - Occupational Therapy
	Linda M. Shires - English
1980-81	Deborah L. Roche - International Affairs
	Alice Reilly - Social Work
	Denise Holmes - Law
	Janice Levine - Child Clinical Psychology
	Carolyn Rumery - Land Resources Regional Planning
1981-82	Josele Arena - Political Science
	Nancy Keller - Medicine
	Janice Prontnicki - Medicine
1981-83	Julie Kaufmann - Medicine
1982-83	Alice L. Dugan - Cancer Nursing
	Eve Lappas - Law
1982-83	Patrice A. Maguire - Law
	Susan J. Sefcik - Medicine
1982-84	Laurel A. Farnham - Medicine
1983-84	Helen A. Campo - Music
	Karen B. Fekety - Pharmaceutical Analysis
	Joanne Kaiser - Osteopathy
	Nancy L. Muirhead - International Law
	Karen L. McQuaide - Research Audiology
	L. Patricia Sampoli - Law

	Susan F. Schauer - Neuroscience/ Psychology
	Ellen H. Zeibig - Medicine
1984-85	Doris Warcholik - Clinical Psychology
	Diane D'Alesandro - National and International Health Law
	Valerie Elliott - Environmental Law
	Bernadine Tucci - Clinical Psychology
	Judith Augustino - Business Mgmt.-
1984-86	Marci Sindell - Business Admin.
1985-86	Bernadine Tucci - Social Work
	Diane D'Alesandro - Law
	Valerie Elliott - Law
	Judith Allen - Dental Hygiene
	Marci Sindell - Business Admin.
	Martha Ramsey - Fine Arts
	Marcia Rappaport - Business Admin. Admin.
1986-87	Judith Epstein - Medicine
	Enechi Modu - Law
	Vanessa Cano - International Rel.
	Shirley Warren - Writers Program
	Julie Kaufmann - Medicine
	Helayne Sherman - Medicine
	Luise Welby - Law
1987-88	Heather Olsen - Speech Pathology and Audiology
	Constance Hills - Mental Health Counseling
	Gloria Samartine - School Psychology
	Morna Sweeney - Nurse/Attorney

	Laura Winters - Education
	Diane Stachelski - Law
	Vicki Peterscheck - Music
1988-89	Maureen Russo - Law
	Janet Biscaha - Chiropractic
	Eileen Huddy - Law
	Phoebe Myhill - Music
	Ellen Hanak - Economics
	Jane Bailey - English Literature
	Lisa Alumkal - Business Admin. and Economics
1989-90	Betty Achinstein - Education
	Barbara Jonsson - Public Health
	Mary Elizabeth Brown - Internal Medicine
	Judy Okawa - Clinical Psychology
	Cynthia Parshall - Educational Measurement and Eval.
	Jennifer Sterling-Folker - Political Science
1990-91	Janet Buscaha - Dentistry
	Cathy Petti - Medicine
	Melissa Cicetti - Architecture
	Joyce Cutier - Chiropractic
	Julie Oxenberg - International Policy
	Kristine Davidson - Clinical Psychology
1991-92	Janet Biscaha - Dentistry
	Therese Barry - Osteopathic Med.
	Mary Clair Coston - Theology
	Kathleen Scaler - Speech Pathology
	Wendy Young - Novel Cancer Design and Synthesis

Carol Larro - Education

1992-93 Anastasia Cochran - Music

Carolyn D. Grace - Clinical
Psychology

Nora Donald - Nursing

Lorraine Jackowski - Medicine and
Dentistry

Nora C. Melican - Ceramic/BioMed
Engineering

Marie M. Caron - Occupational
Therapy

Pamela R. Swanborn - Physical
Therapy

INTERNATIONAL INTERESTS

The clubwomen of New Jersey have displayed interest in the world surrounding them since NJSFWC was very young.

Although not the earliest international project, the establishment of the Pan-American Exchange Scholarship Fund (later named the Louie C. Francisco International Exchange Scholarship Fund in honor of the original Chairman) was a very far-reaching project. The extent of its outreach became even better known in 1992! The first recipient of the scholarship was Senorita Marina Orellana of Santiago, Chile who came to the New Jersey College for Women (now Douglass College) in 1940 where she received her BA in English in 1941. An excellent student, she went on to Smith College to receive an MA in Education in 1942. Senorita Orellana's on-going career spans several decades of outstanding accomplishment. She attended a one-month seminar on world affairs sponsored by the Students International Union in Salisbury, Connecticut during the summer of 1941 where she joined participants from other universities and foreign countries. From 1942 to 1945 she served as an Assistant Instructor in Spanish and Philosophy at Smith College; attended a summer session in Philosophy at Columbia University and was granted a scholarship in Philosophy from 1945 to 1946 at Columbia. From 1946 to 1954 Senorita Orellana was a translator and a translator-reviser for the United Nations in New York City. For the next four years she was a free-lance translator and interpreter during which time she translated Lewis Hanke's book <u>Racial Prejudice in the New World</u>. From 1958 to 1961 she was the translator-reviser for UNESCO in Paris. She continued her work as a translator, primarily with WHO/PAHO in Washington, DC, and was chief of translation services for this organization from 1969 to 1978. She has written a number of books and articles during her outstanding career, conducted workshops on translation and was the keynote speaker at the First Symposium on Translation in San Juan, Puerto Rico in September 1992. For ten years from 1979 to 1989 Senorita Orellana was a columnist on languages for "El Mercurio", the main newspaper of Santiago, Chile. In August of 1992 she received the Danica Seleskovitch prize awarded by ELADI (Latin American School of Languages) "To the Chilean Professional Who Has Made a Significant Contribution in the Field of Translation and Interpretation".

Marina Orellana, 1940

391

Over the years, Senorita Orellana had kept in touch with Douglass College, primarily through the former Assistant Dean, Edna M. Newby. With the thought that Douglass College would be celebrating its 75th Anniversary in 1993 and NJSFWC would complete its first century in 1994, Marina Orellana contacted Miss Newby to ask how she could contribute to these events. In consultation with NJSFWC President, Joan M. Hunt, Dean Newby was instrumental in advising Senorita Orellana of the establishment of a Federation Library at NJSFWC Headquarters and the plans for publishing a history. On September 24, 1992 a letter and a check for $50,000 was received from Senorita Orellana which she said, "Does not cover the debt of gratitude I have for the Federation". This generous contribution made possible the publication of the history and supplied the Federation Library with much-needed equipment. NJSFWC will be eternally grateful to the student from Chile who says, "In my heart I am half Chilean and half American".

Marina Orellana, 1993

Dean Edna Newby, who had been so much involved with the Pan-American Scholarship Program, traveled to several South American countries in 1968 under the financial sponsorship of NJSFWC. She visited former Pan-American scholars, families of current students and other Douglass graduates along with getting in touch with educational institutions which would suggest names for future scholarships. In May 1969, Miss Newby spoke at the Federation Convention in Atlantic City to give a very complete report of her experiences. Her memories of her many years as Dean of Admissions at Douglass and her work with all students, including those from foreign countries, was a highlight of this 75th anniversary of NJSFWC. Looking ahead to the Federation's Centennial, Dean Newby asked, "Shall we meet on the moon in 1994?" Her dedication to the work of NJSFWC will always be appreciated on any planet!

Interest in other parts of the world was exhibited in 1935 - 1937 when 98 Marathon Round Tables were held by study groups which had been formed in the Federation. In cooperation with the Juniors and the New East Foundation, a goal of $1500 was reached in 1938 to rebuild communities in Macedonia. NJSFWC was first in the number of essays on International Relations submitted by high schools students for a GFWC contest in 1937. Monthly seminars were held on international affairs with the New York Times in 1938 and 1939 and the "Good Neighbor Project" of 1938-1941 found a delegation of clubwomen visiting South American countries.

The Federation helped "International Friends" during World War II and the post-war years included projects such as a Philippine Friendly Fund which produced $400 for seeds. Chickens and three tons of clothing were shipped to Holland. A 1947 call for help from GFWC resulted in $1,083.50 and 900 yards of cloth, plus other supplies, for Greece. Five schools abroad were adopted through the Save the Children Federation and individuals were adopted at a cost of $95 per child. Food and blanket packages were sent through CARE and a special United Nations' appeal for the children of the world resulted in over $3,000 in 1948 - 1949. Over 20,000 pounds of clothing and other gifts were presented to a friendship train in 1947 - 1948, the Friends' Service Committee and the Emergency Food Fund were supported and money contributed for youth centers in Greece.

In 1944 - 1947 the Federation was honored by the New York Rotary as the first state organization to include Canada in its study aimed at promoting better international relations. The Community Club of Hastings, New Zealand was contacted through a GFWC project of fostering relationships with clubs in foreign countries. This became the "Sister Club" with which correspondence was maintained for some time.

In 1949 five German women visited NJSFWC to study club operation in a democracy. The Crusade for Freedom and Radio Free Europe were widely supported. In 1957 - 1958 a fund to provide aid for graduate studies by Asian women students was established, and the first recipient was Josefina Phodaca Ambrosio, an attorney. Known in the Republic of the Phillipines as the "Moral Crusader" she became an official observer to the United Nations Commission on the Status of Women and completed a term in the Philippine Senate. The second recipient of this fellowship for Asian women was Och Soon Kim of Korea.

Through CARE two community centers were established in the Philippines with $14,936.83 raised in 1953 - 1956. The centers were constructed with volunteer labor on land donated by Philippine natives. Foreign Student Week was observed with club members entertaining students from other lands in their homes in the 1950's. One club reported having 30 students as guests. Clubwomen have continued to house exchange students from many areas and this is a trend which carries on. CARE has continued to be an agency through which NJSFWC has worked for international understanding and assistance. Thousands of dollars have been contributed along with useful items of all types. "Meals for Millions", which fights malnutrition and hunger throughout the world and some poverty-stricken areas in the United States, has been a popular project since the 1950's. The work of the late Dr. Thomas A. Dooley received Federation support in the 1960's.

UNICEF has been a Federation by-word since its inception. Contributions are given annually for the work of UNICEF. Clubs sponsor the Halloween "Trick or Treat for UNICEF" drives in their communities.

The "People to People" program conducted in 1960 - 1961 provided hospitality and gifts of medical kits etc. GFWC "Dollars for Scholars" received $740 from New Jersey clubs at this time. Books and funds were collected to wage war on illiteracy in Latin American countries through the Pan American Union. The S.S. Hope, Cuban refugees, American-Korean Foundation, Foster Parents Plan, Inc. and many others have been part of the Federation efforts to spread hope and help in far flung corners of the world.

Money was raised to provide a house, furniture and a set of parents for twenty-five Tibetan refugee children in 1963 and redoubled efforts by the same club raised $1400 the following year. An Orphans Home in Seoul, Korea received $100 from a club and another made 100 bandages for a leper colony in Taiwan. A library was started in Ghana and a Zulu Mission in South Africa was aided through other individual club efforts. In 1967 - 1968 an orphanage in Cali, Colombia received over 2000 pounds of clothing from 60 clubs to assist the Cali Woman's Club in their local project. Hong Kong refugees received $2,000 from a club at this time, and another club contributed to relief funds for Costa Rica while other clubs campaigned for funds to help earthquake victims in Sicily. Feeling that athletes can be "good will ambassadors", clubs continue to contribute funds to send the United States participants to the Olympic Games.

A current project, Operation Smile, generated hundreds of soft cloth "dolls without faces" made by clubwomen to be taken overseas by medical teams who perform plastic surgery (without charge) on children of many nations. The small patients draw the face they hope to have after plastic surgery on the dolls and cuddle them during the ordeal. Small cloth bags containing toilet articles and items to help amuse the children are also provided by clubs.

Weaving a network of friendship throughout the world has brought many honors and citations to NJSFWC from the many agencies supported. A wall at the Headquarters Building in New Brunswick is virtually covered with such framed tokens of esteem. There is a big world out there and the clubwomen continue to be well aware of it as they work diligently to expand their horizons and become true citizens of the world.

LOUIE C. FRANCISCO INTERNATIONAL EXCHANGE SCHOLARSHIP

This scholarship program had its beginning when Mattie Eastlack Driscoll was President of NJSFWC (1935-38) and suggested a Foreign Exchange Scholarship as a project to the Junior Membership Department. The Juniors adopted the idea in 1938-39 and exceeded their goal of $500 to provide two travel scholarships .. one for a student from the New Jersey College for Women (now Douglass College) and one for a foreign student to come to New Brunswick.

Louie C. Francisco, who was then State Chairman of International Relations for NJSFWC, suggested that the Federation establish such an exchange scholarship between the New Jersey College for Women and Latin American countries. Approval for this project was given on May 17, 1939, and on January 29, 1940 the Pan American Scholarship Committee met in Trenton and decided that it should be a full scholarship for one year rather than just a travel scholarship. It was believed that the recipients would foster better inter-American relationships having lived together and studied in each other's countries. The slogan "Dimes for Democracy" was originated and it was hoped that every club woman in New Jersey would contribute at least one dime.

By May, 1940 the required $2,000 had been raised, with the Junior Membership Department contributing the first $500.

Two candidates were selected in cooperation with the Institute of International Education and with the approval of the Pan American Union and the Trustees of the New Jersey College for Women. The program was then called the Pan-American Scholarship Award, and was changed in 1968 to its present designation in honor of Mrs. Francisco. The amount of money required for each scholarship award rose consistently over the years. The generosity of the clubs in making contributions to this fund made it possible for the scholarship to continue without lapse from its inception. Complete exchanges between two countries were made whenever funds were available; however, when there was not enough money for a complete exchange, preference was given to bringing a student from South America to New Jersey.

New Jersey is believed to be the first Federation to initiate and to continue this type of project, although other State Federations have since started similar projects as a result of information received from New Jersey.

The scholarships are still being awarded to women foreign students (with those from Latin America preferred) so that they may study at Douglass College during their junior year. If there are no foreign student applicants in a given year, the University is authorized to award the scholarship to an American woman student, perferably from Douglass College, to study abroad. The following women have been recipients of the Louie C. Francisco International Exchange Scholarships:

1940-41	Marina Orellana - Chile
1942-43	Eida Campos - Costa Rica
1943-44	Sara Ayale - Panama

1945-46	Zelia Moretzshon - Brazil
1946-48	Dylma Maryins - Brazil
1948-49	Olga Bravo - Ecuador
1949-50	Mary Tamayo-Lagos - Peru
1951-52	Mary Amador - Costa Rica
1952-53	Rocia V. Echavarria - Colombia
1954-55	Susana Tampieri - Argentina
1955-56	Cillu Cardoso Marques De Souza Brazil
1956-57	Maryssa Navarro - Uruguay
1957-58	Margarida A. Rosas - Brazil
1958-59	Maria Mercedes Jimenez - Paraguay
1959-60	Zelia Pessoa - Brazil
1961-62	Alba Maria Beyhaut - Uruguay
1962-63	Hildegard Wassilowsky - Peru
1964-65	Hortensia Barreyro Salva - Argentina
1965-66	Maria Delores Godinez Serrano Mexico
1966-68	Betty Taylor - Brazil
1967-68	Maria Luisa De Castro - Chile
1968-69	Wania Fonseca - Brazil
1969-70	Patricia Bermeo - Ecuador
1970-71	Yedamarie Moulin Ribeiro - Brazil Norma Teresa Lima - Mexico
1971-72	Lucia Maria Monteiro De Caravalho Brazil
1972-73	Marilda de sa Ribeiro - Brazil
1973-74	Magda Alanon (returned home)
1974-75	Pilar Bascunin - Chile
1975-76	Christina Chavarria - Costa Rica
1977-78	Vania Muniz - Brazil
1980-82	Jocelyn Koifman - Chile
1987-88	Elizabeth Hauschild - Germany Clare Garate-Delgado - France

Sueli Brodin - France

Anna Marie Fattori - Italy

1988-89   Anne deCadaran - France

1989-90   Christine Boucher - France

1990-91   Chiara Cillerai - Italy

1991-92   Geraldine Dibden - France

1992-93   Laurence Fouque - France

DOUGLASS COLLEGE STUDENTS SENT ABROAD:

1941-42   Elinor Dillon - Chile

1943-44   Elsie Braun - Mexico

1944-45   Susan Isaacs - Cuba

1945-46   Amelia Sollito - Cuba

1948-49   Elsie Linser - Mexico

1950-51   Gloria Hoffman - Chile

1953-54   Joy Kaiser - Peru

Judith Anderson - Chile

1955-56   Dolores Kazanjian - Cuba

1956-57   Doris Sohnle - Paraguay

1958-59   Fern L. Mayo - Chile

1961-62   Marie Szymanski - Argentina

1962-63   Louise Ann Ramsey - Mexico

1964-65   Joanne Meyers - Mexico

1987-88   Jean Fugate - Germany

Diane Mather - Germany

Elizabeth Lemesevski - France

Yvonne Montantino - France

Gina DeVito - Italy

1988-89   Melissa Liptak - France

1989-90   Maria Delfino - Italy

1990-91   Carol Schoenfeld - Germany

1991-92   Christine Persche - France

1992-93   Marisa Panzani - England

SOCIAL WELFARE

Members of NJSFWC have always been interested in "Society" in its broadest sense — defining it as "people in general, considered as living in relationships with each other". They consider their social obligations and social concerns as much more than reciprocal dinner invitations! Many of the volunteer efforts are described under appropriate categorical topics dealing with related fields (Health, Education, Safety, etc.). Since it was founded the Federation has always had committees and/or departments concerned with the welfare of others. The earliest one was dubbed Public Welfare Department and this metamorphosed into the Sociology Department, later known as the Child Labor Department. Other names were Civics Department and Civil Service Department, Public Affairs and Social Services.

Quite naturally, clubwomen are interested in the welfare of other women. Since 1900 they have sought to protect "working women" and their children by urging legislation which would assure safe working conditions. In the early 1900's they supported the idea of giving employed women the right to vote. This evolved into support of Women's Suffrage in general.

NJSFWC urged that women be permitted to serve on boards of state and county institutions where women were housed. In 1912 a Resolution requested separate facilities for women in prisons, jails and other detention facilities. They urged that the Legislature of New Jersey appropriate more funds for such facilities and that intellectual and physical training programs be included. The clubwomen studied national and state laws affecting women and children who were incarcerated and asked that a resident woman physician be placed on staffs of such institutions. As a result of Federation effort in 1913, a Bill for police women and matrons in jails went to the New Jersey Legislature and was passed in 1915.

Appeals had been made for methods of helping discharged prisoners of both sexes toward rehabilitation in 1904 - 1906 and, during the next three years, a night school for convicts at the Trenton Prison was advocated. This met with success and by 1911 the clubwomen were visiting the Trenton prison night school, along with writing to the Legislature asking continuance of the $1600 annual appropriation which had been made for this purpose.

Clubwomen worked closely with correctional institutions over the years and were helpful in finding markets for articles made by patients and inmates. In 1928 - 1929 an exhibit of occupational and vocational work was held. The heads of such institutions were encouraged by the Federation's participation since they also thought of their work as "a thankless job". In 1948 - 1949 outstanding service by state institution employees was recognized with awards of "merit" presented by the Federation to encourage such personnel. During this time period, clubwomen were emphasizing "rehabilitation" and visiting state homes and hospitals to give monthly birthday parties to brighten the surroundings (which were best described as "bleak").

Helping other women has continued to be of prime importance as crime on the streets escalated in recent years. Victims of rape and other abuse have been aided with support of WAR (Women Against Rape) and various organizations concerned with assistance to battered women and children. In 1958 the Federation urged commitment of sex offenders to diagnostic centers for examination before sentencing. At that time, there was no law concerning treatment of offenders and the Federation urged that New Jersey have stringent supervision and mandatory treatment of sex offenders by psychiatrists after their release.

In 1964 a NJSFWC Resolution urged a central reporting system whereby schools, doctors, hospitals, etc. could report child abuse. A portion of this Resolution also urged that parents/guardians guilty of abuse be punished and be provided with psychiatric treatment. In 1971 the Federation urged evaluation of New Jersey's shelters and detention centers for neglected, dependent and abused children. In 1978 legislation to protect battered spouses was endorsed; in 1982 support was given to the Crime Victims' Bill of Rights. NJSFWC continued support of a 1968 Resolution which called for the abolition of suspended sentences for previously convicted criminals along with the promotion of stronger parole procedures.

When "car jacking" appeared on the scene in the 1990's, the Federation went on record as urging that this be made a criminal offense with mandatory sentences and ineligibility for parole. The legislation supported was enacted in 1993.

In 1934 the Federation surveyed communities to explore the problems of "slum housing" and cooperated with other agencies to destroy this "blot on civilization". Adequate Federal housing for defense workers was sought in the days prior to World War II and urban renewal programs were supported in the 1960's. In 1949 NJSFWC endorsed a $100,000,000 bond issue to provide housing in New Jersey for middle income families since Federal funds were being devoted to housing for those in the very low income range. At the same time they worked to improve the lot of Native Americans (then referred to as American Indians) in efforts to provide them with better living conditions, full citizenship and the end of discrimination.

In 1950, when the Federal deficit was reported at $5,000,000,000 the Federation endorsed the Hoover Commission Report of 1949 which listed eight steps for deficit reduction. The second Hoover Report was also endorsed in 1958. Since the 1930's, clubwomen have studied taxation of all types and given constructive backing or opposition to legislative action on the tax scene. In 1971 clubwomen urged tax relief in New Jersey for elderly citizens, favored a balanced budget in 1980 and, in 1984, supported phasing out inheritance taxes in New Jersey. They urged that proof of alien status be submitted when applying for a Social Security Number to prevent aliens using Social Security Numbers to collect benefits to which they were not entitled.

In 1978 a Uniform Probate Code in New Jersey was urged to help protect widows when a spouse died without leaving a will. In 1989 Federation support was given to "living wills" in New Jersey and this type of legislation became a reality. In 1992 a Resolution urged New Jersey to adopt legislation (similar to that adopted in 1990 by Pennsylvania) which would prevent physicians from billing Medicare beneficiaries more than the Medicare allowance for covered services whether or not they "accepted assignment" on claims. In 1993 the Federation urged reinstatement of a $2,000 tax deduction on IRA's for all workers.

Legislation in 1993 which would provide immunity from law suits brought by perpetrators against those who used mace or similar chemical substances in self defense was endorsed by the Federation. In the interest of preserving privacy, a Resolution was also adopted in 1993 to restrict use of telephone lines for unwanted recorded commercial messages.

The Federation favored English as the official language of the United States since 1987 and again confirmed its position in 1992 by urging an Amendment to the NJ Constitution. This does not infer that the clubwomen are opposed to immigration. Many projects over the years have helped those newly-arrived in the United States to receive the education necessary to adjust to their new country and to succeed as citizens. Many of the laws that have protected the work force, including support of unemployment insurance in 1929 - 1932, have helped to make lives for such new citizens much more productive.

The Political Science Scholarship was begun in 1979. Awards are given annually to Douglass Colllege students majoring in this field.

On the somewhat lighter side, NJSFWC was proud to sponsor Louise Ferla, President of the Montville Woman's Club, as a participant in the Ms. New Jersey Senior America Pageant in 1993. As winner of the New Jersey pageant,

Louise went on to national competition in Nashville, Tennessee. Although she was not the winner, she did receive the award for the most active volunteerism. New Jersey clubwomen exhibited much pride in "their contestant".

Other items on the list of activities to make for a better country, included the Federation's support in 1990 of a limited term of office for United States Congress. They urged a limit of six terms (twelve years) for Representatives and two terms (twelve years) for United States Senators.

Concern for public safety was voiced in 1927 when the Federation endorsed the control of firearms to reduce crime. By 1964 there was a recommendation that the firearms laws in New Jersey be broadened to require licenses for sale of rifles, shotguns and ammunition and that the application for a permit to carry firearms include a physician's statement as to the physical and mental qualifications of the applicant. In 1983 approval was stated for having a gun in the home to provide self defense. The regulation of sale and use of firearms by individuals is still a controversial topic which has yet to be resolved. The 1993 "Brady Bill" may—or may not—help.

Many of the projects which have been aimed at improving life for others have centered around enhancements in individual communities throughout New Jersey. In 1949 - 1950 the General Federation sponsored "Build a Better Community" which boasted 43 entries from the New Jersey clubs. The first "Community Achievement" contest in cooperation with the GFWC and the Sears Roebuck Foundation was held in 1955 and 51 New Jersey clubs entered. These contests continued as two-year programs under the "Community Improvement Program" (CIP) label.

406

Monetary awards were provided by Sears Roebuck, and by 1968 there were 12,000 entries competing nationally for $100,000 in awards. New Jersey clubs entered and reported, receiving a $500 award for the Federation. The CIP contests have been continued with the General Federation's co-sponsor having changed to Chevron Corporation. The goal has continued to be 100 percent participation of New Jersey clubs. Many of the NJSFWC clubs have received state and national awards over the years with the dollars received having been used to further the prize-winning projects or to start new ones. The Community Improvement Program means that every community where a woman's club is located benefits as a result of the local club's project. CIP projects have touched every aspect of NJSFWC's agenda. They range from unique small projects to massive efforts which have encompassed all of the other organizations, schools and entire population of the communities involved. Seminars and workshops held for participating clubs have greatly improved performance and preparation of the essential reports which are submitted at the end of each two-year contest.

Working within their respective communities is a very popular aspect of club work in New Jersey. Despite the fact that the interests of clubwomen are unlimited in scope and they often "reach for the stars", doing things which will benefit their own neighbors provide a warm sense of personal satisfaction which is unrivaled. Volunteer service is difficult to tabulate because it includes personal involvement and degrees of devotion and effort; however, the number of volunteer hours and amounts of monetary contributions made by united clubwomen are phenomenal!

THE CECILIA GAINES HOLLAND AWARD

Upon her death in 1944 Mrs. John A. Holland, who as Cecilia Gaines had been the Federation's second President (1896-1898), bequeathed the sum of $1,000 to NJSFWC. Her will instructed that this amount be invested in securities by the Trustees of the Federation and that the income from the investment be given annually — either in cash or a medal — to a clubwoman doing outstanding civic work in New Jersey.

The Cecilia Gaines Holland Award has been given annually since its inception. Presented with appropriate ceremonies at the Annual Convention, it is the most prestigious award bestowed through the Federation to "one of its own".

Recipients are selected from resumes of eligible club-women submitted by Federated Clubs each year. The Cecilia Gaines Holland Award Chairman and her committee members "sanitize" the resumes to remove the candidate's name and identifying data, making the qualifications anonymous for the selection process. Until 1994 the winner was chosen by votes of NJSFWC elected Trustees. Currently, the honoree is selected by three or five Past State Presidents of NJSFWC with the winner's name being held in confidence until the Award is presented at the Annual Convention. This procedure retains the impartiality of the selection process and builds an aura of suspense until the exciting moment of presentation.

The following clubwomen have been honored as the recipients of The Cecilia Gaines Holland Award, and have received appropriate mementos along with framed certificates:

1944-45	Helen Purdy Adams
1945-46	Lena Griffith
1946-47	Louise B. Glass
1947-48	Dr. Margaret T. Corwin
1948-49	Clarette Sehon
1949-50	Grace Freeman
1950-51	Dr. Frances Bartlett Tyson
1951-52	Effie M. Morrison
1952-53	Dr. Agnes Wayman
1953-54	Ida Lillian Page
1954-55	Dr. Lillian Moller Gilbreth
1955-56	Mamie R. Stone
1956-57	Adelaide Hoffman Marvin
1957-58	Edna Ames Clark
1958-59	Alice L. Cornelison
1959-60	Florence M. Gaudineer
1960-61	Grace Y. Christian
1961-62	Thyra Stiles Maxwell
1962-63	Edith Asten Kellers
1963-64	Elizabeth Barstow Alton
1964-65	Mary Gindhart Roebling
1965-66	Ernestine Richards

1966-67	Mariamne Bowen
1967-68	Ida Emily Housman
1968-69	Agnes Faherty
1969-70	Lavenia S. Taylor
1970-71	Ilene Evans Fleming
1971-72	Olga Mackaronis
1972-73	Ida P. Edge
1073-74	Ella Harris
1974-75	Louise Scott
1975-76	Lucille M. Dangremond
1976-77	Dorothy B. McGlade
1977-78	Ellen Shiplee
1978-79	Evelyn Preziosi
1979-80	Helen S. Clancy
1980-81	Dorothy Virginia Wescoat
1981-82	Mary E. Volz
1982-83	Phyllis E. Cable
1983-84	Linda Rissel
1984-85	Katherine Everett
1985-86	Eula H. Reall
1986-87	Betty R. Bransdorf
1987-88	Carolyn A. Hartman Lunn
1988-89	Rhoda D'Accurso
1989-90	Mary Lou Sullivan
1990-91	Patricia Leuliette
1991-92	Dorothy M. Waters
1992-93	Maude F. Kenyon

NEW JERSEY WOMEN OF ACHIEVEMENT AWARDS

These awards originated in 1982 as a program jointly sponsored by Douglass College and the New Jersey State Federation of Women's Clubs. Awards are conferred upon women in recognition of outstanding accomplishments and distinguished service in various fields.

By public announcement, individuals and/or organizations in New Jersey are invited to submit nominations. To be eligible, a nominee must be a woman residing in New Jersey who has gained visibility in a broad range of personal and professional qualities and accomplishments. Recipients are selected by a committee of clubwomen and Douglass College representatives.

The first awards were presented in 1982 at a special program recognizing women for their accomplishments. It has become a continuing program with annual awards . The following women have been honored:

1982   Clara Allen
        Elizabeth Alton
        Millicent Fenwick
        Yolanda Mapp
        Claire Nagle
        Adelaide Zagoren

1983	Adrienne Anderson
	Robbie Cagnina
	Olga Mackaronis
	Barbara McConnell
	Lucille Dangremond
1984	Althea Gibson
	Linda Stamato
	Ruth Supp
	Evelyn Witkin
	Joan Wright
1985	Mary Higgins Clark
	Hazel Frank Gluck
	Ellen Levine
	Maria Parnell
	Mary Roebling
	Ruth Parlin Sanborn
	Constance Woodruff
1986	Ruth Ann Burns
	Vera King Farris
	Golden Johnson-Burns
	Irma Mirante
	Belva Plain
	Jean Sidar
1987	Celia Dorantes Abalos
	Marguerite Chandler
	Lena Edwards
	Jeanne Marie Fox
	Kent Manahan
	Dorothy McGlade
	Barbara Boggs Sigmund
1988	Marie Alberian
	Leanna Brown
	Frances Clark
	Theresa Grentz
	Alma Hill
	Esther Hymer
	Wynona Lipman

1989	Mary Lee Fitzgerald
	Maria Hernandez
	Ming Hsu
	Shirley Jackson
	Dorothy LoSasso
	Joyce Carol Oates
1990	Gloria Bonilla-Santiago
	Barbara C. Crafton
	Mary Good
	Marge Roukema
	Linda Volker
	Deborah Wolfe
1991	Anne Dillman
	Dolores Harris
	Barbara Irvine
	Janice Davis Miller
	Cecily Ramos-Ouimet
	Phoebe Seham
	Linda Troeller
	Margaret Varma
1992	Edna Alex
	Fran Avallone
	Francine Essien
	Lisa Klein
	Betty Kraemer
	Rita Newman
	Jacqueline Rotteveel
	Susan Wilson
	Ellen Zavian
1993	Helen Berman
	Zulima Farber
	Elinor Ferdon
	Helen Hurd
	Keiko Harvey
	Penelope Lattimer
	Carol Sas
	Pat Stanislaski

GOOD HEALTH EQUALS BETTER LIVES

The earliest members of NJSFWC knew that improving health care was essential to everyone, and millions of volunteer hours have been devoted to health-related concerns. In 1899 the Federation supported the need for a New Jersey Health Code which was finally established in 1922 and later accepted as a model by other states. The Federation was given credit for being largely responsible for the passage of this legislation. In the meantime, they had endorsed the Pure Food Bill in 1905 and, by 1906, had urged the prohibition of chemicals and dyes in foods, correct labeling and preservation of food and the inspection of slaughter houses and milk.

The Morristown Woman's Club had named a "Sanitation Committee" which organized collection of ashes and garbage in their town and obtained a ruling that dogs and flies should be kept out of food and bakery shops. Clubwomen urged improvement in sanitary conditions in schools and restrooms of local railroad stations. At the same time clubs were asked to form public health committees to study the conditions in factories, public buildings and streets. In 1913 the Federation urged that women be appointed to local Boards of Health and

414

in 1917 conducted a survey of state institutions. The influence of the clubs was being felt by then. The State Board of Health commended the organization by commenting on favorable conditions in the face of increased immigration by saying, "Advances can be attributed to better water, better milk, etc. but most of all to the change of public opinion for which clubwomen can claim much credit." The old universal "public drinking cup" had been abolished by 1911 — a movement sturdily supported by the Federation.

Tuberculosis was one of the first diseases which interested the Federation, and in 1906 they urged medical inspections for TB in schools and the establishment of small sanatoria. Clubwomen volunteered their services and Glen Gardner, a state TB sanatorium, opened in 1907. Clubwomen worked with local TB organizations and held "stuffing parties" in 1917 - 1920 whereby the bulk of the traditional "TB Christmas Seals" reached donors.

Maternal health and child care were always high on the list of priorities established by NJSFWC. In the early 1900's the licensing of midwives was advocated. Local Boards of Health were urged to have "Baby Saving Campaigns" by employing visiting nurses to educate mothers. In 1918 the Federation urged maternity insurance for the working women. Clubs had observed "Baby Week" in 1916 - 1917 to reduce the dangers to maternal and child health, and by 1967 the Federation urged mandatory screening of new-born infants for the metabolic disorder, PKU. The Evening Membership Department raised nearly $30,000 in 1963 for Babies Hospital, Newark, to lower infant mortality rates. The Junior Membership Department assisted "Operation Better Babies" at that time.

As an outgrowth of the project known as "The Pines" (which was begun in 1916) a bed for children was endowed at Burlington County Hospital and a dental ambulance was purchased for use in rural school districts. This vehicle, which was a fully-equipped ambulance originally intended for dental work overseas, was offered to the Federation for $1000 in 1919 after the end of World War I. This amount was raised in one day! This "Dental Clinic on Wheels" was the first of its kind in the country. In February, 1942 the Federation's cooperation in a state dental health program provided a dental trailer which served 123 towns in the state and treated 2607 needy children in its two years of operation. At the end of that time a Bill was adopted by New Jersey to provide dental care for the needy in rural areas. Federation support was voiced in 1954 for the establishment of a New Jersey College for Medicine and Dentistry. This made it possible for New Jersey students to receive this type of training without leaving their home state.

In 1917 the clubwomen urged periodic physical examination for the early detection of disease, and, in 1920, stressed the necessity of a health examination and certification before marriage . They also felt that there should be eugenic sterilization or the prevention of marriages between people with mental illness and venereal diseases. They studied the spread of venereal disease in the late 1930's and, although the dangers subsided with the advent of antibiotics during World War II, they were concerned with increasing problems in this area — especially among teenagers. This subject is again contemporary as VD viruses have become resistant to many of the antibiotics in use.

Work with the blind in New Jersey began in Federation in 1917 when clubs cooperated with the State Department of

416

Health, New Jersey Medical Society, and New Jersey Nurses' Association in a "Prevention of Blindness Campaign". Several NJSFWC Past State Presidents served on the New Jersey Commission for the Blind when appointed by governors of New Jersey. Articles made by blind persons have been sold at club and federation events since 1932 with sales amounting to $7,193 reported in 1959. In March 1934 a demonstration of the work of the blind was held for one week at Hahne and Company in Newark. Clubwomen held neighborhood surveys to bring many blind people to the attention of the State Commission so that they could be helped.

The Junior Membership Department has continuously worked to help the blind as evidenced by the Mobile Eye Clinic, Talking Books Project, support of Overbrook School for the Blind and a camp for blind children. The clubwomen have collected eye glasses for "Eyes for the Needy" in Short Hills, New Jersey and the "Eye Bank for Sight Restoration" has been well-publicized by the Federation. Many clubwomen have pledged to give their eyes at death for transplant purposes. The Eye Institute of New Jersey was the beneficiary of $54,000 collected in 1976 to 1978 as a Special State Project with Marion Graham Arnao as Chairman. State President Virginia E. Zanetich served as a member of the Board of Directors for the Eye Institute at that time.

Many Special State Projects (described under the applicable administration histories of the State Presidents) have been related to health care. Some of these include a volunteer program at the State School for Boys located at Skillman, the Douglass Developmental Disability Center for Autistic Children and St. John of God School for Special Children. In 1990 - 1992 the Special State Project was the New

Jersey Children's Hospital AIDS Program (CHAP) to help babies born with AIDS. The 1992-1994 project will equip the Resuscitation Critical Response Room (RCRR) at Children's Hospital in Newark.

Before NJSFWC Project

New home of Douglass Developmental Disabilities Center

Many other diseases have been attacked by NJSFWC members during its history. In 1946 - 1947 pressure from clubwomen was largely responsible for the establishment of the Department of Health Education and Bureau of Cancer Control under the New Jersey Department of Health. In cooperation with the American Cancer Society, clubwomen have been active in community campaigns for the "Cancer Crusade" and in 1969 the drive was headed in New Jersey by

418

Marjory Bonynge (Fielding) as the first woman to serve in this position.

The 1951 JMD State Project was a Mobile Cancer Education Unit which toured the state for many years, and the EMD provided $28,000 for equipment in use at the South Jersey Medical Research Foundation where much was done in cancer detection and control. In 1991 the Federation supported Medicaid and other insurance coverage for mammograms in New Jersey, and this legislation became a reality.

The Juniors' Mobile Cancer Unit

In 1993 NJSFWC joined the American Cancer Society in petitioning President William Clinton to focus on breast cancer. October and May are observed as breast cancer awareness months and an accredited mobile unit will come to the 1994 Annual Convention to provide mammograms to interested clubwomen at a reduced fee of $79.

Clubs aid groups interested in the fields of heart disease, cystic fibrosis, multiple sclerosis, muscular dystrophy, polio, kidney diseases, cerebral palsy, arthritis, rheumatism and many others. The Juniors established Curative Workshops and the Upper Extremity Amputee Fund to aid the handicapped. The EMD raised money for artificial kidney machines which are supplied for home use.

Mental health is as important as physical health to the Federation which has long worked with agencies and institutions involved in this field. Early clubwomen visited institutions which were then caring for the "feeble minded" and their efforts counted in improving the conditions they found there. Mental hygiene was studied by the clubwomen as early as 1923 when the Federation conducted a campaign for public education regarding the causes, prevention and cures of mental illness in an effort to banish fear and superstition. Mental hospitals have received financial aid from clubs and many hours of volunteer service along with thousands of items to be used for the residents of such institutions. Greystone, Marlboro, Trenton and Ancora State Hospitals received literally tons of comfort items over the years and members "adopted" patients to provide them with useful gifts. The EMD raised money for the State School for Girls at Vineland in 1960 - 1961 and the American Institute for Mental Studies (AIMS) (which was formerly known as the Vineland Training School) has been a special interest of the

Federation since 1934. The Woman's Club of Vineland initiated a project to raise $500 for a laboratory there, and other clubs were invited to contribute. In 1935 the Federation founded the Vineland Research Fund for the purpose of determining causes of mental retardation in children. By 1944 it was reported that 100 percent of the clubs were contributing to this fund and clubs visited the school annually to observe the techniques practiced there. During World War II mental tests formulated by AIMS were used by all branches of the armed forces. Annual contributions to this facility are still made by the Federation. It is now called the Vineland Developmental Center.

New Jersey Juniors were ahead of the times when, in the 1960's, they worked to make everyone aware of architectural barriers in public buildings which precluded access to the physically-challenged. The latest laws mandating such public access did not come about until 1993.

Special attention has been paid to the field of geriatrics by helping to form senior citizen groups — the trend of thought is that "active people are healthy people". With the advent of Medicare in 1966 and the confusing paper work which accompanies it, clubs sponsored speakers from government agencies to explain this medical coverage.   Morale of residents in homes for the aged and convalescent centers is improved by visits from clubs who present entertainment, gifts on special holidays and the ever-popular "Operation Candy Cookie" goodies.

As a carrier of disease, New Jersey's "famous pest", the mosquito, received its share of attention since 1899. Eradicating the mosquito is an on-going project which was started from scratch! Although New Jersey residents are still swatting the mosquito, there have been improvements.

Clubs continue to sponsor blood bank programs in cooperation with the American Red Cross. They contribute to local hospitals, have staffed Sabin Polio Vaccine and Chest X-ray Clinics, held first aid classes, patterned brain-injured children, made cancer dressings and "stuffed" envelopes for hundreds of fund drives in their local communities. Many of the Margaret Yardley Fellowship Awards have been to graduate students in health-connected fields.

Although the "drug scene" may seem to have developed relatively recently, New Jersey clubwomen realized in 1929 that drug addition was becoming a world problem. At that time they cooperated in National Narcotic Education Week and by 1952 the Federation passed a Resolution to limit the production of opium, employ more narcotic agents and prevent drug smuggling. Later the clubwomen urged more severe and mandatory sentences for drug peddlers and pushers, stressed the dangers of LSD and, in 1966, urged action on the non-narcotic but dangerous drugs which were available over-the-counter. In 1971 NJSFWC denounced the use of TV advertising of some over-the-counter drugs which were harmful to young children by giving them the impression that "taking pills is a desirable way to solve problems". Even earlier, in the 1930's, the Federation was warned of the dangers of marijuana. A campaign was instituted to destroy "pot" which was found growing in vacant lots, fields and backyards.

Indiscriminate use of alcohol, especially among teenagers, has been discouraged by Federated clubwomen for many years. They support TIPS (Training for Intervention Procedures by Servers of alcohol), MADD (Mothers Against

Drunk Driving), and S.O.B.E.R. (Slow on the Bottle Enjoy the Ride). The first Allied Youth Posts in New Jersey were established in 1956 - 1958 where young people could learn that "fun" was not dependent upon drinking alcohol. In 1986 the Federation urged banning sale of tobacco products to young people under the age of eighteen.

With national health insurance looming on the horizon in the 1990's, NJSFWC looks back on having studied socialized medicine in 1939 to evaluate it when the President of the United States called a National Health Conference due to changing economic conditions. In 1949 the Federation opposed the compulsory health insurance being considered by Congress at that time because they felt that it would create tax burdens, hamper medical research, interfere with doctor-patient relationships and be subject to undue political influence. Depending upon the outcome of current legislation, this viewpoint could change. Undoubtedly, New Jersey clubwomen will have their opinions and will express them to governing bodies.

SAFETY: ENVIRONMENT AND PEOPLE

The clubwomen of New Jersey have always been concerned with the world around them and the people in it. Protecting the environment and conserving natural resources are issues which surfaced more recently; however, the Federation urged factories and railroads to stop using soft coal as fuel in 1906. As early as 1926 NJSFWC endorsed legislation to conserve trees, water and soil. In 1946, the Federation urged international control of atomic energy and air pollution. In the 1960's the clubs asked for laws to control air pollution in New Jersey and to enforce existing air pollution laws by spending the funds necessary to accomplish this. They recommended tailpipe exhaust suppressors on automobiles and non-diesel trucks and asked that all club members support state and national legislation involving all environmental concerns.

Keeping the water supply free from pollution became an issue as the Federation supported the Model River Program in 1971 when efforts began to clean up the water-ways in the country. The Clean Water Act was supported in 1985 — the Federation had been demanding the elimination of "ocean

424

dumping" since 1977 and they reinforced this viewpoint with a Resolution in 1988 to end the dumping of sewerage and sludge in the ocean. At the same time they asked that the waterways not be polluted by littering of materials thrown from ships and barges transporting waste material. With the increase of medical waste found along New Jersey's beaches, the Federation adopted further Resolutions in 1992 condemning dumping of waste material in all state waterways. The battle continues.

Since 1978 clubwomen have been urging New Jersey to develop a comprehensive, long term practical energy program. In 1981, a Resolution asked that the Federal Government study electro-magnetic pollution to establish legal, safe standards for exposure and emission. In 1986 Resolutions recommended the fluoridation of commercial water supplies and that the Department of Environmental Protection and Energy (DEPE) study the problem of acid rain to try to find a solution. By 1987 the dangers of Radon gas had developed, and the clubwomen were interested in how to test for its presence and eliminate it. Certain pesticides had become known pollutants and, in 1992, New Jersey was urged to ban the use of arsenic-based pesticides and fungicide Daconli on public and private lawns.

Fighting "litter bugs" was a battle in which NJSFWC became involved in 1952 when laws were urged to clean up refuse thrown out of cars on the highways and to make consistent efforts to prevent littering by motorists. Not wanting archaeologists of the future to find us "buried in our own trash", the Federation was an early participant in recycling efforts. In 1985 the extension of the Super Fund for cleanup of landfills and other areas of pollution received attention and a Resolution recommended that the State of

New Jersey use recycled products to encourage recycling efforts. "Saving the Brown Paper Bag" was a project started in the Junior clubs in the 1980's. All club members cooperated by urging local businesses to use paper bags (which could be recycled) instead of plastic bags. This is an on-going project. Many clubs have been responsible for getting recycling started in their respective communities, and "sorting the trash" into several designated containers has become a way of life. In 1992 the Federation adopted a Resolution asking New Jersey to ban the sale of products that were not contained in reusable/recyclable material except where other material is needed for tamper-proof seals or to meet health and safety requirements by Federal law.

The idea of recycling materials undoubtedly comes easily to federated clubwomen. For generations they have been noted for creating unique and beautiful things from "throw away" items. From making papier-mache figures from old newspapers to using tuna fish cans and tissue boxes for attractive centerpieces, they've done it all!

Saving the environment is essential, but so is the safety of the people who live in it.

In 1902, when the private use of fireworks was legal, clubwomen discussed its dangers. In 1905 the Federation sponsored its first campaign for safe, patriotic observances of Independence Day. Dismayed by an increasing number of deaths and injuries caused by individuals setting off fireworks, a Resolution was passed in 1916 urging that fireworks be permitted only at community celebrations and pressed for municipal laws to accomplish this. Efforts in this direction were continued and, eventually, private use of fireworks was prohibited in New Jersey. Other holidays could also present dangers, and clubwomen stressed safety in home decorations and taught their children caution in "Trick or Treat" visiting at Halloween.

As mobility increased and highways were expanded in New Jersey, clubwomen "took to the road". In 1927 the Federation urged statewide traffic regulations to replace individual county or community road rules. This subject surfaced many times and, in 1953, it was still the subject of a Resolution adopted at Convention. In 1929 an endorsement was given to the work of the State Police. As traffic hazards increased clubs began seeking better enforcement of traffic laws and, in 1938, a Safety Committee became part of NJSFWC's program. In 1957 the Federation safety program was cited by the New Jersey Commissioner of Motor Vehicles and by Governor Robert Meyner. An enthusiastic campaign against traffic accidents was waged at this time and the Federation urged the suspension or revocation of licenses belonging to people arrested for speeding. As a result, new traffic laws were passed in January, 1959 and signs proclaiming that "Speeders Lose Licenses" began to appear along the highways. The Pennsylvania Safety Council gave NJSFWC an award for outstanding work in this field.

In 1961 - 1962 clubwomen promoted the nationwide "Women's Crusade for Seat Belts" and endorsed legislation making them mandatory. One of the results was that all automobiles are now being equipped with seat belts. Not everyone "Buckled Up" immediately, but New Jersey clubwomen were among the first to make fastening their seat belts a reflex action when they entered their automobiles. In 1990 the Federation adopted a resolution supporting compliance with the Seat Belt Law and urging that it become a primary action of police in halting motorists. In 1993

NJSFWC won an award for its "Buckle Up" campaign.

In 1959 the Federation urged automobile manufacturers to install the five major safety devices then available as standard equipment in new cars. Federation action also encouraged legislation about passing halted school buses in 1958. The requirement that infants and children be safely transported in appropriate car seats was stressed by clubs. They participated in the "loaner program" through which new parents who did not have an infant seat could borrow one to take the baby home from the hospital. In 1992 a Resolution asked for the elimination of liability from civil damages for organizations who provided "loaners".

Since 1960 clubwomen have asked that laws concerning heavy vehicular traffic on the highways be enforced and that more stringent and continuous checking be done on such vehicles. In 1969 prompt action was urged in clearing highways and restoring the site of an accident to safer conditions, and in 1971 the state was asked to take action on vehicles transporting and dropping hazardous materials on New Jersey roads. In 1992 support was given to establishing wildlife warning highway reflectors in New Jersey, and in 1993 the Federation asked the New Jersey Department of Transportation to require commercial properties located on state highways to make their street numbers visible from the highway. Another 1993 Resolution supported L.I.V.E.S. (Lights Increase Visibility — Enhance Safety), a movement to suggest driving with headlights on at all times.

Driving while intoxicated is condemned by NJSFWC which supports the activities of S.O.B.E.R. (Slow On the Bottle Enjoy the Ride) and MADD (Mothers Against Drunk Driving). In 1974 the Federation urged the reduction of the blood alcohol level which denoted legal intoxication from .15 to .10. This was incorporated into New Jersey law. However, in 1992 a Resolution by the Federation asked that it be reduced to .08.

Automobiles are not the only vehicles that receive attention from clubwomen. In 1958 they were endorsing compulsory licensing for bicycles in New Jersey and, in 1966, sponsored pedal lights on bicycles as the first improvement for such vehicles in forty years. NJSFWC was the only source for this type of equipment at that time. Later legislation was passed requiring that young children riding bicycles wear safety helmets. In 1992 the Federation adopted a Resolution requiring the use of helmets by bikers of all ages.

In 1971 the New Jersey Legislature was urged to control the operation and regulate the use of off-road vehicles such as snowmobiles and all-terrain vehicles which cause air pollution and property damage. Prior to that, the Federation had given its support to a controversial law requiring the installation of safety equipment on motorcycles and the use of helmets by their drivers . This law became a reality.

Water safety in swimming and boating has been taught under the auspices of the New Jersey clubs and many members are qualified in life saving techniques. The safe operation of pleasure boats was endorsed in 1986 as was the "Death by Boat" Bill in 1989 which dealt with deaths caused by careless/reckless operation of boats. In 1992 the Federation urged testing for drugs and alcohol in boating accidents.

Safety in the home has been important to clubwomen since 1913 when members were urged to see that their kitchens were as safe as an inspector would expect a factory to be. Safety Councils and Home Safety Institutes have been held throughout the state by clubwomen since 1937 which, among other things, stressed safe storage of dangerous medical materials to prevent accidental poisoning and the elimination of safety hazards in the home to prevent fires. First aid courses were given for clubwomen, many of whom serve on first aid squads and ambulance crews in their communities. Medical identification cards indicating physical disabilities and drug allergies have been distributed for many years.

As early as 1926 the Federation was urging better supervision of the sale and use of fire arms. National events brought the subject into sharp focus in 1963 and the clubs went on record in 1964 as supporting the request for strong state and federal legislation to control fire arms. As increased crime in the streets is still a vital concern, "Gun Control" continues to be an issue of national importance.

In the Federation archives a report carried a tagline — "Think Safety until vigilance becomes an unconscious reflex". The clubwomen of New Jersey do "Think Safety".

TO PRESERVE, CONSERVE AND BEAUTIFY

Long before "environment" became a modern buzz-word and Governor Thomas Kean created the slogan "New Jersey and You — Perfect Together" the women of NJSFWC devoted time, money and effort to keeping their state in good shape.

In 1896 one of New Jersey's "Natural Wonders" — the towering rocky cliffs bordering the Hudson River, the Palisades, — were in danger of wanton destruction by commercial enterprise which would blast them away. On March 20, 1896 in Trenton clubwomen listened to papers concerning the preservation of state forests and the Palisades. A May 1897 meeting in Englewood devoted an entire day to discussing this absorbing topic, and Federation Board members were later taken on a yacht trip up the Hudson to view the destructive activities.

With customary verve and tenacity the clubwomen decided to "Save the Palisades" for posterity. Since the Palisades constitute a joint scenic asset of New York and New Jersey and the Legislatures of both states had formed a Commission in 1895 to establish a Military Park there, the

Federation decided to work through this vehicle. Governor Voorhees of New Jersey and Governor Franklin D. Roosevelt of New York were persuaded to appoint Commissions with NJSFWC represented on the one from New Jersey. Plan after plan was considered and rejected until only one remained — that of a permanent Commission to obtain an Interstate Park.

Elizabeth Vermilye of Englewood was appointed Chairman of a Subcommittee on the Palisades under the Federation's Department of Forestry. In 1899 the Federation formed a Palisades League outside of its own activities to assist in raising funds for the project. New Jersey appropriated $50,000 followed by a $400,000 grant from New York. J. P. Morgan promised $122,500 contingent upon gifts from the states. The destruction was successfully halted with the women continuing their vigorous work, despite public-spirited men having become discouraged. In fact, Governor Voorhees, when meeting with Federation representatives, had said, "Ladies this is a hopeless task. I have tried for ten years to find a way to save the Palisades; it can not be done." On April 4, 1900 the Palisades Bill was passed by the Legislature — an action which was acclaimed by interested conservationists throughout the United States.

The Federation and the Palisades League continued to raise funds to establish a suitable memorial to commemorate the saving of the Palisades. The League raised $1500 from outsiders and the Federation raised another $1500 from the clubwomen. With this money as a base the Federation consulted with the Palisades Commission. It offered to furnish a strip of land measuring one hundred and twenty five feet on the Hudson River at the top of the Palisades near Alpine where there was a magnificent view. A highway was to be constructed which would make the new Federation Park more accessible and the memorial less liable to vandalism. The intent was to keep this area in its "wild" condition so that future generations would know its natural state at the time of the preservation. A meeting of the Federation was held on this site and plans were made for a monument. A Watch Tower in Federation Park was formally dedicated on April 30, 1929 climaxing over thirty years of effort! NJSFWC has a habit of maintaining its interest in things which it has begun and keeping an eye on the safety of the Palisades exemplifies this. Whenever an issue arose, prompt action was taken to resolve it. In 1964 the Federation supported the preservation of Bluff Point, a Palisades area. In 1993 a Resolution asked that the Palisades Interstate Park be placed on the New Jersey Register of Natural Areas and that the State of New Jersey provide appropriate financial support as well as making a study of the park to determine the impact of public recreation areas and vehicular traffic.

Blackledge-Kearny House (Cornwallis Headquarters)

When the Interstate Park Commission began the restoration of Cornwallis Headquarters (now known as the Blackledge - Kearney House) at the foot of the Palisades, the Federation agreed to furnish the building when the restoration was completed. On June 8, 1933 this historical site was opened to the public. It contains authentic American furniture — the gifts of of 149 clubs and 22 individuals. The search for such collectors' items took many months of work by clubwomen. The most precious relic is the sea chest of Henry Hudson which was donated by the Interstate Park Commissioners. The Federation's interest in this building has continued with visits by clubwomen and financial contributions from clubs on a regular basis.

Greenbrook Sanctuary, located in Palisades Interstate Park, has been supported by clubs since 1958. In 1965, $1,000 was raised by clubs to construct a wooden foot bridge over the Sphagnum Bog in Greenbrook Sanctuary and club contributions continue to support this area with more than $1,000 in gifts each year.

In 1955 - 1956 club groups visiting historic areas became interested in the restoration of the deserted village at Allaire. By 1957 rapid strides had been made with roads built, picnic grounds with outdoor drills established and restroom facilities constructed. The motto: "Virginia has its Williamsburg, Massachussets has Sturbridge Village and New Jersey should have Allaire!" New Jersey's first three-story department store was used as a museum for the many articles connected with Allaire and in 1957 - 1958 a fund was started for voluntary contributions from clubs for the purpose of restoring the Old Bakery Building. Allaire State Park was formally opened on June 1, 1958 and the museum room in the Bakery opened in 1959. Allaire's unique historical background includes the first screw-nail to be made on a lathe, the first enameled cookware, the manufacture of stoves which were carried west by covered wagon trains, the first iron pipes ever designed and made to carry water and many parts of the world's first steamboat created by Robert Fulton. Fulton was a friend of the Allaire family who founded the Village. By 1960 the Federation was raising funds to restore the "Inn" which was on its way to restoration with furniture included by 1962. An annual picnic was held on this site for "Allaire Day" with capacity crowds in attendance.

The Nature Area of Batsto in the Wharton Track was a 1960 - 1962 Federation project. The 51 acre site had been acquired by the state in 1954 and contains rare specimens of many wild flowers and plants indigenous to the "New Jersey Pine Barrens". These may well have been lost to nature lovers for all time if the Batsto Nature Area had not been dedicated on May 27, 1962 as a result of the Federation's action. Nature trails in the area make it possible to present interpretative nature education programs regularly. The First Batsto Picnic was held for Federation members and friends in 1968, and club contributions of more than $1,000 annually have continued.

A 1968 Resolution recommended the establishment of a New Jersey Pine Barrens National Monument and Reserve in support of a movement by the Audubon Society. This area dates back to the Miocene Epoch of some 25 million years in the past and has remained relatively unchanged. At this time the 550 square miles encompassed were threatened by housing projects, industrial complexes and plans for a giant jetport. This would have destroyed for all time the unique environment essential for rare species of flora and fauna, including the Pine Barren's Tree Frog and the Curly Grass Fern found nowhere else in the country. Earlier the Federation had opposed the construction of a global jetport in Morris County in order to preserve important wildlife and historical landmarks in that area.

Preserving Island Beach in its natural state was sponsored by the Federation in 1958 - 1959 and interest in Goose Pond and the extension of the Wharton Tract for water conservation was also manifested. In 1959 - 1960 legislation to preserve the Swamp Lands of New Jersey was urged and in 1963 - 1964 the "Great Swamp National Wildlife Refuge" became a project of the Federation. On September 28, 1968 President Lyndon B. Johnson signed the law which placed the area's 3,750 acres under the National Wilderness Preservation System from which only an Act of Congress can remove it! In 1964 - 1965 the Federation implemented the Tock Island and Sandy Hook State Park Projects and supported agencies and groups interested in the Passaic River Valley area, the "Wetlands" (which are the Salt Marshes) and the Great Piece Meadows. The Green Acres Bond issue was staunchly supported in 1960 - 1962 to purchase lands for recreation, reservoir sites and water uses.

In 1954 - 1956 New Jersey clubwomen supported the General Federation project to restore the interior of Independence Hall in Philadelphia and New Jersey clubs contributed

$13,320 — the second largest amount raised. More recently, in 1986, the Federation supported the restoration of the Statue of Liberty and Ellis Island with significant contributions. The clubs were heavily involved in 1975 and 1976 when the nation celebrated its Bicentennial. Clubs sponsored programs in their communities, joined in parades and participated in an untold number of events which helped to celebrate the U.S.A.'s 200th birthday.

Probably because they do so much traveling on them, clubwomen have always been interested in keeping New Jersey's roadways not only safe but attractive. Since 1906 the Federation has been in the forefront in many movements to abolish unsightly signs and billboards along the state's highways. Resolutions concerning this subject have been adopted and/or reaffirmed at least nine times over the years. When a law concerning highway billboards was passed on March 25, 1930 it was felt that progress was being made. Club members have fought the repeal or amendment of this law for many years and the struggle will probably continue. It seems to have been successful along the New Jersey Turnpike and the Garden State Parkway as well as the newer Atlantic City Expressway. NJSFWC has continued to urge plantings and landscaping along the major state highways, and this appears to have been somewhat effective.

Currently the NJSFWC Board of Directors participate in the Adopt-A-Highway project by caring for an area near Federation Headquarters. Many New Jersey clubs share in this activity in their communities.

Trees have come in for their share of support by New Jersey clubwomen. As early as 1908 the Federation was concerned about the national danger of "A Forest Famine" and urged

437

that America protect its trees. In 1926 New Jersey was urged to use a $250,000 appropriation to acquire 1,400,000 acres of idle forest lands for use as a state forest. In celebration of NJSFWC's Seventy-Fifth anniversary in 1969 over ninety percent of the clubs planted trees in their communities. Clubs take Arbor Day seriously and sponsor programs where residents and school children plant trees in their towns. In 1945 - 1947 support was given to the New Jersey Federation of Garden Clubs' project planting dogwood trees along Blue Star Drive as memorials to men and women serving in the military. In 1964, in observance of New Jersey's Tercentenary celebrations, clubs planted over two thousand Red Oak and dogwood trees. Back in 1937 the Federation went on record as being opposed to destroying the flowering cherry trees for construction of the Memorial at the Washington, DC Tidal Basin. They felt that this was not only an area of great beauty but was a symbol of international understanding with Japan! No one can always be right!

Although accused of being "Tea-Drinking" Ladies wearing flowery hats (an image which the Federation has fought hard to discourage over the years), the members of federated clubs have always cherished flowers and been noted for having "green thumbs". Many early clubs started as garden clubs and groups concerned with the beautification of their communities through landscaping. In 1906 Resolutions were adopted to save wildflowers in New Jersey and to choose a State Flower. The purple violet was named in 1913. The Federation favored the selection of laurel as the National Flower — a movement endorsed by Mrs. Woodrow Wilson — and was instrumental in having a bill for this purpose introduced in Congress in 1916.

Club garden committees still engage in many activities

such as organizing flower shows, conducting classes in the growing and arranging of flowers and corsage making and participating in many projects to beautify their communities. NJSFWC has had award-winning exhibits at the New Jersey Flower and Garden Show on many occasions as well as in many other well-known programs of this nature. The District Achievement Days held each year include a plethora of flower arrangements, potted plants and other unique exhibits using flowers. Federation Day at the New York World's Fair in 1939 included "Gardens on Parade" as part of the New Jersey Exhibit. In 1958 - 1959 two planes filled with clubwomen flew to Europe on a Federation Garden Tour. School gardens were sponsored in 1907, essay contests on horticulture and conservation were held for eighth grade students in 1958 and "Litterbug" campaigns in communities are a way of life. Municipal landscaping projects are prominent in club calendars and, when the Federation Headquarters was built, funds were raised for landscaping with a plan developed by Rutgers University and the Laughing Boys Club utilized.

As early as 1915 the Federation had the Governor of New Jersey proclaiming the last week in April as "Clean Up Week" to make community surroundings more healthful and beautiful. Many clubs enter competitions sponsored by GFWC and business firms. In 1971 the Woman's Club of Lincoln Park won First Place in the nation for the CITGO Business for Beauty Project and received a $2,000 check at the GFWC Convention. A similar contest to conserve gasoline was sponsored by GFWC and the Shell Oil Company in 1981 - 1982 with the Dover Junior Woman's Club being a winner in this "Every Drop Makes A Difference" competition.

The preservation of birds and animals is a concern of

NJSFWC which has cooperated in many projects conducted by the Audubon Society. At the request of the Federation, Governor James F. Fielder proclaimed April 3, 1917 as "New Jersey Bird Day" in the interest of conserving the state's song birds. Way back in 1906 the clubwomen were urged to stop wearing plumage in their hats to prevent the extinction of the birds which supplied the plumes. Support was also given to the endorsement of a law to prohibit live pigeon shooting, and children have been educated in good outdoor manners to protect wildlife and birds.

Like most women, New Jersey clubwomen enjoy wearing furs; however, they voiced their opposition to the use of inhumane animal traps as early as 1935. Of course, they are not going to wear furs obtained from animals on the endangered species list and many of them have supported faux furs in place of animal fur. Although the Federation as an organization has not yet taken a specific stand on "animal rights", individual members have freedom of choice and may have been numbered among the more recent demonstrators.

All "rights" are important to NJSFWC women; however, it must be confessed that they have worked earnestly for the irradication of the mosquito and poison ivy since the 1930's. The boy who won the Federation's $10 prize for collecting 800 tent caterpillars in the 1920's must have missed a few of them since they still make their appearance in the spring each year. The gypsy moth which destroyed a lot of New Jersey foliage in recent years is also on the list of nature's creatures which the Federation does not care to preserve.

In the midst of busy lives, New Jersey clubwomen do try to "Take time for all things" and that includes an opportunity to stop and smell the flowers.

440

HOME AND FAMILY LIFE

The New Jersey clubwoman of 1994 is most likely to be working at a full or part time job along with being a homemaker. Although a clubwoman does not deny that "woman's place is in the home" she is proof positive that she can create an excellent homelife for her family while bringing home the bacon before she fries it up in the pan!

The earliest members of NJSFWC were less likely to have careers outside of their homes; however, many of them were professional women and/or volunteers for excellent causes. As early as 1896 a state-wide meeting was held in Trenton to discuss "Household Economics" and at the 1899 Federation Convention the women voted to cooperate with the Consumers League through which they demanded that manufacturers produce articles of good quality under clean, healthful working conditions. The inclusion of Domestic Science courses in the public schools was urged in 1900 and many young women eventually went into the field of Home Economics as a career. Some of them were helped in this undertaking by scholarships offered by the Federation. The Home Economic Scholarship established in 1953 became

441

known as the Nutrition-Management-Sciences Scholarship in 1992 for Douglass College students majoring in nutrition studies of the 1990's.

It appears that the original clubwomen in New Jersey may have had some kind of household help and the welfare of these domestic workers became a concern. The Federation tried to make housework as attractive as factory work to young immigrant girls who filled many of these positions. The methods adopted may not have been completely successful since a committee compiled a pamphlet entitled "Hints to Housekeepers Without a Maid or Easy Methods of Housekeeping" for club distribution in 1906. A committee planned a demonstration center designed to eliminate the drudgery of housework. It was non-profit and non-commercial, termed "An Objective Study of Efficient Management with the use of Modern Apparatus to Replace the Average Inefficient Servant" and was financed without aid from the Federation treasury. (At that time the Treasury was suffering a fifty-two cent deficit!)

State President Mary Pattison made a four-room wing of her home in Colonia available and on June 9, 1910 the "Household Experiment Station" was opened. Thousands of letters of inquiry were received and more than 3,000 persons visited the site within the first year. Clubs came en masse to spend the day observing the approved routines and operation of new appliances. They even brought the traditional "box lunches" for which NJSFWC is famous. Over 12,000 from 123 clubs attended sessions at the station. A report in 1913 stated that 30 people had been fed for a total of $5, which would indicate that a great deal was learned.

Protection of family life and family values has been a

priority since 1899 when the Federation adopted a Resolution to outlaw polygamy. In 1900 a Constitutional Amendment to ban plural marriages was studied and consensus was that polygamy should be a "national crime". In 1920 clubwomen urged that a health certificate be obtained before marriage and in 1923 - 1926 Federation support was given to bills for uniform marriage and divorce laws, compulsory physical examination before marriage and the prevention of marriage between those who were mentally deficient or infected with venereal diseases. In 1992 the Federation urged laws to keep divorce and custody documents private and in 1993 a Resolution supported "Parental Advisory and Warnings" to appear on labels of music items containing lurid lyrics etc.

The health and well being of families have always been important issues to women everywhere and New Jersey clubwomen have done battle since 1902 when they supported the Pure Food Bill in an effort to insure the availability of healthful food stuffs. Pure Food and Drug legislation had been consistently endorsed and by 1911 the Federation was demanding inspection of slaughter houses. In 1961 - 1962 they supported the Humane Slaughter Bill. In 1913 clubwomen began urging the inspection of milk, and in 1923 the Federation was credited with being largely responsible for the passage of New Jersey's Pure Milk and Cream Bills.

The 1920 - 1923 clubwomen served as "reporters" to keep the Port Authority advised on prices. At that time produce raised in New Jersey was being shipped to New York, trucked to market and often trucked or ferried back to New Jersey for sale. This resulted in an increase in price and deterioration of quality. These efforts were felt to be largely responsible for the Port Authority Bill which corrected the situation being passed without a dissenting vote! In more recent years clubs supported a wide variety of legislation such as the cooking of garbage used to feed hogs and a more recent provision of uniform meat inspection. In the 1950's the Federation was on record as being opposed to government crop control since it tends to create artificial scarcities and increased prices.

Along with food and shelter, women are always interested in clothing. The homemakers of 1906 agreed to refrain from using Aigrette plumage on their hats to keep the bird which supplied the plumes from becoming extinct. They also disapproved of killing baby lambs for their skins and agreed to refrain from wearing coats made of this material. In 1914 clubwomen endorsed "simplicity in dress" — perhaps because these ladies were expert seamstresses and made many of their own clothes. New Jersey Federation Day at the 1939 New York World's Fair was enhanced by a floral map done in needlework by club members. Participation was high in the Vogue Pattern Sewing Contest from 1956 to 1963 when more than 500 club members enthusiastically entered the competition. Since that time the American Home Department has held dress-making competitions and other contests for needlework at District Achievement Days. Top prize-winning entries are proudly displayed at the Federation's Annual Conventions.

During the major wars in which the United States was engaged the women of the Federation prepared and served food at depots as troop trains arrived and departed. The kitchen and its food service chores were an important part of "The Haversack" in World War I and during the World War II years, the clubwomen of the 1940's planted their share of Victory Gardens and preserved crops from their agricultural adventures.

A part of good home management involves the handling of money and, in 1920, a Department of Practical Finance was organized by the Federation to outline the study of financial affairs as they touch the home, municipality and state. With the objective of teaching the clubwomen how to get the most for their money, a Thrift Committee was formed to educate members in keeping household accounts and to urge them to stop unnecessary buying which raised prices. They supported the government's anti-inflation program during World War II and worked to combat the sale of "black market" items. In 1952 they were still fighting inflation, banning the "black market" and avoiding waste etc. With the economy crunch of the early 1990's wise clubwomen became expert "coupon clippers" and more efficient shoppers.

As women learned more about handling their own funds in the 1920's they visited the New York Stock Exchange and began learning about investments. Clubs were building/ buying club houses and the knowledge of how to finance them was important. In the 1950's women were controlling even more money and Banking Seminars were held at local banks through the cooperation of the New Jersey Bankers' Association. Finance Forums were popular club programs throughout the years. In 1993 a very successful Financial Seminar was held at Headquarters in New Brunswick. With an increasing number of clubwomen becoming widows, the need for dealing with the legal aspects of wills and inheritances was added to their financial responsibilities. Learning the rudimentary facts of financial life is a "fringe benefit" of Federation membership.

With many clubwomen widows and single parents a Displaced Homemaker seminar was held in March 1994 at NJSFWC Headquarters under the direction of Dolores

Farrelly, Home Life/Social Services Department Chairman.

Creativity is high on the list of accomplishments among the clubwomen. The American Home Department held many classes over the years in rug making and braiding, lamps and lamp shade making, furniture refinishing, ceramics, china painting, candle making, jewelry design, egg decorating and needlework of all types. The results are astounding and the talent evidenced by the items displayed at District Creative Arts Days and at the Annual Convention is unsurpassed.

A home needs to be beautiful as well as comfortable, so the Federation provided opportunities for interior decorating. In the 1960's clubwomen were able to find an outlet for their love of "doll houses" when they produced exquisite miniature rooms of all types (including a New Jersey kitchen circa 1664 when the state celebrated its 300th birthday in 1964).

Religion is a subject close to home and family life. NJSFWC members have made several studies in this area which began with a detailed study of the great religions of the world 1966 - 1968. They placed prayer cards obtained from the General Federation in restaurants, hospitals and other institutions and went on record at that time as being opposed to the Supreme Court's decision to ban prayer in the public schools. Several times the Federation has adopted Resolutions urging a Constitutional Amendment to permit optional prayer in schools and to restore Bible reading and the privilege of individual prayer in New Jersey schools. NJSFWC is non-sectarian with the membership composed of women of many faiths.

Looking after businesses in the state has also been a

446

concern of clubwomen from time to time. In 1912 the Federation pledged support of closing stores at 5:00 p.m. on week days and on Saturday afternoons in July and August — they volunteered not to shop "after hours". Times change, and the busy working women of today would probably find it difficult not to be able to shop in the supermarkets during the more expanded hours now available. In 1939 the Federation opposed race track betting in New Jersey because it would tend to divert money from legitimate business and create hardship on merchants located near race tracks. They also felt that most of the money would go to the tracks and not to the state budget. They quoted a State Constitution provision of 1897 which prohibited race track betting. As we know now, this was a battle lost and the State Constitution was amended.

In 1900 the Federation records indicate cooperation with the Mothers' Congress. Motherhood is enjoyed by a large percentage of clubwomen with many of the Junior Clubs holding the record for the most small children. In 1964 a clubwoman was chosen as the "New Jersey Mother of the Year" by the American Mothers' Committee. Undoubtedly the hand that rocks the cradle is still doing its share in today's world.

Federation members have been very vocal in opposition of violence against women. In 1982 support was given to rape crisis centers and in 1990 the Federation went on record as asking that bail and parole be denied to rapists who may be afflicted with AIDS. It also recommended mandatory sentences on first offenders who have committed sexual assaults and/or rape. In 1992 support was given to the Violence Against Women Act.

Since 1989 the Federation has urged the FDA and the DEPE to clean up food supplies, test pesticides for health effects and to issue clear guidelines in this field. This was reaffirmed in 1992.

Another labeling issue came to the fore in 1988 when the Federation urged national action to label materials used for arts and crafts so that users would be aware of possible hazardous contents. Since 1990 the clubwomen have been urging the return to unit pricing on items in supermarkets so that they can keep better track of their purchases at the checkout counter when scanning is used on Bar Codes.

Although clubwomen, as "Professional Volunteers" and busy members of today's labor force, may not spend as much time in their homes as they did in 1894 there is no doubt that they care just as much about home and family life.

FOR THE YOUNGER GENERATIONS

NJSFWC is a firm believer in "building with youth for a better world"; therefore, much volunteer effort is devoted to raising funds and providing services for the young (and sometimes restless) components of society. Working with children and youth is a facet of club activity which helps to bridge the generation gap.

In 1900 juvenile delinquency was already a concern of the Federation and it endorsed a national movement for a Juvenile Court. The custom at that time of placing the young offenders beside adult criminals in the same court room was deplored. Juvenile Courts became a reality and clubs continued to study laws in 1910 - 1911 which affected children in jails and detention centers. Clubwomen were interested in the work of probation officers and the rehabilitation of youthful criminals. Unfortunately, "crime in the streets" continued to increase to the serious problem it has become in the 1990's. In 1963 the Federation urged improved street lighting to combat juvenile delinquency in support of a GFWC movement. The Federation recommended New Jersey laws to hold parents financially responsible for property damage done by juveniles and, in 1968, urged the publication of the names of young offenders upon conviction of more than one offense. In 1976 it took the position that the age whereby juvenile offenders could be tried as adults should be reduced from 18 to 16 when violent crimes such as murder, assault, and armed robbery were involved.

The clubwomen of the early 1900's realized that stemming the tide of juvenile crime could best be tackled at the local level. They took the approach of keeping young people constructively occupied with the purpose of brightening their long winter evenings and bringing new life to a monotonous existence by teaching crafts such as sewing and basketry. These efforts were expanded and developed into clubs opening community youth centers and youth hostels. Clubwomen worked with schools in their communities to encourage expansion of programs in art, music and sports — all of which helped to fill idle hours.

An early project to aid in the rehabilitation of young law breakers was support of the George, Jr. Republic of Freeville, New York. From 1903 to 1909 clubs financially sponsored boys sent to the Republic for help. The New Jersey branch of the Republic was opened in April, 1909 at a farm near Flemington, and clubs continued to contribute to the support of boys and girls there until 1916 when it was closed. Ranch Hope in Alloway, New Jersey was founded by the Rev. David L. Bailey in the early 1960's to help delinquent boys become better citizens. This is still an active, successful facility which has continued to receive assistance from the Federation. Robins' Nest, a home for teenage girls in the southern part of New Jersey, became a Federation project in the 1970's when the Junior Woman's Club of Woodbury "adopted" it and was one of ten national finalists in the GFWC Community

Improvement Program (CIP). NJSFWC clubs have continued their support of this project also.

Child labor, which is now a thing of the past, was a serious problem in 1902 when the Federation first went on record to support laws which would eliminate the flagrant abuses of the time. In 1906 a Resolution was adopted urging Federal Child Labor Laws and the creation of a Children's Bureau. The clubwomen had learned that newspaper and telegraph boys in Washington DC worked all through the night and young boys also worked at night in New Jersey's glass factories. By 1909 - 1911 the Federation endorsed laws to restrict child labor at night in all types of factories.

Now that harmful labor by young children is properly restricted and working conditions are governed by law, clubwomen have turned their attention to assisting young people in finding appropriate gainful employment through youth employment services which attempt to match ambitious young workers with suitable jobs. In 1964 - 1966 the Federation supported the Job Training Center at Camp Kilmer were young people were trained and placed in suitable employment so that they could earn a living.

A 1959 Resolution of the Federation asked New Jersey to review its Child Labor Laws to permit local autonomy allowing those between the ages of 14 and 17 to find part time work in non-hazardous jobs. With the steadily increasing cost of higher education part time work for teenagers has become a way of life. These ambitious youngsters are encouraged in their efforts by clubwomen; however, the Federation is still watchful over their welfare.

In 1932 - 1935 the needs of the State Home for Girls in

Clinton was studied. A JMD project in 1960 raised funds to build and equip an athletic field at the Trenton State Home for Girls. The Vineland State School also receives attention from the clubwomen and, in all of these facilities, club members have provided individual involvement by adopting residents and supplying them with gifts and personal needs throughout the year.

Babies and young children are always of interest to the clubwomen. In 1916 it was learned that 7,000 New Jersey babies were dying in their first year of life. "Baby Week" as part of the "Better Babies Campaign" was supported to educate mothers on child care. As a result of the Federation work at this time the Division of Child Hygiene and Nursing was created in Trenton with a woman physician in charge. At this time NJSFWC petitioned the New Jersey Legislature to amend school medical examination laws so that no school girl would be examined in the nude or in a semi-nude condition except by a woman medical inspector or in the presence of a woman.

In 1919 clubwomen urged physical and health education in public schools to improve physical fitness — a need was discovered when one-third of the men drafted for World War I were found to be unfit for service. With more women entering the work force in the 1970's, clubs urged support of day care centers for the children of working mothers. Many clubwomen served as volunteers in centers operating in their own communities. In 1968 a Resolution urged that sex education be provided in New Jersey schools, and in 1990 the United States was urged to ratify the United Nations Convention on The Rights of the Child.

New Jersey clubwomen have aided local "Head Start"

programs since their inception and the problem of the high school "dropout" has been tackled with enthusiasm. Youth activities sponsored and aided by clubs include Scouting for both boys and girls, YMCA and YWCA groups, youth canteens, teenage forums, 4H groups, Little League Baseball and Midget Football teams, the "Helping Hand" and other variations on the block parent programs to prevent child molestation and abuse. Clubs sent children and young people to summer camps, established teenage book corners in local libraries and conducted children's story hours. They support driver education in the schools and organize school safety campaigns which include bicycle inspections and encourage the wearing of helmets while riding bicycles — a procedure which has recently become state law.

Realizing that there are many influences on children and young people, clubwomen in 1918 asked that motion pictures be improved to eliminate scenes of war, violence and vulgarity. In the 1950's a concentrated effort was made to get obscene literature such as pornographic magazines etc. off the news stands. In 1921 the Federation opposed "secret societies" in public schools as being undemocratic, and in 1924 clubwomen voiced their opposition to "beauty contests" as a menace to the ideals of young women. This may have had some part in making competitions of the 1990's geared to "scholarship" contests at a higher level.

Mental health of children and young people has been a Federation concern since 1926 when a child welfare luncheon was sponsored with speakers appealing for the founding of a psychiatric clinic for children in New Jersey. In 1934 the Vineland Research Fund was established for the purpose of determining the cause of mental retardation in children. Work done by the Federation at the American Institute for

Mental Studies (AIMS) (which was formerly the Vineland Training School and now the Vineland Developmental Center) has been a well-loved project which continues to the current date. A Special State Project in the 1980's, the St. John of God School in Westville Grove, New Jersey, (where young children who are mentally-challenged receive special instruction) is still dear to the hearts of clubwomen. They continue to provide financial aid, volunteer services and labels from the Campbell Company products to support this facility. More recently clubwomen have been collecting Scott Paper Company product symbols to assist the Ronald McDonald houses throughout the country where parents and children can find a home-like atmosphere near hospitals while children are receiving treatment.

Alcohol and drug abuse are serious concerns to everyone and the clubwomen of New Jersey share this concern. In the early 1950's, and for several years after that, NJSFWC was represented at National Allied Youth Conferences where teenagers learned the facts about the consumption of alcoholic beverages. The first Allied Youth Posts in New Jersey were chartered at Somerville High School and at Collingswood High School. In 1959 - 1960 the Federation supported raising the legal drinking age and urged New York to raise its drinking age from 18 to 21 to coincide with New Jersey law because so many young people from New Jersey were crossing the state line to consume and purchase liquor. The Federation reconfirmed its position on the drinking age in 1982 and clubwomen are pleased that New Jersey has established 21 as the legal age.

The Federation ideas for providing young women with opportunities have been firmly entrenched since the earliest days of the organization. In the 1930's NJSFWC began holding "College Day" at Douglass College. This provides young women entering their junior year in high school to spend a day on the Douglass College campus where they attend seminars conducted by faculty members, tour the college and become acquainted with the curriculum offered. The event has become increasingly successful over the years and a portion of the attendees have later become Douglass College students.

A program begun in 1947 was a unique part of NJSFWC. Originally called Girls' Citizenship Institute (GCI) the name was more recently changed to Girls' Career Institute which provides a better description of the current format. Young women completing their junior year in high school are sponsored by federated clubs throughout New Jersey to attend this four-day event held in June each year. A committee from the sponsoring club usually interviews applicants and selects a delegate and an alternate based on their qualifications. These include scholastic ability, school activities and community involvement. The delegates live in Douglass College dormitories with clubwomen serving as "house mothers". Well-known speakers from many fields conduct lecture sessions, forums and panel discussions during GCI with more recent emphasis being on career fields open to women. Entertainment is provided throughout the sessions — often by the delegates themselves who exhibit a wide variety of excellent talent. Sports such as swimming, tennis, volleyball, softball etc. are available to the delegates and they are provided with free time for getting acquainted with each other while exchanging views and ideas. "Fun Night" on the final evening is a popular event with dormitory sections presenting skits and other acts in hilarious form.

A wise combination of education and recreation has made

GCI a valuable experience for attendees and it is a great honor for a high school student to be chosen as a delegate by her local club. She reports on her week's experiences to the sponsoring club during the following year. Approximately 400 young women attend GCI each year at Douglass College and their enthusiastic reports indicate that it was a "time to remember".

The clubs provide the funds to send their delegates to GCI. In 1947 the first session, which was held at Montclair State Teachers College with 100 outstanding high school girls attending the two-day session, cost $5.25 (which included everything). From 1948 on (when GCI has been held at Douglass College) the costs have risen to $140 and most clubs include a little "spending money" for their delegate in the event that she wants to visit the college bookstore etc. Since 1954 when there were some excess funds in the account, a GCI Scholarship has been offered at Douglass for an incoming Freshman who attended the Girls' Career Institute during her high school days. The scholarship fund has been augmented by direct contributions from clubs and, when funds permit, several scholarships are given annually. GCI delegates also issue their own newspapers during the session. These publications are often dedicated to the the GCI committee and to the house mothers who attended. Several reunions of former delegates have been held, and many of the students find themselves keeping in touch with their fellow delegates for many years.

A more recent youth program has been HOBY (The Hugh O'Brien Youth Foundation) which is a General Federation Program. Clubs sponsor outstanding high school sophomores for a Leadership Seminar spanning a spring weekend held in all 50 states, the Bahamas, Canada, Jamaica, Japan and

Mexico. HOBY has been gaining delegates in New Jersey with more than 50 students being sponsored each year. The cost to the sponsoring school or organization is $150 for each delegate.

NJSFWC clubwomen who are "young at heart" continue to support children and youth in all that they do.

Emily Strakosch   Hugh O'Brien   Joan Hunt

Joel Lomberg, Motivational Speaker, and HOBY students

ARTISTIC ENDEAVORS — Picture This!

It is said that "a picture is worth a thousand words", but it would take millions of words to paint a full picture of the comprehensive art activities of NJSFWC!

Since 1898 New Jersey clubwomen were interested in art and in 1899 the interest was extensive enough to hold a Ceramics Exhibit in Atlantic City. By 1906 the Art Department was officially designated to follow the GFWC pattern. Currently it is part of the broader Arts/Creative Department conforming to the General Federation structure.

From the early 1900's club members have studied the history and theory of art, including research of art in nearly every country throughout the world. Those with artistic talent applied their knowledge to every facet of artwork including crafts, painting, sculpture and other media from stained glass to paper collage. Since 1920 special interest was shown in living artists, particularly those from America and especially those from New Jersey.

Not content with advancing their own knowledge,

458

clubwomen have sponsored art classes for others from tiny tots to senior citizens. Many clubs claim the honor of being responsible for having Art taught in the public schools even before the "Help Youth" drive of 1944-1947 which insisted on instruction in all public schools and raised funds to advance this cause. Even the comics interested the earlier clubwomen when, in 1909, they protested the quality of the artwork, the atrocious colors and the vulgarity of the texts which perverted the art tastes of the young comic strip readers.

Art exhibits of every type have been sponsored through NJSFWC and its clubs. From clothesline displays, formal gallery exhibits and one-woman shows — they've done it all! New Jersey as a pottery center stimulated clubwomen to become experts in this subject. Over the years several thousand clubwomen have attended art symposia, Federated Art Days, and special exhibits at the Metropolitan Museum of Art in New York, the Newark Museum, the Trenton State and Montclair Museums and galleries in Philadelphia and New Hope, Pennsylvania.

By 1935 exhibits of clubwomen's art work became a regular feature at District Conferences. These springtime events in the eleven districts are now known as "Creative Arts Days". Winners of the competition in many categories continue to compete on a state-wide basis at the Annual Conventions.

In 1923 - 1926 New Jersey women did their full share of campaigning via letter writing which resulted in Congress appropriating $2,500,000 for the National Gallery of Art. The Federation art enthusiasts recognized their civic responsibilities by efforts to restrict unsightly roadside advertising in the rural and residential areas of New Jersey.

The art-oriented clubwomen did their part to help during two World Wars and the conflicts in Korea and Vietnam. They used their talents in arts and crafts to become "reconstruction aides" to help in the rehabilitation of hospitalized military personnel. They provided artwork to brighten military recreation rooms in hospitals, and established an Art Studio at Camp Kilmer where art supply kits were given to service personnel.

From 1934 thorough 1938 NJSFWC was the first Federation to publish a monthly Art Calendar which was distributed without charge. The calendar provided information on what to see in New Jersey in the art field. Art Week was established in 1936, and by 1958 the Governor of New Jersey proclaimed the first week in November as American Art Week. Many clubs were successful in having the Mayors of their respective towns follow suit. The New Jersey Tercentenary found club members serving as costumed hostesses for the Historymobile which toured the state. Club Art Departments decorated floats for local parades and special art exhibits depicting New Jersey history were held.

Nellie Wright Allen served as NJSFWC Art Chairman in 1919. She inaugurated the unique idea of asking clubs to contribute one penny per member to establish a special fund. This money was used to purchase paintings by New Jersey artists for presentation to clubs doing the most to stimulate art, especially among young people. This idea was enthusiastically supported and was called "The Penny Art Fund". This continuing fund was renamed the Nellie Wright Allen Fund in 1928 to honor its founder. At the end of that year, a permanent fund in Mrs. Allen's name was established with the principal being invested and the interest annually transferred to the Penny Art Fund. In 1938 the fund was closed to further contributions. The amount of $1,000 left in this permanent fund is still receiving interest which augments the Penny Art Fund each year. Mrs. Allen had actually begun a national movement. In 1929 the General Federation Art Chairman began to institute Penny Art Funds in other states. The Art Scholarship, begun in 1954, now receives the Allen Fund interest along with club contributions which supply several scholarships to Douglass College students.

Other art scholarships have been awarded under the auspices of NJSFWC for many years. In 1958 Mary Roebling of Trenton presented a $750 Art Scholarship to be given through the Federation to a senior high school student in an public, private or parochial school in New Jersey. There were 22 finalists whose work was exhibited at the Trenton Museum. The 21 who did not receive the award were given a signed piece of porcelain sculpture created by Edward Marshall Boehm, noted sculptor of Trenton.

In 1960 an additional $750 scholarship for sculpture was presented by Helen F. Boehm and the program became known as the Roebling-Boehm Scholarship Awards. In 1967 this program became known as the New Jersey Fine Arts Scholarship Awards to assist promising artists to further their education in their respective fields.

In 1970-71 the NJSFWC mural by Michael Lenson was dedicated at Federation Headquarters, and two gold frames were presented to hold the pictures of NJSFWC Past State Presidents. This has grown to a three-frame display.

Throughout the century of its existence, the art-consious members of the Federation have been responsible for giving thousands of dollars in art-related scholarships and in support of the Yard School of Art, a facility for training the handicapped. Original projects have been continued and many innovative and creative ideas have been added. Art is, indeed, alive and flourishing at NJSFWC.

Bronze figures by Gladys Cordts

After Play

Japanese Dancer

National Art Week

462

CLUBWOMEN "ON STAGE"

Displaying the customary female flair for the dramatic, New Jersey clubwomen became interested in being thespians early in NJSFWC's history. In September 1915 the Federation formed a Pageantry Department in conjunction with the Civics Department to stimulate participation in community celebrations and patriotic events. This later became the Drama Department which, for a time, was combined with the Literature Department. In 1942 the Drama Department became a separate entity. In 1992 — to fall into the GFWC pattern — Drama became a part of the new Arts/Performing Department.

During World War I and the post-war area of 1917-20 better use of national holidays to increase historical knowledge was stressed. A Play Exchange Bureau was maintained with income devoted to war relief projects.

In 1916 the Shakespearean Tercentenary Festival was observed with six clubs presenting "Masque of Psyche". Instinctively knowing that "all the world is a stage", clubs expanded their interest in drama by exchanging plays, costumes and scenery until 1925 when the Little Theater Tournament was founded. By 1928 this became an annual event with an ever-increasing number of entries until 1934-35 when the volume of plays being presented made it necessary to hold District Drama Festivals. The winning clubs competed for the honor of performing at the Annual Convention. The 1941 club year found 39 clubs participating and New Jersey was the winner in a second inter-state festival held with the Connecticut Federation. (New Jersey lost the first inter-state festival in 1940 by three points!) The larger drama of World War II resulted in Drama Festivals being cancelled due to transportation difficulties; however, clubs still "got into the act" by producing plays and other entertainments for USO centers and other groups which entertained service personnel. War Bonds and Stamps were sold at these performances with one club selling $570,000 in bonds by presenting an original play 11 times.

Drama Festivals were resumed after World War II and attracted large audiences each year. Clubs held classes in every phase of stage craft and became interested in puppetry and pantomime. Workshops on make-up, directing, acting and all other production aspects were popular events. A lending library of plays and other material was established in 1944, and by 1960 a record was set of circulating over 800 plays and books to clubs by mail.

A contest for writing original plays failed to generate enough interest in 1944-1947, although five plays were submitted to a similar GFWC contest. Twenty-five years later the amateur playwrights were ready with 20 entries — by 1964 the contest had become an annual event. In 1967 the Bea Rothwell Award for novice playwrights was given for the first time, and a $50 Bond was given to an aspiring playwright at Douglass College. In 1953 a $100 contribution given to the Federation in the name of Jessie Alexander Ropes, a former State President, established a Drama Scholarship. Club contributions and proceeds from Drama Festivals have continued the Drama Scholarships with well over $1,000 being awarded each year to Douglass College students.

In observance of the New Jersey Tercentenary in 1964 an historical pageant entitled "No Summer Soldiers These" was presented at Convention. The play was written by two clubwomen and portrayed by five clubs. The production was later given at the Fine Arts Conference of the GFWC Convention as a fitting tribute to New Jersey's 300th Anniversary.

At the 1969 Convention, when the Federation celebrated its 75th Anniversary, three Elizabeth B. Alton monetary awards were given for pageants, plays, or plays with music which were based on the history of a federated club or the history of NJSFWC. Miniature stage sets and costumed dolls depicting characters of stage, screen and television became a part of the Drama Department competitions in the 1950's. The Federation's 75th Anniversary Convention in 1969 included a special category of dolls representing actresses of the 1890's. Clubwomen have continued to demonstrate their creative abilities in these costumed doll competitions each year.

Drama devotees in NJSFWC clubs do more than enhance their own abilities on the stage and behind the scenes. In 1966 the efforts of the Drama Department purchased and installed a complete sound and public address system in Headquarters. This included a Stromberg-Carlson amplification system with built-in interior speakers, a portable outside speaker with connections, three microphones, stands and a tape recorder. It was successfully used at the dedication ceremonies when the Headquarters' Building was officially opened. As the system aged, it was replaced by a more modern system which was a gift of the Fourth District clubs in honor of their DVP, Jane Smith.

There is no doubt in the mind of NJSFWC that "the play's the thing"!

"Showboat" Minstrel Show
Penn's Grove / Carney's Point Woman's Club

LITERATURE, LIBRARIES, AND LITERACY

The written word was a primary interest in women's clubs 100 years ago, and it has continued to be a vital part of their activities. The names of many of the original clubs included "reading" and "literary" which indicated that their major purpose was getting together to read and discuss books. In the 1906-1909 time period the Literature Department was created. In 1992, in order to conform with the GFWC structure, it became a Division under the broader Arts/Performing Department where it continues to flourish.

In 1912 this Department was already interested in suppression of crime news and joined the Art Department in its objections to the comics appearing in newspapers. Efforts to "clean up the comics" was a continuing crusade given further impetus in 1935 -1938 when a Resolution was presented to "Foster the Habit of Reading Good Literature". Again in 1942, horror comics and porn magazines were denounced as a detrimental influence on young people of the country. Support was given to a General Federation movement in this area, and in 1949 - 1950 a Resolution urged stronger laws to control the circulation and sale of "Lurid Literature". Members were urged to attack this problem at the level of their local news dealers. Far from being prudes, NJSFWC clubwomen still seriously object to pornography when it affects the lives of young people.

In 1921 an Original Work Department conducted creative writing contests among clubwomen. By 1926 interest in this had grown and 1,000 poems were submitted during the next three years. Interest in the Creative Writing Contest has grown each year and there are now eight categories for entries which include short and short short stories, book reviews, essays, reports, serious verse, light verse, and Haiku. In 1929 100 poems written by clubwomen were published in a book entitled "Verses by New Jersey Clubwomen".

From 1930 through 1933 a literary supplement to the "New Jersey Clubwoman" magazine was published and contained the winning entries in the Creative Writing Contest. These supplements were financed by theater parties, but in 1933 the proceeds of the theater parties were not sufficient to meet the cost of publication. In 1934 it was necessary to initiate small entrance fees paid by those entering the contests. The fees are used to purchase awards for the winners and to meet the expense of professional judging. In 1969 the entry fees were used to publish a small volume, <u>Diamond Harvest</u>, which contains women's entries from 1968 - 1969 and previous years.

Former State President, Lavenia Taylor, enriched the Federation with an anthology of poetry assembled in 1927 and a literary map of New Jersey was compiled by the

Woman's Club of Merchantville. Elizabeth Clark of East Orange presented the Federation with her mother's copy of "New Jersey's Scrapbook of Women Writers" which had been compiled by Margaret Yardley. Older clubs assembled literature material with historic value for addition to the Federation archives.

For several years club Literature Departments have participated in "Creative Writing Days" in their respective Districts. Women read selections, many of which are their own original writings. These events are now incorporated in the Arts/Performing Festivals held in each District.

The GFWC sponsored an essay competition through the "Atlantic Monthly" on the subject of "The Modern Woman's Place in the Home" during 1944 - 1947. Thirty-three New Jersey clubwomen entered this competition, and in 1959 they participated in the "Creativity" contest.

Individual clubs give many English awards and scholarships to their local high school students under the auspices of their Literature Departments. Scholarships have been given by NJSFWC regularly as part of the Literature Department activities. Douglass College students benefit from the Literature/Journalism Scholarships amounting to well over $1,000 annually.

New Jersey clubwomen have been interested in working for libraries of various types since NJSFWC's inception. One of the five initial departments in the Federation was "Libraries" and in 1895 a committee was appointed to urge legislation for a state commission to promote traveling libraries. The legislation was finally enacted in 1899 and the Federation was asked by the State Librarian to suggest a list of books to be purchased. The first boxes of books were contributed by clubs and in February, 1900 the Federation's Board of Directors donated a complete library to be circulated in the name of the Federation. The state assembled sixty-two traveling libraries but, due to poor publicity concerning the procedure to be followed by towns to apply for their use, only five were circulated. In 1901 the Federation conducted an educational campaign to "get out the books". In 1904 a study was made regarding the need for more traveling libraries and clubs were loaned libraries for one year at a cost of $2.

One of 4,655 traveling libraries or book wagons in operation in the early 1900's.

Although there was an urgent need for trained library workers, club members served as volunteer librarians — a service function still being performed by clubwomen throughout New Jersey. "Bookmobiles" were organized by clubs in the early years and set a pattern which is still followed by many libraries throughout the state to reach the rural areas.

NJSFWC is very proud that a high percentage of the local libraries in New Jersey were organized through the efforts of clubs. Support of local and school libraries is still an on-going activity in nearly every club in New Jersey.

In 1949 - 1950 a project to establish a library in the Walt Whitman Home in Camden was highly successful. "The Good Gray Poet" spent the last years of his life in southern New Jersey and is buried in Camden's Harleigh Cemetery. Clubwomen study Whitman's works extensively and many have made pilgrimages to the home in Camden and the Stafford House and Spring in Laurel Springs where he visited and rested after having served as a male nurse in the Civil War. Whitman's home is maintained as a shrine by the state; however, a Federation project begun in 1965 (and continued to date) has resulted in contributions which assist in its rehabilitation and maintenance.

In 1984 the General Federation opened its History/ Resource Library at its Headquarters in Washington, DC. Carol B. Hancock (currently Third Vice President of NJSFWC) reported on the gala opening. She served as a Chairman from New Jersey.

Several years of effort went into the establishment of NJSFWC's Library in the Headquarters Building. Many gifts and contributions were received from clubs and individuals for this purpose. The Library became a reality in 1990, and is continuing to grow. Gail C. Shast, who served as the appointed Librarian from 1990 to 1994, has been largely responsible for this project by cataloguing books and materials, arranging for needed equipment and generally overseeing the birth of this new resource. Having "a library to call its own" is a vital addition to the life and history of NJSFWC.

A special interest in the continuing self-education of New Jersey clubwomen has been participation in Epsilon Sigma Omicron, better known as ESO. This program is officially recognized by colleges, state universities and state libraries and, when New Jersey received its charter in May 1977, it was the 37th state to have formed a chapter. Irma Mirante was Chairman at that time.

ESO was founded in 1928 in Indiana. It stimulates systematic home reading and study, encourages reading group study and the establishment of home libraries, encourages participation in college courses (both credit and non-credit) and opens new channels of thought to meet the challenges of today. Participants choose books from categories of choice set up by ESO and read at their own speed. When they have completed twenty books, they send brief reports to the organization. Awards are received by participants as they reach specified levels of achievement. In 1990 ten Federation members received Century Awards for having read and reported on 100 books. At this same time, two members received special awards for having completed the 1,000 book level. This honorary sorority sponsored by GFWC offers all club members an excellent opportunity to continue their education through reading. Taking the motto "Enlighten Your Own Pathway" very seriously, ESO is steadily gaining in popularity.

In 1992 - 1994 a GFWC project was SOAR (Stories Offer Adventure - Read!). Participation in this was through NJSFWC's Education Department chaired by Betty Bransdorf. It featured sponsoring books through RIF (Reading is Fundamental); a "Books for Babies" feature where material was distributed to new parents at local hospitals and sessions of telling stories to young children. These activities went along with the clubwomen's interest in literacy. Learning that there was a percentage of residents in the United States of America who could not read spurred clubwomen to take action which would help to resolve this situation. In its earlier years, NJSFWC urged more evening classes for immigrants so that they could learn to read English and become better-informed when they exercised their right to vote. Many clubwomen have joined the literacy program to teach reading to adults. They also urge reading to small children to establish good reading habits at an early age and to better prepare them for entrance into school. Reading and writing are still important concerns to all those who are a part of NJSFWC. This is seen as a growing emphasis in the work of New Jersey clubwomen.

THE SOUNDS OF MUSIC

In the Victorian Era when NJSFWC was born, the "ladies" were expected to have music as one of their accomplishments. The clubwomen of New Jersey have always considered this an important part of their agenda.

In 1897 the first official Federation song was chosen. The original words were written by Marion Couthey Smith of Orange and sung to the tune of "America". In 1913 a contest was held and the winning song was "On New Jersey Daughters" which was written by Mrs. Allen Smith of Ridgefield Park and sung to the tune of "Onward Christian Soldiers". In 1924, Mary J. S. Moore of the Haddon Fortnightly offered an award of $50 for a new Federation song. The winner was a composition by Dr. Lavina Baily Clement and Ellen Vinton Ford. The Woman's Club of Raritan Township won first place in the 1959- 1960 contest with "Club Women of New Jersey" which became part of the Federation's repertoire. As the years rolled on creative ability was developed through competition and in Music Departments' annual contests for vocal and instrumental compositions.

474

The meaningful words of the "Collect for Club Women" written by Mary Stewart in 1904 have been set to music and this is often sung at Federation events. First District Clubs will always remember the late Mary Oleksa's rendition in March 1993.

"Federation Spirit" with words and music by Karen L. Edson, a former State Music Chairman, is the NJSFWC Centennial song for 1994.

"Federation Spirit"

In eighteen ninety four they came from near and far,
They had one purpose to unfold in eighteen ninety four;
Our FEDERATION then was formed with dreams and
        goals aglow,
We teach, we share, we lend a hand, we're women strong
        you know.
State Presidents led us and Boards kept us strong,
All of this still happpening in nineteen ninety four!
Volunteering is our motto through courage and steadfast
        love,
"A GLORIOUS PAST A BRILLIANT FUTURE" remains
        our dream you know.
Federated women hold their heads up high,
For N.J.S.F.W.C. is never going to die!
Douglass College is our pride, our Headquarters makes
        us glow,
The State Projects remain to show we care, we all must
        grow!
Federated women hold their heads up high,
For N.J.S.F.W.C. is never going to die!

476

In 1909, when the Music Department was still young, clubs urged sight-reading classes and other musical courses. An attempt was made to raise funds for a Music Scholarship. During World War I clubs entertained the troops with musical programs, sent musical instruments and sheet music to military installations and contributed 100,000 phonograph records to military bases.

"Let's Sing Our Way To Victory" became the theme as World War II found Music Departments studying music of other nations, entertaining military personnel and sending CARE packages to needy musicians in Europe. As an associate of the New Jersey Federation of Music Clubs, NJSFWC received a citation for participating in "Ward Music in War Hospitals". Sunday supper musicales emphasized current events in the world of music and the wounded in the hospitals had their hours brightened by performances of clubwomen.

In 1919 Mrs. Edward MacDowell spoke to the Federation to tell the story of the MacDowell Colony in Peterboro, New Hampshire. This was established in 1907 as a memorial to her husband, an American composer of note. The Colony offers a sanctuary for creative artists in all fields by giving them an atmosphere of peace and quiet in which to pursue their work. Accomplishments brought to fruition in this rustic haven have built a significant record of immortality. The Federation's Music Department became interested in building a studio at the MacDowell Colony, and $1,500 was raised for this purpose very quickly. In May, 1920 the State President and the Music Chairman visited Peterboro to place a plaque on the door of the New Jersey Studio identifying it as a gift of NJSFWC. The cottage was described as "one large room with a big fireplace and windows on three sides". The

MacDowell Foundation supplied a piano but the rest of the furnishings were gifts of the Federation.

Contributions are received for the MacDowell Fund each year and used to provide maintenance for the New Jersey Studio. Later, the studio was electrified and provided with plumbing. In 1968 a contribution of $900 was used to install a heating system and floor insulation which makes possible year-round use. Clubs continue to send contributions for the MacDowell Fund making it possible to give this project more than $1,000 each year. NJSWC members felt even closer to this project when they learned that Mary Higgins Clark, a 1993 Convention speaker, wrote one of her suspense novels at the MacDowell Colony.

Clubs had formed Music Departments and Club Choruses for several years, along with studying the music of America and other countries. The Pilgrim Tercentenary was celebrated in 1920 with a "Pilgrim's Canticle". Choral contests were held at this time with 11 choral groups competing for a silver cup. As a result of the interest generated, 35 new choruses were formed and Community Christmas Carol Sings were organized. A Schubert Centennial was celebrated in 1928 — 1929, and clubs made radio broadcasts. By 1958 — 1960 District Music Festivals had increased and there was a growing interest in opera. "Cheer Groups" worked with the sick and aged with more than 50 club choruses working hard to entertain at hospitals, nursing homes, children's homes, and civic events. In 1959 the Music Department gave its first concert at the Annual Convention of the Federation.

The State Chorus was organized in 1960-1961 with 75 voices from 12 clubs coming from seven Districts. Participation increased throughout the years, and the State

Chorus Concert is an anticipated event at Convention. In 1968 an evening's entertainment at Convention was presented by the Music Department which produced "A Showcase of Clubwomen Stars". Early morning "sing-alongs" have been part of Convention agendas.

An Exchange Library for Choral Work was organized in 1935 with a circulation of more than 7,000 copies of music. A state-wide Music Festival held in 1938 in New Brunswick found 14 clubs entertaining an audience of 600. The state-wide chorus of 200 voices was organized to sing on New Jersey Day at the New York World's Fair of 1939. A special milestone was reached when a Golden Jubilee Chorus of 950 women from all parts of the country sang on May 21, 1941 with the New Jersey State Chorus as a nucleus. This group was an important part of the GFWC Convention held in Atlantic City that year.

Music Scholarships became a primary interest of the Federation with two scholarships being given in 1932 to students at New Jersey College for Women (now Douglass College). Modest profits from all contests made it possible to establish the Meta Thorne Waters Music Scholarship at this time. A continuing fund, contributions from clubs make it possible to provide nearly $2,000 each year in scholarships for Douglass College students. Recipients of these awards have often been enthusiastic performers at the Federation's Annual Conventions.

A Baldwin Acrosonic Piano was placed in the Federation Headquarters Building in October, 1966 as a result of a special Music Department Fund which was over subscribed. The balance of $125 remaining in the fund provided maintenance for the piano. In 1993 Doris and Ken Malle presented a "piano caddy" in honor of State President Joan M. Hunt. This will make possible easier movement of the instrument within the Headquarters Building.

In 1969 a Music Library was started with material made available to clubs at nominal fees. Song sheets have been produced since 1928 and are consistently updated.

With the many activities of club Music Departments, it is a sure bet that New Jersey clubwomen will always have "A Song in the Air".

A Convention Concert by the State Chorus

MEDIA COMMUNICATION

The earliest clubwomen who described the Victorian Age as one of "Pride, Prejudice, and Exquisite Discomfort", believed that it was necessary to explain NJSFWC to the general public. Making sure that people understand and appreciate the fact that women's clubs are service organizations — rather than tea parties and sewing circles — is still a difficult task.

We can visualize the first clubwomen laboriously preparing press releases manually long before typewriters and word processors became equipment taken for granted by nearly everyone. Early clubs were often able to get their news published in local newspapers — most often in the "social columns". Press releases of a more general nature did not receive equal attention from editors in the 1890's.

In 1902 the Federation appointed a Press Committee to formulate state-wide releases. In 1906 to 1909 a weekly column in the Jersey City Journal carried "official" department news for the Federation. The State Chamber of Commerce gave a page to club news for several months in the

1913 - 1915 years. In 1918 a Publicity Committee was established and it functioned until 1922 when its work was combined with the Education Department.

A separate Publicity Committee emerged in 1926 - 1927, sending monthly bulletins to 35 newspapers. In the next five years the number of newspapers being contacted had grown to 45. The "Depression Years" resulted in there being much less space available in the newspapers for club news; however, 1500 words were sent each week to 18 large and 45 small newspapers. A Sunday issue of the Herald Tribune in 1932 - 1933 carried 66 columns of news, plus pictures, to cover a special Federation feature story. During World War II the "home front" activities of 301 clubs were compiled and reported.

As part of the educational process, clubwomen have long been instructed on quality reporting and establishing closer contacts with the local media. By the late 1970's Federation news was going to 38 daily newspapers and 260 weekly newspapers. Currently known as the Communications Committee, the women involved in clubs and at the Federation level have continued to "tell it like it is", and newspaper coverage has definitely gone beyond the social pages.

The Federation was quick to take advantage of other mass media. On November 21, 1928 the first radio program under NJSFWC auspices was a broadcast over WOR. It was called The Club Woman's Hour and reportedly heard as far away as Puerto Rico. It was a regular feature for ten years, dropped for a year and then picked up by WOR as a program entitled The Woman's Club of the Air. About 30 meetings of this unique hypothetical organization were aired. The program's time slot was pre-empted in 1938 by Benito Mussolini voicing his approval of Adolph Hitler's actions! These broadcasts were a "war casualty" with the advent of World War II.

By 1948 three Federation programs were heard over a Newark station and, in 1950, the Second and Third District Clubs had radio programs connected with their activities. In the 1949-1950 club year, clubs reported 16 other broadcasts connected with their work. During 1956-1958 the Federation's Civics and Legislation Department cooperated with the New Jersey Broadcasters' Association in a state-wide "Register and Vote" campaign. Twenty-five affiliated stations carried spot announcements as often as 18 times each day for two months prior to election. An award for this project was received from the American Heritage Foundation. In 1964 - 1965 all of the clubs in the Eleventh District were invited to broadcast over station WKER. Lucille Dangremond, State President, taped a radio show with the Governor of New Jersey which was carried on 26 stations. By 1968 it was reported that 74 clubs had obtained radio time and three had appeared on television.

Television became an excellent method of spreading Federation facts and figures. In 1957 the General Federation International Affairs Department and the NJSFWC International Relations Chairman, along with two club chairmen, appeared on the nation-wide "NBC Home Show" with Arlene Francis and Carlos Romulo (of the Phillipines). In 1963 Margaret Wagner, State President, appeared on NBC-TV for the "Community Checkers" program and Lavenia Taylor was a frequent television personality during her administration. While serving as Southern Vice President in 1967, Dorothy McGlade appeared on the Helen Meyner Show over Channel 47 in Newark. This twenty-minute show included a former GCI delegate giving her impression of her week at Douglass College. The increased use of television and the inauguration of cable TV has made it possible to "spread the word" with many Federation women appearing on the "tube".

The Publicity Committee became the Public Relations Committee in 1967. Prior to that time, Federation publicity had been expanded as a result of educational programs in this field. In 1930-31 the Federation was represented at a Herald Tribune Conference for the Club Press Chairmen from six states. The topic was "Federation Page". In 1936 - 1937 over 700 women attended the seven schools for press releases which were held with this newspaper's cooperation. In 1937 - 1938 Club Chairmen attended a roundtable program, luncheon and tour conducted by a newspaper. This is a courtesy now regularly extended by many newspapers throughout the state. Workshops are held at NJSFWC Conferences and the Annual Conventions with professional newspaper people on hand to explain the mechanics of preparing usable material for the mass media. By 1956 it was noted that members of the Fourth Estate were covering District Conferences and other Federation events — a trend which continued to grow as clubwomen learned the value of good public relations to spur the success of club projects and events.

In the 1950's Press Books became a part of club life, and contests were held with professional judging and awards at Convention. Collecting newspaper clippings and other evidence of media coverage are regular club activities. The Press Books are valuable sources of material for members who are asked, "just what does your club do?"

Clubs in other states and throughout the world know about the work done by New Jersey clubwomen through articles appearing in the General Federation Club Woman magazine to which clubs and state committees contribute material. An article on the formation of the Evening Membership Department (which is unique to New Jersey) received national recognition in 1938. In 1968 two Communications Forums were attended by representatives of NJSFWC along with GFWC representatives and those of 177 other organizations. The discussions at these events concerned "the influence of the communications media on the caliber of American civilization." New Jersey also participated in the Citizens' Media Ballot which gave members an opportunity to record opinions of mass media and the Good News Program where news was obtained from all possible sources for distribution to news channels.

In September 1983 the Courier-Post newspapers of Camden produced a three-page spread on President Gloria Malasky and NJSFWC. In 1986 - 1987 New Jersey was commended for obtaining the most coverage because of its activity in the "Lady of Liberty" project and support of S.O.B.E.R. (Slow On the Bottle Enjoy the Ride). New Jersey governors have been supportive of NJSFWC activities. On April 24, 1985 Governor Thomas Kean proclaimed GFWC/NJSFWC Day in New Jersey. Statewide Recognition Day for NJSFWC began on September 26, 1987 in shopping malls throughout the state. This has been a continuing event which creates good public relations and gives the clubs an opportunity for increasing membership.

Since 1963 clubs have been urged to purchase GFWC Roadsigns to be erected at various entrances to their communities. In many towns the familiar international symbol tells the general public that there is a Federated Woman's Club located in the community. These signs often join those of other familiar service organizations such as Lions International, Kiwanis and Rotary.

By becoming more visible in the mass media the Federation's "image" has come a long way in its first century of existence. But the job is far from being completed. There was not enough information on the NJSFWC available to those who are not familiar with the scope of the organization and its fascinating history. A CENTURY OF CHALLENGE was written to provide clubwomen, students, historians and the general public with a detailed record (and a reference source) of the activities and achievements of this very special group of women— a segment of New Jersey's population which has had a definite impact on life in the community, state, nation and the world.   THE FIRST CENTURYANS prepared the book with "Pride in Membership".

A LOOK AT NOW AND THE FUTURE

The "Profile" of New Jersey clubwomen has constantly changed, often reflecting the society in which they live. Carol B. Hancock, NJSFWC Third Vice President 1992-1994, conducted a survey of members which revealed that most of them (excluding Juniorettes and Juniors) are in the "over 40" age brackets, married or widowed, work at full or part-time jobs, continued their education in various ways beyond high school and volunteer time to a great number of organizations in addition to NJSFWC. They hold many elected and appointed positions within their communities and counties and belong to more than one Federated Women's Club in the state. Regardless of their age and economic situation, they are actively meeting the challenges of today! Clubwomen do want to continue "to make a difference" !

Members surveyed want NJSFWC to move into its next century by advocating women's rights, attracting younger women into the Federation, working for World Peace, making and accepting changes and GROWING individually and collectively.

Membership has fluctuated over the past century (as it has in all service organizations), often due to the more mobile population experienced since the World War II era. Clubs have disbanded due to circumstances beyond their control; however, new clubs are consistently being organized. Those received into NJSFWC in 1992 and until December 31, 1994 will be designated "Centennial Clubs" — as this book went into publication they included:

Middlesex Area Woman's Club
GFWC Bayshore Woman's Club
Jefferson Township Woman's Club
Women in Community Service (Glen Rock)
Middlesex Area Juniorettes
Long Valley Juniorettes
GFWC West Deptford Woman's Club
Clearview-Wenonah Junior Woman's Club
Hunterdon Hills Contemporary Club

The future is bright and NJSFWC will continue to be a vital force among volunteer service organizations as it enters its second century.

Carol B. Hancock   *Dorothy Lowe Greene*   *Cathy Southwick*

Collect

Words by Mary Stewart

Music by Dodie Waters

Keep us, O God, from petti-ness; Let us be large in thought, in word, in deed. Let us be done with fault find-ing, and leave off self seek-ing. May we put a-way all pre-tense and meet each other face to face With-out self pity & with-out pre-ju-dice. May we never be has-ty in judge-ment and al-ways gen-er-ous. Let us take time for all things, Make us to grow calm, ser-ene, (and) gen-tle. Teach us to put in-to ac-tion our bet-ter im-pul-ses, straight for-ward and un-a-fraid. Grant that we may real-ize it is the lit-tle things that create dif-fren-ces; that in the big things of life we are at one. And may we strive to teach and know the great common human heart of us all, (and) O, Lord God! Let us for-get not to be kind

Bibliography

History of the Women's Club Movement in America
        —J. C. Croly
History of the General Federation of Women's Clubs for the
        First Twenty-Two Years of Its Organization.
                — Mary I. Wood
Reaching Out - A story of the GFWC
                — Mary Jean Houde
Unity and Diversity - Volume I
                — Mildred White Wells
The Clubwoman as Feminist - True Womanhood Redefined
1868-1914
                — Karen J. Blair
Memories of Jane Cunningham Croly - "Jenny June"
                — Caroline Morse
Crusades and Crinolines
                — Ishbell Ross
Herbert Croly of The New Republic
                — David Levy
The Beauteous Jenny June
                — Henry Ladd Smith
The Nineteenth Century Woman's Dilemma and Jennie June
                — Elizabeth Bancroft Schlesinger
Report of the Twenty-First Anniversary of Sorosis
                —NY Styles and Cash Printers
Memorial Dedication of Jane Cunnigham Croly's Grave -
1990   — Ann Quinn
Early History of the New Jersey College for Women
                — Mabel Smith Douglass; Student Annual 1929
History of New Jersey State Federation of Women's Clubs
                — Ada D. Fuller 1917 and 1927

History of New Jersey State Federation of Women's Clubs
— Helen Esther Marsh (1947)
History of New Jersey State Federation of Women's Clubs
— Mrs. Frederick C. Wurtz (1958)
Federation Milestones - NJSFWC's 75-Year History
— Grace Mathis Williams (1969)
Past and Promise - Lives of New Jersey Women (1990)
—Women's Project of NJ - Joan Burstyn,
Editor-in-Chief
From the Beginning - A Page of History
— Published by NJSFWC - 1979
The New Jersey Club Woman and Even'Tide Magazines
Tel-A-Junior (New Jersey Juniors Newsletter)
Minutes of NJSFWC Board of Directors Meetings
NJSFWC State Yearbooks
NJSFWC Annual Convention Programs
Cecilia Gaines Holland's 1933 speech
Elizabeth B. Alton's Notes on Headquarters Project
The ALMANAC (1968-1994)
Video Tapes of Past State Presidents of NJSFWC
Correspondence from Past State Presidents of NJSFWC
and Others
Pictures, Reports and Other Documents from NJSFWC
Archives

504

NEW JERSEY STATE FEDERATION OF WOMEN'S CLUBS

NEW JERSEY STATE FEDERATION OF WOMEN'S CLUBS

NEW JERSEY STATE FEDERATION OF WOMEN'S CLUBS